Ref

VISITOR'S GUIDE: NORWAY
World Traveller Series

Ringve Musical Instruments nr. Trondheim

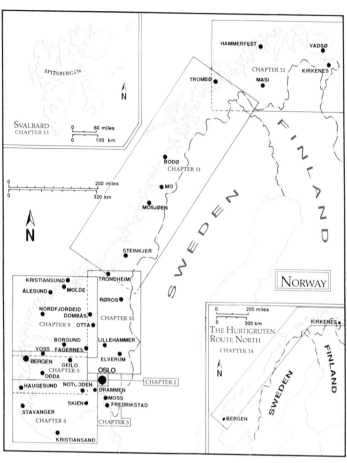

SVALBARD
CHAPTER 13

SPITSBERGEN

0 —— 60 miles
0 —— 100 km

N

0 —— 200 miles
0 —— 320 km

N

HAMMERFEST
VADSØ
TROMSØ
CHAPTER 12
MASI
KIRKENES

FINLAND

BODØ
CHAPTER 11
MO
MOSJØEN

SWEDEN

STEINKJER

KRISTIANSUND
MOLDE
ÅLESUND
NORDFJORDEID
DOMBÅS
CHAPTER 9
OTTA
BORGUND
VOSS FAGERNES
BERGEN
GEILO
CHAPTER 5
ODDA
HAUGESUND NOTODDEN
SKIEN
STAVANGER
CHAPTER 4
KRISTIANSAND

TRONDHEIM
RØROS
CHAPTER 10
LILLEHAMMER
ELVERUM
OSLO
CHAPTER 2
DRAMMEN
MOSS
FREDRIKSTAD
CHAPTER 3

NORWAY

THE HURTIGRUTEN
ROUTE NORTH
CHAPTER 14

0 —— 200 miles
0 —— 300 km

KIRKENES

FINLAND

SWEDEN

N

BERGEN

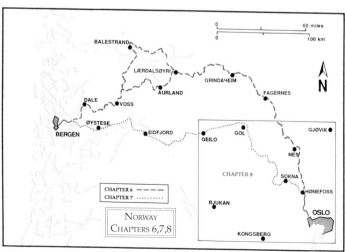

0 —— 60 miles
0 —— 100 km

BALESTRAND

LÆRDALSØYRI
GRINDAHEIM
AURLAND
FAGERNES

N

DALE
VOSS
ØYSTESE
BERGEN
EIDFJORD
GEILO
GOL
GJØVIK
NES
CHAPTER 8
SOKNA
HØNEFOSS
RJUKAN
OSLO
KONGSBERG

CHAPTER 6 — — —
CHAPTER 7 ....

NORWAY
CHAPTERS 6,7,8

VISITOR'S GUIDE
NORWAY

Don Philpott

MPC
HUNTER
PUBLISHING INC

Published by:
Moorland Publishing Co Ltd,
Moor Farm Road West,
Airfield Estate,
Ashbourne,
Derbyshire
DE6 1HD
England

British Library Cataloguing in Publication Data:
Philpott, Don
    The visitor's guide to Norway.
    1. Norway - Visitor's guides
    I. Title
    914.810449

ISBN 0 86190 424 9

Colour origination by:
Scantrans, Singapore

Printed in the UK by:
Butler & Tanner Ltd, Frome, Somerset

Published in the USA by:
Hunter Publishing Inc,
300 Raritan Center Parkway,
CN 94, Edison, NJ 08818
ISBN 1-55650-450-0

Cover photograph: Romdalsfjorden (*International Photobank*)

Illustrations have been supplied as follows:
A. Lawrenson: p222; Marit Graff Hagen: pp 15 (both), 163 (top), 195 (bottom); MPC Picture Collection: pp 18 (both), 26 (bottom), 34, 43 (bottom), 51 (top), 59 (top), 71, 79, 82, 83, 87, 90 (both), 98 (top), 107 (top), 142 (both), 143, 155 (top), 158 (bottom), 163 (bottom), 166 (bottom), 175 (both), 178 (top), 179, 186, 187, 190, 227; Norwegian Tourist Board: pp 10, 11, 22, 35, 51 (bottom), 98 (bottom), 103, 107 (bottom), 115, 122, 130 (bottom), 150, 155 (bottom), 182, 183, 195 (top), 198, 199 (bottom), 210 (bottom), 211 (bottom); D. Philpott: pp 43 (top), 99, 178 (bottom); B. Pyatt: pp 26 (top), 54, 59 (bottom), 130 (top); M. Rogers: pp 158 (top), 159, 162, 166 (top), 167 (both), 199 (top), 210 (top), 211 (top), 230.

Acknowledgements
The author would like to thank Marit Graff Hagen whose friendship and help has made this book possible and the Norwegian National Tourist Office, London.

MPC Production Team:
Editor: Tonya Monk
Designer: Jonathan Moss
Cartographer: Alastair Morrison

Contents

Key to Symbols Used in Text Margin and on Maps

⛪	Church/Ecclesiastical site	🚶	Recommended walk
🌳	Parkland	⊞	Building of interest
ᴨ	Archaeological site	🏰	Castle/Fortification
🏞	Beautiful view/Scenery, Natural phenomenon	🦌	Nature reserve/Animal interest
🏛	Museum/Art gallery	⛷	Skiing facilities
☀	Other place of interest	🦆	Birdlife

Key to Maps

● ⬠	Town/City	·—·—·	National boundary
═══	Motorway	------	Regional boundary
——	Main road		Rivers
——	Minor road		Lakes

How To Use This Guide

This MPC Visitor's Guide has been designed to be as easy to use as possible. Each chapter covers a region or itinerary in a natural progression which gives all the background information to help you enjoy your visit. MPC's distinctive margin symbols, the important places printed in bold, and a comprehensive index enable the reader to find the most interesting places to visit with ease.

At the end of each chapter an Additional Information section gives specific details such as addresses and opening times, making this guide a complete sightseeing companion.

At the back of the guide the Fact File, arranged in alphabetical order, gives practical information and useful tips to help you plan your holiday — before you go and while you are there.

The maps of each region show the main towns, villages, roads and places of interest, but are not designed as route maps and motorists should always use a good recommended road atlas.

FOREWORD

N orway has a magic and charm all of its own. It is a huge country of constant contrast and change and it would take a lifetime to explore it fully. The magic, however, keeps calling you back. There is the breathtaking scenery of the fjords, the wonders of the Midnight Sun, beautiful mountains to enjoy all year round, the forests and lakes, the bustling towns and sleepy hamlets and the quite magnificent ancient timber buildings. Whether you are interested in history or the countryside, sunbathing or walking, ferry hopping or reindeer spotting, Norway has more than enough to offer.

This guide sets out to help you make the most of the time you have for your holiday. Apart from suggesting tours along the most interesting routes, I have tried to include places off the beaten track; those that are not so frequently visited but which give an insight into Norway, its customs and its warm, friendly people.

The three great assets of Norway are the people, the scenery and the country's incredibly efficient travel network. You can drive or cycle, or hop on a bus, train, plane or ferry. Virtually every part of the country is served by land or sea and both afford a marvellous way of seeing Norway in all its splendour.

Norway is a country long accustomed to looking after its guests and there is accommodation ranging from campsites to log cabins, youth hostels to five-star hotels. Most towns and districts have their own tourist offices and you can usually find someone who speaks English if you need help.

There really is something for everyone in Norway. I hope this guide gives you a flavour of what to expect, helps you plan your trip and allows you to get the maximum enjoyment out of your trip while you are in Norway.

1

INTRODUCTION

History

Norway has a rich history with the first traces of human settlement dating back to 9000BC. Little is known about these first settlers but it is likely that they were from German tribes which started to migrate northwards in the late glacial period as the ice cap that had covered the Norwegian mountains and coastal plains started to melt and retreat.

The first settlers were hunters and would have hunted the massive reindeer herds that roamed the area. The hunters would have settled in small groups and they left proof of their occupation in flint tools, clay vessels and rock carvings. Throughout the country there remain specimens of their art. The carvings show their prey: reindeer, moose, deer, bear and fish.

The transition to agriculture started about 4000BC and by the start of the Iron Age, farming and fishing had become the main occupations throughout most of the country. Because of the latter the Norwegians developed their boatbuilding, navigation and seamanship skills which were to stand them in such good stead.

By the Bronze Age most parts of the country as far north as Tromsø had been settled by the Germanic migrants although the major communities were established, as they still are, along the coast or along fjords.

During the Roman period Norway established trading links with countries to the south, and utensils of bronze and glass, as well as weapons, have been discovered in graves and excavations. It was during this period that the art of writing, in the form of runic letters, was first introduced into the Nordic countries.

The Viking Period

The next main phase in the country's history started in about AD800. The Norwegians were great traders and explorers and their skill as boat builders had enabled them to produce ships that could sail the oceans. By AD800 the Norwegians had already settled peacefully in Shetland and the Orkneys but the next two centuries were to see a rapid, and not so peaceful, territorial expansion.

Few historical records remain about this transition from prehistoric Norway to the Viking Age apart from archaeological discoveries and the sagas. It is known, however, that Norway was still divided into a number of kingdoms at this time and they joined forces to attack and conquer the Isle of Man, the Hebrides, north Scotland and most of Ireland. They settled in parts of England and Normandy, Iceland and Greenland.

The two major events during this period, however, were the unification of Norway, and its conversion to Christianity. Harald the Fairhead defeated the local chieftans in a major sea battle in Hafrsfjord, near Stavanger, in about AD885 to become the first king of a unified Norway. He created 'national' laws which were upheld by nobles appointed to govern the different districts.

Before his death Harald bequeathed the country to his son Eirik, soon to acquire the name of Bloody-Axe, and in doing so established the principle of dynastic rule. He succeeded in having his authority recognised in most parts of the country so that after his death and right up to the union with Sweden in 1319, the kingdom of Norway became an inheritance of the Harald family. This concept of the inherited right of the Harald dynasty took deep root and explains why the royal family is respected so highly.

The following century Olav Haraldsson (St Olav, Norway's national saint), invited the Catholic Church into Norway and by the time of his death in 1030 much of the country had been converted to Christianity.

It was a period of rapid expansion. King Harald Hardrade was killed in 1066 at the Battle of Stanford Bridge in a bid to conquer England, and this is now regarded as the date that signalled the end of the Viking Age. He founded Oslo in about 1050 and Bergen was established about 20 years later. It saw the beginning of the great building period when the first of the magnificent timber stave churches were built and was a period rich in story-telling and the sagas recorded and embellished the history, merging fact and folkore.

Civil War and Danish Rule

Rivalries between tribal chiefs quickly developed into Civil War and the country was split by intermittent fighting for the next three centuries.

Because Norway was weakened, it fell prey to the Scandinavian Union of Sweden and Denmark, and lost much of its national identity. Many of its trading outposts abroad were taken over by the Hanseatic League and a near fatal blow was inflicted in the mid-fourteenth century when the country was struck by bubonic plague.

In 1380 Norway joined a union with Denmark and in 1397 through the Union of Kalmar, Sweden became the third member of the Triple Union. In the 1530s the union had broken up and Norway became part of Denmark and was governed by the Danish king. The two countries were often referred to as the 'twin realms'.

In 1537 the Danish king introduced the Lutheran religion as the official religion of the state and it has remained the State Church ever since. Despite Danish rule and thanks to the relative isolation of much of the country, the Norwegians retained a great deal of their national spirit, culture and language, and were able to develop their own industries. Timber mills and shipyards flourished, iron works were established and the Norwegian middle class grew and began to prosper.

Denmark surrendered large areas of Norway after being defeated by Sweden in the 1640s and 1650s and at the Assembly of the States General in Copenhagen in 1660 Frederik III was acclaimed heir to the throne and given the task of producing a new constitution for the two countries. For the first time Norway was subjected to an absolute monarchy which more often than not was in no position to rule.

From the Napoleonic Wars to the Present

Denmark entered the Napoleonic Wars on the side of France, drawing Norway into the fighting alongside her, while Sweden, her former ally, sided against the French. Because of the continental blockade, enormous damage was inflicted on Norway's shipping and trade.

Deep in the grip of winter

Sweden attacked and defeated Denmark and in the Kiel peace settlement that followed Napoleon's defeat in 1814, was given Norway. The Norwegians, who had had no say in this, were furious and rose up in rebellion. Delegates were elected to a constituent assembly at Eidsvoll, to the north of Oslo, and on 17 May 1814 they adopted a constitution for a free, independent and democratically governed Norway.

The constitution adopted that day is still in force and is based on three principles — sovereignty of the people, division of powers and inviolable human rights. It provided for a national assembly (the Storting) elected by the people with the executive power in the hands of the king who was to elect his government.

The foundation for modern industry in Norway was laid in the 1840s with the establishment of the first textile factories and engineering workshops. The merchant fleet expanded rapidly but there were still hard times.

In 1905 the union with Sweden was peacefully dissolved after a referendum in which the overwhelming majority of Norwegians voted for independence. The Treaty of Karlstad was signed in October and Norway became an independent state.

Prince Carl, a member of the Danish royal family, was invited to become king of Norway and he took the name Haakon VII when he ascended the throne in November 1905. The new king became the country's symbol of unity during the construction of independent modern Norway. Norway was neutral during the Great War although the merchant fleet suffered heavy losses because of the submarine war.

Norway is the home of skiing

In 1920 Norway became a member of the League of Nations but the depression hit the country hard and unemployment was severe until the outbreak of World War II.

The German armies attacked Norway in April 1940 and stayed as an occupying power for 5 years. After 2 months of war against the much more powerful army, King Haakon VII and his government escaped to London from where they continued the struggle.

The Germans maintained an army in Norway but the Norwegian resistance movement continued to fight them until the country was liberated on 8 May 1945. The king returned to Norway on 7 June 1945 to towns that had been bombed and many northern provinces razed to the ground. The next 30 years saw sustained growth as industry, the merchant fleet, farming, fishing and forestry flourished, helped largely by North Sea oil and natural gas.

The king died in 1957, aged 85, and was succeeded by his only son, King Olav V, who was born in 1903. He married the Swedish Princess Martha (who died in 1954) and has three children, the Princesses Ragnhild and Astrid and Crown Prince Harald, who is heir to the throne. In 1968 the Crown Prince, through a special act of parliament, married Sonja Haraldsen, who is now the Crown Princess.

National Independence Day (17 May) is Norway's major national holiday and every year wreaths are laid on monuments and church services are held before the celebrations begin. In every town there are colourful processions led by bands and schoolchildren.

Norway joined NATO in 1949 and was a founding member of EFTA in 1969. Despite two applications to join the Common Market — in 1962 and 1965 — the Norwegian people voted against full membership in a referendum in 1972.

Climate

The two most surprising aspects about Norway's weather are that it is much milder than one would imagine, and that it can change very quickly. Even in the far north, despite the latitude, one can get a glorious tan during the never-ending summer days. Temperatures between 25 °C and 30 °C are not uncommon in northern Norway. There are enormous climatic differences because of the sheer size of the country, but the influence of the warm Gulf Stream which raises the temperature of the sea, means that even during winter Norway's harbours are ice-free.

The prevailing, moist westerly winds reach further north in Norway than anywhere else in Europe and deposit a lot of rain, especially in the south and south-west. Inland, however, it can be quite dry in the summer because most of the precipitation falls on the seaward side of the mountains as relief rain.

The mountains and steep sided fjords also have tremendous effects on the weather, and one fjord can be enjoying bright sunshine, while its neighbour is experiencing a downpour. Altitude also affects weather conditions and you can drive from sun-drenched valleys up into thick mist, and then out of it again just as quickly.

The coastal climate is less changeable than inland and in the far north. Coastal summers tend to be cooler because of the higher rainfall and accompanying cloud. Bergen can be very wet but the rain clouds can blow away as fast as they arrive and be replaced by beautiful sunshine.

Summer

During the summer the days are long and in the north there is permanent daylight. Even in Oslo in mid-summer it does not get dark although the sun ducks down behind the horizon and there are 4 or 5 hours of twilight before the very early dawn. July and August are the busiest months and it is advisable to book accommodation in advance for this period.

The Midnight Sun is a phenomenon only found in areas close to the poles. Because the earth moves on an axis, the northern hemisphere is pointed nearer to the sun during the summer and pointed away during the winter. The most northerly latitudes are closest to the sun in the summer, so close in fact, that the sun never really sets below the horizon so there is permanent daylight. The exact opposite is the case during the winter leaving the most northerly latitudes in permanent darkness for much of the time.

The Midnight Sun is a glorious spectacle in its own right but is also a very useful phenomenon because it allows you to see and do so much more. Few people have difficulty adjusting to so much sun and in the far north it is easy to drop into a routine so that you travel and explore when you feel awake, and then sleep for a few hours when you feel tired, irrespective of what time it is, day or night.

These long days of sun in what is a comparatively short summer have an almost immediate effect on plant life. Everything happens much faster than elsewhere, the flowers and plants suddenly burst into life and their life-cycle is speeded up so that they can blossom and shed their seeds in time.

All places north of the Arctic Circle enjoy permanent daylight on Midsummer Day (23 June) the further north one travels, the longer this period extends.

The best time to see the Midnight Sun is the early season and high summer. The sun does not sink below the horizon at the North Cape from the second week in May until the last week in July.

The Midnight Sun can be experienced in:

Svalbard	from 20 April-21 August
North Cape	14 May-30 July
Hammerfest	17 May-28 July
Tromsø	21 May-23 July
Narvik	26 May-19 July
Bodø	5 June-9 July

Autumn

Summers in Norway can linger on well into September, and late summer and early autumn are ideal times to go mountain walking. The crowds have disappeared, the weather is cooler but still not cold, and the colours are magnificent.

Winter

This is the season for skiing in Norway. The best skiing is usually had between Christmas and the end of April although there can be heavy falls both before and long after this period. Weather conditions are usually dry and pleasant in the resorts. The air is crisp, clean and dry. Although the far north may be in permanent darkness (just a couple of hours of twilight a day in mid-winter) and bitterly cold, the southern ski resorts enjoy between 5 and 7 hours of daily sunshine in January, 7 to 10 hours in February, and 12 to 15 hours in April.

Winter is also the time to see that other great phenomenon of the Arctic Circle — the Aurora Borealis. The Northern Lights, as they are also called, can usually be seen between November and February although this is dependent on certain meteorological conditions — it is thought they are connected with periods of intense solar activity when sun spots bombard the earth with protons. The protons are deflected towards the North and South Poles as they hit the earth's magnetic fields creating fascinating patterns of colour and light. It is a sight that can best be witnessed north of the Arctic Circle.

Although the winters are dark they are not depressing. There is an abundance of electricity for street lighting and the Norwegians love light.

The period of winter darkness is:

Svalbard	25 October-16 February
North Cape	18 November-24 January
Hammerfest	20 November-22 January
Tromsø	25 November-17 January
Bodø	14 December-28 December

Spring

Easter provides the last chance for many people to ski in the mountains, and it is the favourite holiday period. A growing number of tourists are now travelling to Norway in May and June to take advantage of the warmer weather. It is not as hot as the summer, but statistics show that these months are drier in Oslo, Bergen and Trondheim than the following two months, the traditional peak tourist season.

	Average temperatures (°C)			Average rainfall (mm)		
	Oslo	Bergen	Tromsø	Oslo	Bergen	Tromsø
January	-5	2	-3	49	179	96
February	-4	1	-4	35	139	79
March	0	3	-3	26	109	91
April	5	6	0	44	104	65
May	11	10	4	44	83	61
June	15	13	9	71	126	59
July	17	15	12	84	141	56
August	16	15	11	96	167	80
September	11	12	7	83	228	109
October	6	8	3	76	236	115
November	1	5	0	69	207	88
December	-2	3	-2	63	203	95

Norway's changing landscape: from cold inhospitable high plateaux to dramatic mountains, forests, glaciers and fjords

Geography and Geology

The Oslo area which accounts for almost a third of the country's population, consists of four regions — Oslo city, Vestfold, Akershus and Østfold.

The eastern half of Norway comprises the regions of Buskerud, Oppland and Hedmark, and is noted for its valley chains, mountains and huge forest areas with excellent walking. It has the country's largest massifs.

Sørland and Telemark make up the southern part of Norway. Sørland has many beautiful little coastal towns and resorts with beaches, while Telemark is famed for its scenery, forests and hills rising up to the southern mountains covering the regions of Telemark, Aust-Agder and Vest-Agder.

West Norway is fjord, mountain and glacier country and comprises Rogaland, Hordaland, Sogn og Fjordane and Møre og Romsdal. It is also the country's main fruit growing area — the region's capital is Bergen.

Trøndelag, consisting of Nord-Trøndelag and Sør-Trøndelag, is the country's historic heartland with Trondheim, Norway's old capital, as the main city. It is an area of deep forests, barren mountains and fertile plains.

The country narrows as you travel northwards through Nordland, then Troms to Finnmark in the far north. These three regions are known as northern Norway and most is above the Arctic Circle. It is the most northerly part of Europe and easily accessible by both car and public transport.

Norway, which means 'the way to the north', stretches along the western coast of the Scandinavian peninsula in north-west Europe. It is a country dominated by mountains, lakes, fjords and forests. Almost half the country lies above the Arctic Circle.

Norway is long, stretching almost 1,800km from south to north and tapering as it goes so that it is barely more than 6km wide at its narrowest point near Narvik. It is one of the largest countries in Europe because of its length and is bordered by the North Sea and the North Atlantic on the west and north, by Sweden to the south and Finland and Russia to the east. The most northern territory is Svalbard, an arctic archipelago which came under Norwegian sovereignty in 1920. Norway also controls Jan Mayen.

About a quarter of the country is more than 1,000m above sea level and the highest peaks — Galdhøpiggen (2,469m) and Glitterinden (2,465m) — are in the great massif of Jotunheimen in the central part of southern Norway. Galdhøpiggen is also the highest mountain in northern Europe.

Norway can lay claim to many other records. Jostedalsbreen in Sogn og Fjordane, is the largest glacier in mainland Europe covering 486sq km; Sognefjorden is the world's longest and deepest fjord. It is on the western coast and runs for 204km from Solund to Skjolden, and it is more than 1,300m deep. Hornindalsvatn is the deepest lake in Europe (500m), and the Hardangervidda, covering 12,000sq km is the largest plateau in Europe.

There are a huge number of waterfalls in Norway which play a vital role in Norway's economy. Because so many plunge such great distances, they have been tapped to provide hydro-electric power for industry and local communities. All the country's electricity comes from this source. There are no nuclear power stations and no plans to construct any. Ironically, while the Norwegians go to great lengths to protect the environment, it is their reliance on hydro-electric power that has done a great deal to mar the countryside as pylons and cables from poles criss-cross the countryside. After Sykkjed-alsfossen (300m), the tallest waterfalls are Vetisfossen in Ardal (275m), Søre Mardalsfoss in Nesset (250m) and Feigumfossen in Luster (200m).

The fjords and lakes, apart from their natural beauty, are also important because they allow access to many parts of the country which would be very difficult and time consuming by road. After Sognefjorden, Hardangerfjorden is the next longest running 179km from Bømlo to Odda. Trondheimsfjorden is 126km long, Porsangen 123km, Nordfjord 106km, and Oslofjorden 100km.

Norway has established 16 national parks and 675 nature reserves, 57 protected reserves and 29 other protected areas covering about 3,000sq km.

Geology

Most of Norway is mountainous and much of the rock can be dated back to the Fenno-Scandian Shield, up to 3,000 million years old. The present-day mountain ranges are remnants of greater chains that dominated the countryside.

Between 400 and 500 million years ago Britain was part of the continental land mass, with the east coast of Scotland approximating roughly to that of western Norway. Because of pressures exerted on this area, the land was forced up producing a mountain range, mostly of ancient granite and known as the Caledonian Fold. Part of this mountain range slowly sank separating the two countries by sea. The mountain range that was left formed the western coast of Norway and over millions of years was subjected to erosion and the action of the sea which produced the fjords. The fjords were originally valleys which flooded as the coastal land sank, and were then gouged even deeper as the glaciers occupied them during the various ice ages. The action of the glaciers on the already sunken valleys explains why they are so deep.

About 50 million years ago, during the Eocene part of the Tertiary Period, the whole landmass was lifted step by step and a new landscape was created. From an undulating landscape with isolated rounded mountains, the countryside of Norway emerged as a huge area of flat-topped highlands with steep escarpments rising from wide basins.

Over the last two or three million years there has been repeated glaciation with massive ice-shields covering most of Scandinavia. The glaciers and ice streams carved out steep-sided deep valleys, while mountain glaciers cut through the massifs leaving the sharp ridges and peaks that can be seen today. Where the glaciers passed over the tops of the mountains they rounded them and left behind the huge plateaux especially in the south of the country.

The largest glacier is Jostedalsbreen covering almost 500sq km, making it the largest glacier on mainland Europe.

Flora and Fauna

Norway is rich in trees and forests cover almost a quarter of the country. The most common trees are spruce, fir and pine, but deciduous trees such as birch are also widespread, and at quite high altitudes.

The vegetation is richest in the south, south-east and south-west parts of the country, regions of dense forests and broad valleys. These valleys often have fast flowing rivers used by the timber men to float the logs down to the mills and the sea. This area is also fertile and the country's main arable region. There are large fruit orchards and cereal farms. Potatoes, other vegetables and fodder crops are grown wherever possible, and well above the Arctic Circle although the growing season is very short. Crops ripen because of the length of the summer days which makes almost continuous growth where there is perpetual daylight possible.

The south of the country has a typical temperate central European vegetation while the north has an arctic flora. On mountain plateaux you can find a vegetation of shrubs, bushes and dwarf trees. The far north has a vegetation mostly of mosses and lichens and ground hugging plants.

The warmth of the Gulf Stream has led to a rich marine life along the west coast and fishing is important both economically and socially. There is concern, however, that some of the world's richest fishing grounds may have been over-fished in recent years, and government measures have been introduced to try to conserve stocks.

The most important species of fish in Norwegian waters — the eastern North Sea, the Norwegian coast, the Barents Sea and the polar front in the Norwegian Sea — are cod, herring, mackerel and capeline, saithe, haddock, torsk, ling, halibut, red-fish, prawns, sprats, squid, blue whiting, sand eel and Norway pout.

The British nobility came to Norway more than a 100 years ago to fish for salmon. There are about 100 good salmon rivers, some of them world famous.

Seal stocks seem to be recovering after the mysterious pneumonia-like virus which decimated their numbers on both sides of the North Sea at the end of the 1980s. Walrus can also be spotted in some areas.

Flowers add a splash of colour to the scenery of Norway

On land, the bear is almost extinct while the elk — the Norwegian moose — is mainly found in southern Norway and Trøndelag. In the summer the elk retreat deep into the forests but it is quite common for them to come into towns during the winter as they forage for food.

The reindeer perhaps conjures up the most evocative pictures of Norway. Huge herds still roam the north under the watchful eyes of the nomadic Lapps who for centuries have earned their living from nomadic reindeer husbandry. The reindeers usually spend the winter grazing on the vast expanses of the Finnmarksvidda, and are driven to the coast for summer grazing. The largest stock of wild reindeer can be found on Hardangervidda. Wild reindeer can still be found in the central mountains, while roe and red deer can be seen in some coastal districts and less often inland.

Bird Watching

There are many excellent areas for birdwatching, some only a few minutes from the centre of Oslo. The capital is surrounded by woods which attract large numbers of birds during the summer, while a number of islands in Oslofjord have bird reserves. Other areas of particular interest are:

Kløfjellet-Hellestrøm: There are bird reserves on the western and northern sides of this region, and on Grasøyane. There are restrictions during the breeding season.

Nordland: Most famous for the bird reserve on the island of Røst which can be reached by either plane or daily car ferry which takes between 4 and 6 hours depending on the weather. It is 97km out to sea off Bodø and south of the Lofoten Islands. The island is 6km long and between 3 and 4km across, and teems with bird life. Details from Polarsirkelen Reiselivslag (tourist board), Postboks 225, N8601-Mo i Rana, ☎ 087 50 421 Other areas of interest in Nordland are Vaerøy, Lovund in Helgeland and Træna. Lurøy has one of Norway's biggest populations of white tailed eagle.

Oppland: Fokstumyra is near Dombås in Dovrefjell and was declared a nature reserve in 1969. There are many paths and marked trails to follow, and species to be seen include crane, ruff, red necked phalarope, blue throat, hen harrier, bar tailed godwit, brambling and blue headed wagtail. Guided tours can be arranged and the best times to visit are in the spring and early summer. Contact Fokstua Fjellstue, N2660 Dombas, ☎ 062 41 497.

Østfold: A bird reserve on Øra outside Fredrikstad.

Rogaland: A number of good bird watching sights here include the remote island of Utsira. It is one of the largest bird reserves along the entire Norwegian coast and there are good boat connections with Haugesund. The best known bird-watching area is on **Revtangen** on the western side of Jæren.

Runde in Møre og Romsdal: The island of Runde has a bridge to the mainland and is about $2^{1}/_{2}$ hours by car from Ålesund. Bird watchers and experts use the Goksøyr campsite and you can gather information from here. Also contact Herøy og Runde Tourist Office, N-6096 Runde, ☎ (070) 85 905.

Some of the bird colonies along the coast have earned the name of bird mountains because every crevice seems to be occupied by one species or another. The two best known bird mountains are Røst and Runde where thousands of gulls and auk breed. Other inhabitants of the seventeen or so bird mountains are kittiwakes, cormorants, puffin, shag, razorbill, black guillemot and herring gull.

Runde, a few kilometres off Ålesund and easily accessible over a bridge, is an ornithologist's paradise. Until recently it was the only place on the Scandinavian mainland where the fulmar and gannet bred — both species have now spread northwards and breed in a number of locations along the Norwegian coast.

There are many excellent bird watching areas including the Dovrefjell National Park. Most of the park is above the tree line and here you can see black throated diver, golden eagle, alpine and willow grouse, arctic skua, golden plover, bluethroat, Lapland and snow bunting and shore lark.

Fokstumyra is a protected area rich in marsh birds although there is a footpath around the reserve. You can see trumpeting cranes, hen harrier, rough-legged buzzard, short eared owl, golden and ringed plover, dunlin, redshank, ruff, wood sandpiper, ring ouzel, fieldfare, Lapland bunting and bluethroat. Great snipe and broad-billed sandpiper have also been seen there.

The snowy owl has nested in the Hardangervidda area, and in Norway's largest primeval coniferous forest, Øvre Pasvik on the Russian border can be found Tengmalm's, short-eared and hawk owl, capercaillie, goshawk, broad-billed sandpiper, jack snipe, waxwing and Siberian jay.

On the Varanger peninsula, a flat, fell landscape with harsh climate there are nesting red and black-throated divers, long tailed duck, smew, peregrine and gyr falcon, rough legged buzzard, falcon gull, arctic skua and common gull, Temminck's stint, dunlin, ringed plover, purple sandpiper, turnstone Mornell plover and raven. Varangerfjord attracts bird watchers from around the world as there are a wide range of species.

For further information contact the ornithological Society:

Norsk Ornitologisk Forening,
Olav Tryggvasons gt 2B/4,
N-7000 Trondheim,
☎ (07) 52 51 42.

The Norwegian People — Their Culture and Heritage

With Sweden, Norway has the largest fair-haired population in Europe and most of the population have blue eyes. Norwegians also have the highest life expectancy of any nation in Europe, and one of the highest in the world.

The Norwegians love the outdoors and most spend much of their free time in the countryside. Cross-country ski trips or summer walks can take several days through remote countryside as the Norwegians enjoy soltitude and the peace and quiet of their country.

Despite centuries of domination, the Norwegians are fiercely patriotic. Flag poles can be found even at the remotest cabin, and the Norwegians will fly the national flag with its blue cross outlined in white on a red background at every opportunity.

The Lapps

The Norwegians descended from Germanic tribes with their fair hair, blue eyes and are easily distinguishable from the Lapps who live in the far north.

Today the Lapps (or Sami as they prefer to be called in English) are found throughout the northernmost parts of Europe, scattered in small groups from the east coast of the Kola peninsula and north Fenno-Scandia to Femunden and Idre in the south. They have managed to retain much of their traditional culture, which often reflects their close involvement with nature and the harsh environment of which they have become masters. They have their own Finno-Ugric language called Sameh which reflects their close links with Finland dating back many centuries before Christ.

Their origins are still not clear but it is thought they have always been nomadic, and are probably descended from a tribe which arrived from central Russia, possibly Siberia. From their settlements in the far north, they gradually moved southwards and before the Viking Age they had already reached Namdalen in Norway and travelled into Sweden. There are even references in the sagas of the Lapps having travelled as far south as Dovre and beyond.

It was not until the beginning of the twentieth century that the Norwegians started to colonise the far north in large numbers and came in contact with the Lapps. The Lapps learnt about animal husbandry and arable farming, how to make flour, how to spin wool and weave, and these skills were passed to other communities. They also started to make boats from wood and the skills of the Sea Lapps were such that they soon became important boat-builders supplying craft throughout the north of Norway.

Attempts by the Scandinavian countries and Russia to tax the Lapps long delayed attempts to settle the various national borders and it was not until 1751 that the border between Norway and Sweden was finally determined, and 1821 between Norway and Russia.

Despite the formalisation of boundaries, the Lapps continued to travel with their herds across frontiers and they retained their own traditions and social structure. Each group had its own territory and clear demarcation of tasks to be done by men and women.

The Lapp's religion is based on 'the freedom of the soul, reverence of their forefathers and Nature's life-giving or destructive powers'. They worshipped thunder, wind, the sun and moon. The bear was thought to be semi-divine, and strangely-shaped rocks were believed to hold power over the success or failure of a hunting or fishing expedition.

Each community had its *shaman, or noaide*, the go-between of the human world and the supernatural. The *shaman* was believed to be able to travel, often in the guise of an animal, to the spirit world to get advice, or help in order to cure the sick. The *shaman* usually 'travelled' while in a trance induced by tribal singing and the beating of a drum. The magical drum skin was painted with figures depicting their gods, and during seances, a piece of horn would be placed on the drum skin and its movements used to foretell the future.

In the eighteenth century, many Lapp communities were converted to Christianity, largely due to the work of Thomas von Westen, the 'Apostle of the Lapps', but they retained many of their beliefs and incorporated them into their new religion.

Today, there are three distinct Lapp groups — the Mountain Lapp, the River Lapp and the Sea Lapp. The Mountain Lapps are the most widespread and can be found anywhere between Varanger and Femunden. Their main livelihood is reindeer husbandry, they are still semi-nomadic although many have acquired houses where their families live for much of the year.

The River Lapps live along rivers in the interior of Finnmark and earn their living from agriculture and animal husbandry, although hunting, fishing and berry picking add considerably to their income.

The largest group of Lapps are the Sea Lapps who live on the North Norwegian fjords between Varanger and Tysfjord. They mostly fish and farm and their lifestyle now closely resembles that of the Norwegians who settled there at the turn of the century.

The pressure on the Lapps has never been greater, nor the threat to their language and culture. They have had to enter the commercial world and many have adopted the trappings of twentieth century living. Great efforts are now being made to preserve the Lapp identity and their rights. Lappish has been introduced in all schools as an optional language, and courses are run at many colleges and universities. There is now a Lapp museum (in Karasjok), the first Lapp language newspaper *Sami Aigi* (Lapp Times), and a committee for the promotion of Lapp literature.

Bright, traditional costumes contrast sharply with the snow

Every 3 years Lapps from Norway, Finland and Sweden meet for the Nordic Lapp Council, and this set up the Nordic Lapp Institute to carry out research into and to protect Lapp cultural traditions and rights.

The Lapps are gifted artistically as can be seen from their elaborate carvings, embroidery, and the clothes they wear. Their art, both carvings and paintings, is now being appreciated more, and there has been a revival in traditional lapp music and song, especially among the young Lapps.

Today Lapps can be seen throughout Norway but many of those in the south have discovered the advantages of tourism, and they have set up their tents and stalls alongside popular routes to offer their goods for sale. The further north you travel, the more likely you are to see Lapps in their normal habitat, and the better able to understand the lifestyle they choose to follow.

Architecture

The most striking aspect of Norwegian architecture is its use of wood. Timber has been the building material for thousands of years and the Norwegians have perfected the art of creating homes that are both very functional and aesthetically appealing.

As you drive through the country you are constantly reminded of how durable wood is as a building material if used correctly. The marvellous stave churches (dealt with on page 41) are still standing in all their glory although some are more than 800 years old. Ancient farmsteads are still lived in and centuries-old store barns (*stabburer*) and other old buildings are generally not left to fall into disrepair but are faithfully restored.

There are numerous outdoor rural museums throughout Norway which are often collections of the oldest houses and barns in the district. As with the Norwegian Folk Museum in Oslo, these buildings were carefully dismantled and then painstakingly rebuilt on a site where they could be both visited and protected.

Most towns consisted almost entirely of wooden buildings and over the centuries, many have witnessed massive fires which have destroyed whole quarters, but surprisingly old houses still remain, a testament to the skill of their builders.

It was not until Norwegian Independence in 1814 that there was a sudden increase in demand for new buildings to house the administrators and legislators and this sparked a wave of construction using stone. Stone also enjoyed popularity because of the fire risk from timber buildings. As there was little expertise in these building methods, foreign architects were employed, but their skills were quickly picked up by Norwegians, many of whom went to Germany to qualify. The old Oslo University is the best surviving example of this period.

The Norwegian's love of wood saw a resurgence of timber buildings in the latter half of the last century and the emergence of the distinctive 'dragon' style, inspired by the secular log houses and stave churches of the Middle Ages. Since the last war the need for urban housing has led to large-scale brick building although the interiors are often finished in wood. Pine-panelled walls, pine floors and elaborately-carved pine stairs and bannisters can be found in many homes.

Art and Culture

Art and culture have always figured prominently in Norwegian life, from the earliest rock drawings painted more than 5,000 years ago. Today museums abound throughout the country, music concerts take place in the smallest communities and almost any scene can provide the inspiration for a writer, artist, composer or sculptor.

For many years the national policy has been to preserve as much culture as possible. As well as national ballet and opera and a number of permanent theatres, there is a national touring theatre. The main cities have their own symphony orchestra and these are supplemented by national touring orchestras. In addition there are museums and art collections, also supplemented by travelling exhibitions, and public libraries.

The most ancient literary remains surviving are runic inscriptions on tombstones and the history of Norwegian literature can then be traced in a number of steps. The first great literary period was between AD700 and 1300, the age of the sagas when the country's history, legends and folklore were recorded. Many of these works as now regarded as world classics.

The period under Danish rule, often referred to as the 'four hundred years' night', saw little literature produced although the priest-poet Petter Dass lived in Norway in the seventeenth century. The Age of Enlightenment from the late eighteenth century to the mid-1850s, produced literary giants such as Ludvig Holberg and Henrik Wergeland.

The second half of the nineteenth century is known as the Golden Age. It is best remembered for the works of world-famous playwright Henrik Ibsen (1828-1906), and Nobel prize winning dramatist Bjørnstjerne Bjørnson (1832-1910), who wrote the words of Norway's national anthem. Other great names from this period are Jonas Lie and Alexander Kielland, who were followed by Arne Garborg and Hans Kinck.

Two of the most outstanding writers of this century were the lyricist Knut Hamsun (1859-1952) and historical novelist and women's rights champion Sigrid Undset (1882-1949) who both won the Nobel Prize for Literature.

There has been a further renaissance in Norwegian literature since World War II. Many of these authors such as Dag Solstad, Kjartan Fløgstad, Tor Obrestad, Cecilie Løveid and Knut Faldbakken were born in the 1940s and 1950s and their writings reflect the freedom and optimism as the country recovered after the war. Popular modern writers include Edvard Hoem, Peder W.Cappelen and Arne Skouen.

Norway's first dramatist was Ludvig Holberg who was born in Bergen at the end of the seventeenth century although he wrote all his comedies in Denmark. Norway's first theatre opened in Oslo, or *Christiania* as it was then called in 1827, and in 1850 the Norwegian Theatre opened in Bergen and Ibsen was one of its first artistic directors (1851-6).

Theatre tickets throughout Norway are heavily subsidised by the state. Opera is relatively new to Norway and although small companies were established at the turn of the century, Norwegian Opera was not established until 1957 with Kirsten Flagstad, one of the world's leading interpreters of Wagner, as its first director. It is financed entirely by the government.

Norway's first independent professional ballet company, Ny Norsk Ballett, was established in 1948 although it did not have its own theatre. In 1958 it merged with the Norwegian Opera Company. Bergen became home to a new ballet company in 1989.

Folk music in Norway can trace its roots back to Viking times and it represents an unbroken tradition as popular today as it was 1,000 years ago. There are more brass bands in Norway as well as hundreds of choirs, rock and pop groups and jazz bands. The jazz festivals at Molde and Kongsberg attract international artists and fans.

Bronze horns dating from between 1500 and 500BC show that song and music have long traditions in Norway. Scaldic poems of the Viking Age and carvings on the stave churches show that the music played in the Middle Ages in Norway was very similar to the musical traditions of central Europe. The first descriptions of church organs in Norway date from the early 1300s and it was the church and ecclesiastical organisations that maintained the musical tradition during the next 450 years of Danish rule.

It is because of this Danish rule that the history of classical music is comparitively recent and dominated by the composer Edward Grieg (1843-1907), one of Norway's most famous sons. A visit to Bergen and Grieg's beautiful hilltop home is essential, as is a visit to the city's Grieg Hall, which attracts world famous musicians.

The Musikselskabet Harmonien Orchestra, now the Bergen Philarmonic, was founded in the city in 1765 and is one of the oldest orchestras in the world. The Oslo Philarmonic Orchestra, which has developed an international reputation is based in the modern concert hall in the capital and many of its musicians come from the State Academy of Music. The Norwegian Chamber Music Orchestra is considered one of the four best worldwide.

Norway has produced many world class soloists, the first being the nineteenth-century violinist Ole Bull, whose virtuosity was often compared with that of Paganini. Ole Bull is virtually unknown outside Norway but as a composer and violinist, he was one of a small group of international musicians who shaped the cultural profile of Europe and North America in the 1800s.

Other internationally-famous performers include the soprano Kirsten Flagstad, violinist Arve Tellefson, and the singers Ingrid Bjoner Edith Thallaug, Knut Skram and Ragnar Ulfung. World class pianists include Robert Riefling, Eva Knardhal, Einar Steen-Nøkleberg and Kjell Baekkelund.

Other composers include Sparre Olsen, Eivind Groven, Geirr Tveitt and Harald Saeverud, the most notable modern composer is Arne Nordheim.

Painting and sculpture are as old as Norway itself. Today's handicrafts frequently reflect styles and images first used by the Vikings, while the Lapps' carvings stick faithfully to age-old designs and patterns.

The art of painting was not really practised until after 1215 when skills were brought back to Bergen from England. During the Middle Ages these skills were mainly used to produce frontals, a painting depicting Christ or one of the saints which was stood in front of the altar. Several of these dating back to the mid-thirteenth century have been preserved.

The most famous artists in Norway, especially those in the nineteenth century, took nature and rustic life as their subjects. They included Johann Dahl, the most famous of Norway's romantic painters, Hans Gude, August Cappelen, Adolph Tidemand and Lars Hertervig.

Edward Munch (1863-1944) stands out as the greatest twentieth-century artist with his vivid expressionist style. He was a prolific artist depicting haunting scenes of loneliness and death, as well as vibrant pictures bursting with life and health. The Munch Museum, donated by the artist to the City of Oslo, opened in 1963 and houses more than 2,000 of his works.

Norway has produced many other outstanding painters this century such

Wood has always been an important building material in Norway

as Harald Sohlberg, Halfdan Egedius and Nikolai Astrup, and more recently Jean Heiberg, Jakob Weidemann, Franz Widerberg, Henrik Sørensen, Axel Revold and Per Krogh. Hannah Ryggen is noted for her unique tapestries.

Oslo's first art exhibition was held in 1818 and the National Gallery was founded in 1837. In 1882 Norwegian artists organised their own exhibition there, and 2 years later the event was taken over by the government and is now held annually.

Norway has two state galleries, the National Gallery and the National Museum of Contemporary Art, as well as numerous private and muncipal ones. The government, through the Norwegian Cultural Council, provides funds for the decoration of public buildings throughout the country, and purchases Norwegian art so that it can be distributed and viewed nationwide.

The building decoration or 'monumental' art was particularly popular between the two world wars, and perhaps the finest example can be seen in the figures decorating Oslo's City Hall. The artists involved included Per Krogh, Anne Grimdalen, who created the statue of King Harald Hårdråde on the west wall, and Emil Lie, responsible for the bronze and granite statues in front of the building. The most famous statues in Norway, however, are those found in Oslo's Vigeland Park, part of Frogner Park.

Another typical Norwegian folk art is *rosmaling*, the painting of rose patterns. These patterns can be found on almost anything. *Rosmaling* is now a term used to describe rustic painting in general not just the reproduction of roses and other flowers. It can include a wide range of figure motifs, geometrical patterns, and sometimes even landscapes.

The oldest rose painting dates from around 1700 but the practice reached its peak at the end of the eighteenth and beginning of the nineteenth centuries although the art survived in many areas until the 1850s.

Rosmaling as an art form was really restricted to the districts of Telemark and Hallingdal. Red, blue, green and white are the favourite colours on a blue, green or white background, and at first just utensils were decorated, and then walls and finally whole buildings.

The Telemark rose painting borrowed a lot from the Rococo style and many of the earlier artists such as Ola Hansson, Thomas Luraas, Talleiv Maalar and Thomas Blix who decorated many Telemark churches, show a strong urban influence. Telemark consists of valleys, which in those days would have been relatively isolated, so there is no such thing as a Telemark style, rather a series of schools, following the same ideas but showing different development.

Customs and Traditions

Most Norwegians take keep fit very seriously. Those living in built up areas go walking, jogging or cycling during the summer, and all ages don skis during the winter. Even in Oslo itself there are wooded trails to follow.

The Norwegians love the countryside and look after it. There is hardly any litter, walks are well signposted and on the many public holidays and flag days you can mix with the thousands of locals who will be enjoying themselves in the open air whatever the weather. They like skating and sailing, fishing and hunting and going to their cottages.

The Norwegians are also very hospitable and friendly. Many speak English, especially the younger people who learn it at school so communication is not a problem except in isolated areas.

The Norwegian's generosity may well lead to an invitation to visit their homes and if so it is customary to follow the rules of etiquette. You should always take a gift for the hostess — or host if he lives alone — the first time you are a guest in their home. This is usually a box of sweets, some flowers or a speciality from your own country. As a new male guest you will be seated at the head of the table, as the guest of honour, with the hostess on your right.

The other tradition which should be followed is that when dessert arrives, you should say thankyou to her on behalf of all the guests for her hospitality. The speech should be brief and humorous, and end with a toast to the hostess. It is also custom that each guest will shake hands with the hostess as they leave the table. They usually say *takk for maten* (thank you for the food), and if you can remember to repeat this you will leave a good impression.

The Norwegians love dinner parties and tables are usually graced with candles which play an important role in many of their celebrations. There are a number of special occasions to celebrate during the year. Many of these are religious festivals such as Palm Sunday, Easter, Ascension Day and Christmas. Others are Flag Days such as New Year's Day, Liberation Day, National Independence Day and the birthdays of members of the royal family, and then there are public holidays. These special days provide another excuse for them to wear their national costume, which varies from area to area. It is another symbol of their independence and they wear it as often as possible.

Most Norwegians like to be with their families for these special festivals whether it be in the family home or the cottage. Many people ski during the Easter holiday. Apart from its religious importance, Easter is also seen as a celebration of the end of winter, and for many it is the last chance to get their skis on before the warmer weather melts the snow.

Midsummer Eve holds a special place in Norwegian's lives. It is a time when people take to their boats with a picnic basket and blankets, and as the boats bob in the water, other people light huge bonfires along the shore.

Christmas is the biggest festival of the year. It is the time for special foods and preparations start weeks before the holiday. The special Christmas beer *juleøl* is brewed, and traditional pork dishes, and many different kinds of cakes and biscuits are prepared.

In the windows of houses burn seven advent candles although Christmas trees are not put up until Christmas Eve. On 24 December the church bells start to peal vigorously around 5pm to ring in Christmas and then most people go to church before sitting down to a special Christmas dinner and then exchanging presents. In some districts the Christmas festivities do not officially end until 13 January — the twentieth day of Christmas and the Feast Day of St Canute. There is an old Nordic saying that 'on the twentieth day Canute drives Christmas away'.

Food and Drink

The Norwegians take their food seriously and there are very many traditional dishes. While there are international restaurants, cafés, burger bars and pizza restaurants in the major towns and cities, traditional cooking still thrives, especially in the countryside and a meal in a private home is usually a very enjoyable experience.

The Norwegians enjoy a very healthy diet and have one of the world's highest consumptions of fish, milk and cheese. They love berries and again there are many special dishes using the various wild berries that can be harvested and reserved for particular occasions in the year.

The day starts with *frokost* (breakfast) which is usually substantial as the Norwegians normally have a very light lunch. Porridge is very popular, as well as other cereals. This may be followed by smoked fish and cold meats, assorted cheeses, a variety of breads and jams. Marinated herrings are delicious with brown bread, but one may also be offered crispbreads, oatmeal biscuits, potato scones, flat bread and waffles. Salads may be offered together with fruit juices, milk and coffee. The Norwegians love good coffee and fine tea. It is possible in hotel restaurants and cafés to have a continental breakfast by asking for *kaffe-complet*.

Lunch or *middag*, is usually little more than a snack. It is possible to get a more substantial meal in a restaurant. In cafés and smaller restaurants lunch is usually served up to 4pm and consists of soup, a fish or meat course and dessert. Of course, it is also possible to order à la carte. In larger restaurants and hotels, lunch is generally served from 1pm and a cold buffet is very popular, although this usually includes some hot dishes as well. Open sandwiches are available throughout the day.

Most working Norwegians, however, stop for only half an hour or so. They usually have a sandwich of cold meats, fish or cheese and build up their appetite for their evening meal. The large hotels offer both set dinner menus and à la carte, while smaller hotels tend to offer a cold table with a choice of a few hot dishes. The main meal of the day (*middagsmat*) is usually eaten in the early evening.

Fish is fresh, plentiful and excellent. Salmon (*laks*) and trout (*ørret*) can be served in a number of ways. *Gravlaks* is salmon marinated in dill, sugar, salt and pepper and is usually served with boiled potatoes, or hot potato salad. One of the fascinating things about eating in Norway is that recipes change as you move from one county to another, and every family has a slightly different way of preparing traditional dishes.

There is marvellous halibut (*hellefisk*), plaice and sole, crawfish and lobster (*hummer*) in the late summer, and cod (*torsk*) which is served in countless different ways. Bergen is famous for its fish soup.

There is *klippfisk*, which is dried, salted cod; *lutefisk*, cod steeped in potash and a prized delicacy; and *torsk med eggesaus* — cod poached and served with chopped, hard-boiled egg, tomato, parsley and chives.

Cod is often served with plain boiled potatoes and the Norwegians have learnt not to waste anything. Many dishes include fish heads, the liver which can be boiled and sliced, the roe and the tongue — all now regarded as delicacies.

Other fish to try include eel (*ål*), mackerel (*makrell*) which are often smoked (*røket*), *rakørret* which is fermented trout, *rekesaus* a shrimp or prawn dish in a cream, milk, lemon juice, dill and butter sauce, and herring (*sild*), which is served in innumerable ways. *Spekesild* is salt herring, *skalldyr* shellfish, and *tørrfisk* dried fish. You can also try Norwegian caviare which comes in tubes and is spread on sandwiches.

Fiskepudding is ground fish flakes, flour, milk, butter, cream and seasoning, baked in a mould, while *fiskeboller* consists of the same ingredients which are moulded into fish balls. *Fiskesuppe* is a filling fish soup which may have carrots, parsnips, leeks, potatoes, onion, celery and bay added, and is then thickened using cream and egg yolks.

Pork (*svinekjøtt*) is the most popular meat, and pork spare ribs provide the traditional Christmas dinner in most Norwegian homes inland, while *lutefisk* is generally eaten along the coast. Try elk (*elg*) or reindeer (*reinsdier*) or any of the game birds such as ptarmigan (*rype*), grouse and *capercaillie* which can be served fresh or smoked. There is plentiful mutton, beef (*oksekjøtt*), lamb (*lammekjøtt*), chicken (*kylling*), veal (*kalve*) and venison (*rädadyr*).

Betasuppe is a farmhouse mutton soup, and *fenalår* is dried, salted leg of lamb, while *dyrestek* is roast venison, often served with a sauce of goat's cheese and redcurrant jelly. Whole sheep's heads (*smalahovud*) are a great favourite, especially around Voss.

Får i kål is a Norwegian speciality, a stew of mutton and fresh, crisp cabbage seasoned with salt and black pepper. Other meat dishes include *kjøttkaker med surkål*, meat balls with sauerkraut; *kongesuppe*, a thick soup with meat balls, peas, onions and carrots; another speciality *lapskaus* which is a thick stew of chopped meat and vegetables and *pinnekjøtt*, salt cured dried mutton ribs traditionally steamed over birch twigs, and eaten with the fingers. Another treat is *juleskinke*, boiled ham which is then marinated for 2 or 3 weeks.

The Norwegians love warming stews and sausages (*pølser*), and almost any kind of salted, dried or smoked meats. Game is often served with cranberries, linganberries or snowberries, and these figure in a number of desserts. There are blueberries (*blåbær*) and raspberries (*bringbær*), cloudberries (*multer*), and cranberries (*tyttebær*).

Dravle is a mixture of curds and whey sweetened with syrup; *bløtkake* is a speciality, a cream-filled sponge with fresh fruit or jam and covered in cream; and *eggedosis* is a rich, sweet egg sauce which can have brandy or rum added, and which is eaten alone or poured over bilberries.

Fløtvafler are waffles made with a sour cream, ginger or cardamom batter; *himmelsk lapskaus* (which means 'heavenly pot-pourri') is fresh fruit and nuts served with *eggedosis*; and *kransekaka* is a cake of layered marzipan rings made for special occasions. A very interesting dessert is *lompe*, a pancake made from mashed potato, cream and flour, grilled and served with sugar and jam.

There are many different types of cheese made from cow and goat's milk. Some to watch out for are *gammelost* which has a sharp taste and an even sharper smell; *gjetost* a sweetish goat's cheese; *nøkkelost*, a semi-hard cheese with cloves and caraway seeds, and *pultost*, a soft cheese, sometimes with caraway seeds. Jarlsbergost and ridderost are very popular cheeses, with a caramel-like taste, which are great with bread.

A few words that may be helpful when consulting the menu, or asking for something in a restaurant, are: *brød* : bread, *fisk* : fish, *fløte* : cream, *grønnsaker* : vegetables, *kaffe* : coffee, *kjøtt* : meat, *melk* : milk, *ost* : cheese, *poteter* : potatoes, *regning* : bill, *smør* : butter, *spisekart* : menu, *sukker* : sugar, *te* : tea, *vann* : water, *vin* : wine, and *øl* : beer.

Drink

Drink in Norway is expensive and at times difficult to come by. All wines and spirits are sold through state-owned shops (Vi*nmonopolet*) which can be found in most towns and larger villages. They are heavily taxed and you normally have to join large queues waiting to be served although the system is very efficient. As you enter the shop you take a number and then wait for that number to come up at one of the serving points.

Beer is good and available in a number of strengths from *pils*, a light lager style, *brigg*, which is almost non-alcoholic and *bayer*, a light dark beer. Export is the strongest *pils* type of beer and *bokkøl* is the strongest dark beer. Try the excellent *mackøl*, from the world's most northern brewery.

Akevitt is the only spirit produced in Norway. It is not unlike vodka, is drunk neat and often accompanies traditional Norwegian food. It is a strong liquor distilled from potatoes.

Alcoholic beer is not always readily available in country areas, and in some shops it has to be ordered for delivery up to a week ahead. Most restaurants and hotels are licensed to sell wine and beer, and the larger hotels will serve spirits as well, but only between 3pm and 11pm outside tourist areas. Measures are about double those in England. On Sundays and holidays hotels and restaurants are not allowed to sell spirit.

Glögg is a mulled wine traditionally offered by hosts to their guests as they arrive on cold winter nights. It is mulled red wine with cloves, cinnamon, raisons (occasionally fortified with something stronger) and has the power to warm and revive quickly no matter how cold you may be.

Government

Norway is a constitutional monarchy with a parliamentary system. The constitution was approved at the Constituent Assembly in Eidsvoll in 1814 and apart from occasional amendments, is still valid today making it the oldest written constitution in Europe. A large painting depicting the Assembly now hangs behind the President and the Speaker's chair in the Storting.

Executive power is formally vested in the king, but is exercised through a Council of State (the Cabinet), which can only operate with the backing of a majority in the Storting, the National Assembly. The king, who is also Commander in Chief of the armed forces and head of the church, has sole power to appoint the government, but in effect this is always done with the advice of the leader of the winning party or coalition.

All legislative and taxation powers are vested in the Storting to which representatives are elected by proportional representation every 4 years in a general election. The Storting had 165 members in 1990 although the number of representatives has steadily increased over the years. It cannot be dissolved until it has run full term.

The Storting is divided into two chambers, the larger Odelsting and the Lagting. The former vets all proposed legislation, and its findings then have to be endorsed by the latter. The largest political parties are Labour and

Conservative, followed by Party of Progress, Christian Democrat, Centre and Socialist Left. The right to vote was extended to all men in 1898 and to women in 1913. The voting age is 18.

Norway is divided into 19 counties and 454 municipalities, with an extensive system of local government at both county and local level. Representatives are elected every 4 years, midway between the national elections.

Norway's foreign policy is based on active involvement in international cooperation, through membership of the United Nations, NATO and the OECD. Great emphasis is also placed on Norway's relations with the Third World, and the country is the world's largest contributor per capita of development aid.

As the northern flank of NATO, Norway has general conscription for men, although women can volunteer to serve. The 50,000-strong army includes about 12,000 civilian employees, but when fully mobilised with Reservists, it numbers about 320,000.

Language

More than a thousand years ago the first Nordic settlers all spoke the same language whether they were living in Russia, Scandinavia, the Orkneys or Greenland. There were modest differences in dialect but it was not until the late Middle Ages that major changes took place emanating from southern Denmark. As Norway was the country furthest away, it retained the roots of the earlier common Nordic language the longest. Ironically this ancient Nordic language could be written down but it was gradually submerged as Danish became dominant.

The Norwegian language that gradually evolved was closely related to Swedish and Danish which explains why people from all three countries can usually understand each other. Traditionally the language spoken in the towns and cities was Riksmål (now called Bokmål), which was very similar to written Danish because of the countries close ties. In the mid-nineteenth century the gifted linguist Ivar Aasen (1813-1896) developed the Norwegian written language Landsmål, which literally means 'country speech', as an alternative. Bokmål reflected the dialects of the towns, while Landsmål — now called Nynorsk — reflected the dialects of rural areas which were less influenced by Denmark. It is difficult for outsiders to understand why a country which 150 years ago possessed no written language of its own, and relied on Danish, now has two.

Both languages now have official status. Broadcasters are obliged to use both according to an agreed ratio, while municipalities can choose which one is to be used in schools. About 16 per cent of schoolchildren are taught in Nynorsk — new Norwegian.

Whichever Norwegian language the schoolchildren are taught in, the other is taught as a second language and children in secondary schools have to demonstrate a reading and writing ability in both.

Repeated attempts have been made to try to combine the two languages into one called Samnorsk but has been unsuccessful so far. At present maps and road signs for example, can be in either language.

The country's third language is Sámi, or Lappish, used by the Lapps in the north. It derives from the same root as Hungarian, a clue to their probable ancestry.

Trade and Economy

Norway has been a trading nation since the time of the Vikings and its boat-building skills have produced the craft needed to transport its goods and purchases across the seas. Today Norway has the fifth largest merchant navy in the world although many vessels now fly under foreign flags.

For centuries Norway relied heavily on agriculture and fishing for exports but access to plentiful hydro-electric power through harnessing waterfalls, and then the exploitation of its North Sea oil and gas, transformed the country's economy and boosted its industrial growth.

Small coastal towns mushroomed during the oil boom, and many switched from traditional industries to servicing the oil fields. Others, such as Stavanger, specialised in building the giant oil rigs needed for the North Sea and elsewhere, and became the country's oil capital and headquarters of Statoil, the national oil corporation.

Today, falling oil prices around the globe, have hit Norway's economy and measures have been introduced to restore the equilibrium. The oil boom led to inflation and higher wages; Norway was pricing itself out of international markets. The package of austerity measures introduced by the government in the late 1980s was aimed at redressing this and 'will remain in force until Norway has regained its competitive ability on the international market'.

The policy is working and with wage rises severely limited, inflation and interest rates have been falling. At that same, however, Norway is still one of the world's richest countries. It was recently second only to Switzerland in the rankings of highest gross national product per head of population.

The merchant fleet is still very buoyant, North Sea oil production is ten times Norway's own requirements and still increasing. All this is backed by enormous resources of cheap hydro-electric power. About a fifth of the power produced goes to the electrochemical and electrometallurgical industries. Norway is Europe's main producer of unwrought aluminium and ferro-alloys.

Oil extraction, mining, quarrying and manufacture, especially metal products, machinery and equipment, are the major employers outside farming, forestry and fishing. The electronic intelligence sector is growing fast, as is Norway's petrochemical and oil refining industry.

Agriculture

In no other country in the world is commercial farming carried out as far north as it is in Norway. The country's agriculture comprises farming, forestry, horticulture and reindeer keeping, with farming representing the most important sector. Agriculture and farm-based activities are the most important industries in many communities, and in districts where there is little industry, two in three people are engaged in farming.

The best farming areas are in the south-east, south-west and in Trøndelag in central Norway, where these regions enjoy a relatively favourable climate, flat fields and fertile soils. Field sizes tend to be small because of the nature of the land. Part-time farming is very common, especially in areas with relatively good employment prospects in other industries. More than half of all farm families receive more than half their income from non-farming jobs.

Dairying is the most important sector, followed by meat production, cereals and horticulture. Most of the arable land is best suited to grass and other fodder crops which explains livestock's dominant position, and they can be grown even at high altitudes.

Most cereal production, barley, oats and wheat, is in the south and around Trøndelag. Potatoes are grown almost everywhere, while commercial production of vegetables and berries is restricted to the south and south-west corners of the country which have the mildest climate. Reindeer farming is concentrated in the four northernmost counties and in a few areas in the south.

Norway is working towards a production goal of meeting the domestic demand for milk and milk products, meats, eggs, potatoes and storable vegetables, and to produce as much as possible of other vegetables, fruits and berries. The policy is also to support agriculture so that rural populations are maintained, and jobs provided for them, and to protect the environment and husband resources as efficiently as possible. In agriculture, only forestry and fur production are export-orientated.

Three important features of Norway:
the oil industry, passenger ferries and watersports

Fishing

Norway has jurisdiction over some of the world's richest fishing waters. The North Sea, the Norwegian coast, the Barents Sea and the polar front in the Norwegian Sea are some of the most highly productive marine environments in the world's oceans.

Large fisheries have their spawning grounds right off the coast and the relatively cool North Atlantic waters also provide excellent conditions for producing top quality fish catches.

Norway has superb fishing rivers

Through most of its history, fishing has been among the most important of Norway's industries and provided jobs for most of the coastal population. Today, only 2 per cent of the population is directly involved in fishing with about the same percentage engaged in fish processing and exports. Many more people, however, are employed in secondary industries, such as fishing equipment and service sectors.

Because of the economic importance of oil and the growth of land-based industry, fishing now contributes less than one per cent of Norway's gross national product although it is still extremely important to the country.

Along large areas of the coast, especially in the north, the industry is vital to isolated settlement for employment. There are about thirty coastal communities where fishing and fish processing accounts for almost a third of all jobs.

In 1977 Norway established a 200 nautical mile economic zone around its coast to protect stocks and the livelihoods of the fishermen. This has subsequently been extended to include the Spitsbergen Islands and Jan Mayen Island. These huge marine resources are managed either directly by Norway, or in cooperation with other nations, with the aim of controlling fishing to conserve stocks.

Fish farming has evolved over the last 20 years and is now economically the largest single sector of the fishing industry. The main species raised are salmon and trout. Research is now concentrating on new fish to breed and raise. A small quantity of mussels and oysters, crawfish, cod and turbot is already being produced, although the main aim is to bring halibut into commercial production by 1995. Other candidates include plaice and wolf-fish.

Forestry

The forest is one of Norway's most important sources of raw materials and the basis of the country's most important land-based industries.

The best timber is cut into lumber. The rest of the wood goes mainly to the wood processing industry. Cellulose and paper, mostly newsprint, are the most important products and are mainly exported.

Oil

The discovery of huge oil reserves in the North Sea led to many traditional fishing areas being closed to trawlermen but the benefits to Norway have been phenomenal. Exploration for oil only started in 1966 and the first results were all disappointing. The breakthrough came on 23 December 1969 when workers on the drilling rig Ocean Viking smelled oil. Further drilling revealed what the president of Phillip Petroleum called 'a giant oil field'. That was in May, 1970 and the field, directly north of the border with Denmark and at the southernmost point of the Norwegian continental shelf, was named Ekofisk.

Throughout the 1970s new oilfields were discovered. Statfjord, discovered by Mobil, was the world's largest offshore oil field, and the French oil company Elf found the gas field Frigg. Shell discovered another gigantic gas field north-west of Bergen which they called Troll.

Within 4 years of the discovery of Ekofisk, a pipeline had been laid across the North Sea to Teesside. By 1975 production was so great that Norway started oil exports and in 1977 gas was exported, both to West Germany and Scotland.

Although the first discoveries were made by foreign companies, three Norwegian concerns were established to continue exploration and develop finds. These were Statoil and saga and a company established by Norsk-Hydro. All are now major forces in the North Sea oil and gas industry.

Oil production has steadily increased and is set to continue at least until the late 1990s but Norway is confident that new fields will have been discovered by then. Gas reserves will last for at least 100 years and Norway has been exporting gas to West Germany, France, Holland and Belgium for more than 10 years. Water power for electricty is so common in Norway that the country has had no need for gas so almost all has been exported.

National Parks and Nature Reserves

The government has a vigorous environmental protection policy and to date sixteen National Parks have been established to safeguard areas of the countryside which have distinctive characteristics. In addition, areas of special scientific value are also being identified and protected.

A National Park is usually a large area of mainly untouched land and its landscape, plant and animal life, natural and cultural landmarks, are all protected against development, construction work, pollution of all kinds and other encroachment. Special regulations apply to the National Parks, nature reserves and protected areas, and detailed information about each of them can be obtained from regional commissioners or borough conservation officers.

Special reserves have been established along the coast to protect nesting birds. It is forbidden to drive in these areas between 15 April and 15 July and people must keep at least 50m away from the land in these areas. It is also illegal to camp, light fires or let dogs off leashes in these areas which are clearly signposted.

A Look At Some Of The National Parks

BØRGEFJELL, which covers 1,087sq km on the boundary between Nord-Trøndelag and Nordland, was established by Royal Decree in August 1963. It is a highland area with differing landscapes and full of lakes, rivers and streams. The major part of Børgefjell mountain is alpine terrain with high peaks, ice quarried cirques and deep valley gorges. The highest peak is Kvigtind (1,703m).

Granite dominates the stark, impressive features of Store Børgefjell, while the Raines mountains and some other areas have huge slopes of coarse rocks and no vegetation. There is evidence throughout the park of glacial activity with glacial deposits, debris left by avalanches and heaps of moraine material.

Børgefjell, however, is not a lifeless desert of stone. There are fertile hillsides and broad sheltered valleys which support a rich flora and fauna, as do the marshes in the low lying areas which are an important feature of the park's landscape.

The largest lake is Simskarvatn and the main rivers running south are Jengeland Orr, while the water from Lake Sipmek runs eastwards over the border into Sweden. North of the watershed the rivers run into the Tipling valley and emerge to form the Susna. The rivers are large and torrential and in flood can be very difficult and dangerous to cross. There are some wonderful waterfalls towards Namsvatnet.

The park enjoys a suboceanic climate with parts having quite high humidity and cold winters. The high mountain ridges act as an effective barrier against moist sea winds so the eastern side of the park gets partial protection from the rains sweeping in from the west. The most stable weather period is during August. Winters are hard with very heavy snowfalls.

A large part of the park lacks vegetation because many areas were until quite recently covered by glaciers. Vegetation cover, however, is developing and spreading fast. The coniferous tree line is about 600m and the little evergreen forest in the area is mostly restricted to the south and south-west.

Most of the forests are of birch and elsewhere heath vegetation dominates, mostly sedge grass and blueberry. Snow-bed society plants are plentiful as are dwarf willows. The waters are too cold to produce rich vegetation and there is no river moss anywhere in the park. To date almost 300 species of vascular plants have been recorded. The park is of great zoological interest with large numbers of birds around the lower end of the Simskar river and western Tiplingen.

Access: There are no roads into the National Park and the usual route is to walk in from Majavatn, Susendal or the Fipling valley. A good place to start your explorartion is the Lapp camp at Fagerneset on Namsvatnet, which is no longer regularly used, although to get there you will have to cross the lake by boat. From Smalåsen in Namsskogan there is a path into the National Park which bridges the Storelva.

There are no marked paths or trails in the park although some of the rivers are bridged, and the only accommodation is three rather dilapidated reindeer herders' cabins, one in the Lotter valley, one at the mouth of the Guikare and one at the lower Båttjern, south-west of Tiplingen. Many of the cabins marked on the large scale maps no longer exist or now belong to hunting and fishing associations and are locked. Camping is allowed in the park and there are mountain inns at Harvasstua and Kroken outside the park's north-east boundary, and Smalåsen and Majavatn to the west, and Gjersvik in Røyrvik.

ØVRE ANARJÅKKA, a 1,390sq km area covering the southernmost part of Finnmark, was founded in 1975 forms a huge area of unspoilt northern latitude forest and plateau. The area is very remote and there is hardly any tourist traffic. The park provides an ideal opportunity to study a flora and fauna that has remained virtually unchanged for many centuries and unaffected by civilisation other than the grazing of domestic reindeer.

The park is a gently undulating plateau with many low hills. The lowest point is in the east about 215m above sea level, and the highest peak, Muoddahasoai've (591m) is in the west. About half the park consists of bogs and treeless plateaux, although overall it looks like an area of forest.

The west is mainly granite lacking in nutrients and a poor base for vegetation, while to the east of Bavtajåkka most of the rocks are of volcanic origin.

Much of the ground is covered by scree and loose rocks which, like the rivers, can be gold bearing but not in quantities large enough to make prospecting worthwhile.

The park has more than 700 lakes, large and small and the Anarjåkka is the main artery and the largest river in the area. The deep pools are home to many grayling, pike and trout, while young salmon and whitefish can be found in many of the rivers. The lakes support pike, perch and char.

The park has cold, dry winters, down to -45°C, and warm, wet summers. Most rain falls between June and August and while summer temperatures can reach 30°C, the average is 12°C and night frosts can occur in mid-summer.

About five-sixths of the forest consists of birch with the rest made up by pure and mixed Scots pine. The forests are very old with huge trees which restrict new growth. Any young saplings that do establish themselves are usually eaten by the foraging elks. Fire is a constant threat and large areas are frequently destroyed. Although the flora of the park is still being studied, more than 244 species have already been identified.

Access: There are no roads in this wilderness area. The Lapps roam with their reindeer herds and some of their cabins are available and open in the summer. There are no paths in the park. The nearest road runs from Karasjok southwards to Is'kuras by the border, and a forestry road runs along the Anarjåkka to Caskenjåkka. From there it is a 10km walk to the National Park.

HARDANGERVIDDA covers 3,430sq km and extends into the regions of Buskerud, Telemark and Hordaland. It was established in 1981 and is unusual in that about half the land is privately owned. Skaupsjøen/Hardangerjøkulen and Møsvatn/Austfjell have also been established as landscape conservation areas.

The mountain plateau park is rich in flora and fauna and contains a number of important natural and cultural monuments. It is still used for agriculture, outdoor recreation, hunting and fishing, as well as education and research activities.

Most of the park lies on Pre-Cambrian bed rock, calcareous shales and lava. In the north-west the rocks are rich in nutrients while in the south-east there is little to support vegetation and it is mostly barren bedrock. In the south-west there are lots of reminders of the volcanic activity in the area with lava deposits. The Hårteigen mountain is an example of this volcanic upheaval where the lava was thrust up through the layers of shale. There are also lots of large gravel ridges, formed by meltwater during the last Ice Age. The landscape towards the west is more rugged with peaks rising to 1,700m sloping steeply down towards Sørfjord and Eidfjord. Hårteigen, the hat-shaped mountain, dominates the landscape to the west and on clear days, acts as a beacon to people on the plateau. The flat mountain plateau is the major feature of the centre and easterly parts of the park.

Main rivers in the park are the Kinso, Ops and Veig in the west, the Dagali in the east, and the Kvenna to the south. The park is packed with lakes and has long been recognised as one of southern Norway's best fishing areas, especially for mountain trout.

The western part of the park is wetter than the east but warmer. Winter temperatures in the east can fall to -40°C while in the summer they can top -

20 °C, although the average summer temperature is around 10 °C. Snow can often lay on the ground until late spring and in some areas until mid-summer.

The park is a botanist's dream with a wide range of flora. Species of vascular plant have been identified and there are numerous species of mosses, lichens, fungi and algae. The plateau represents the southern limit for many of the plant species, and the vegetation becomes denser and more luxurious as one travels further west. The large lichen heaths on the barren bedrock in the eastern part of the plateau are of vital importance as winter grazing for reindeer. The park is also the southernmost nesting area and home range for a number of arctic species. Hardangervidda is also the home of the largest flock of wild reindeer in Europe and every year thousands of animals migrate east to the winter grazing grounds.

Access: The park can be entered from the north by boat from Halnefjord, and from Dyranut/Tråstølen and Garden; from the west by Hudsalen, Lofthus, Espe and Tyssedal; from the south at Valldal, Haukeliseter and Møsvatn (by boat); and from the east from Kalhovd, Imingfjell, Solheimstulen, Setersdalen and Tuvaseter.

There are a number of well marked trails through the park marked with cairns and rocks painted with red. A map showing all the trails and tourist cabins is available from the Norwegian Tourist Association and the local tourist information office.

There is plenty of accommodation available both within and outside the park. There are fourteen cabins in the park — Stavali, Torehytten, Hedlo, Hadlaskard, Litlos, Hellesvassbu, Besså, Sandhaug, Hellehalsen, Trondsbu, Stigstuv, Rauhelleren, Lågaros and Heinseter. The cabins are owned privately or belong to associations, and some are staffed while the others are self-service.

REISA (803sq km) is in Nordreisa borough in Troms, about 60km from its border with Finnmark. It was founded in 1986 and is an almost untouched mountain and valley area and is open to the public for outdoor recreation.

The Reisa runs through the entire valley which tapers as it travels south. In the north the valley is wide and surrounded by tall peaks but in the south it narrows as it cuts through a broad mountain plateau. The whole area is indented by narrow valleys and gorges. To the west the landscape is dominated by Ráisduottarháldi (1,365m).

The area is rich in rivers and lakes. The largest tributary of the Reisa is Mollisjokka. There are many waterfalls including Mollisfossen which plunges almost 270m, the last 140m of which are uninterrupted fall. The Reisa runs through an impressive 1km long canyon at Imo which contains Imofossen, the largest waterfall on the main river. The Reisa is also one of the best salmon rivers in the area.

The park experiences huge extremes of climate. The winters are very cold with heavy falls of snow to the west. The sea influence means that some western parts of the park have up to 400mm of precipitation a year. There are about 200 days of winter and less than 60 days with an average temperature above 10 °C, although some summer days can be much warmer.

The area has a rich flora including many rare species. All vegetation zones from lowland to high mountain are represented although the majority consists of heaths with downy willow and rather taller than usual dwarf birch. In the valleys birch forests dominate while pine forests are not so common. In the south there are large areas of bogs and marshes, especially south of Raisjavrre.

The park supports a large moose population, several species of carnivore and there is thought to be a viable bear population. Wolverines, arctic foxes, lynx and pine marten have all been spotted.

Reisa is one of the richest bird areas in northern Norway. The steep rock faces of the valley sides provide good nesting sites for many species of birds of prey.

Access: From the north access is along highway 865 from Reisafjorden and up Reisadalen to Bilto. From here the road continues as a forestry road to Sarelv. In summer you can hire a boat to travel further up the river, usually as far as Nedrefoss. Access from the south is along national highway 92 through Kautokeino which goes as far as the Raisjavrre area. From the north-west you can drive from Kåfjordbotn into the Raisduoddarhaldde landscape conservation area to Guolasjávre.

There is a marked summer path up Reisadalen, passing through Imo and from there across the mountain plateau to Ráisjávre, ending at Dier'bavarri. In winter a marked snow mobile track leads from Grappuns to Somajávri.

There are a number of unattended cabins in the park. Those owned by the Troms Touring Association are locked but the key can be obtained from the local official. The cabins are equipped with pots and pans and mattresses but you have to take in your own food. There are unlocked cabins at Sieima, Somajávri, Sidosgohppi and Deatnumuotki.

Stave Churches

There are thirty-two of these ancient, magnificent wooden churches left and all are worth making a detour to see.

Most of these churches were built between 700 and 800 years ago at a time when the rest of Europe was turning to stone for such buildings. The Norwegians, however, had mastered the art of preparing timber that could withstand the ravages of time, and the medieval stave churches still bear witness to this today. They are by far the finest examples of wooden architecture in Norway.

Centuries ago there were several hundred stave churches throughout Norway but most fell into disrepair or were demolished so that the wood could be used for other buildings. Many more recent churches were partly built with boards and panels from the stave churches.

Most of the stave churches are found in central and southern Norway although the remains of one have been found at Greensted in Essex on the site of an ancient Viking settlement, and there is another near Gothenburg in Sweden.

It is only relatively recently that great efforts have been made to protect and restore the remaining stave churches. Although a great deal is known about most of the stave churches, when they were built and their subsequent history, there is still some uncertainty about how their strange structure developed in the first place. It is suggested that the basic structure, a large wooden hall, was copied from the meeting places used by the chiefs and elders of the Germanic tribes living to the south. How the amazing and complex mass of supporting columns developed, is the subject of great speculation. The large wooden halls are reminiscent of those that used to be found on the large farmsteads in the south, and they also resemble the early pagan temples built to worship Tor, Odin and other gods from Norse mythology.

The earliest stave churches were built 'palisade' style. The walls consisted of upright planks buried in the ground. As the technique became more refined at the end of the twelfth century, the Norwegians incorporated many of their ship building methods to construct the stave churches. Four massive corner timber pillars (staves) were erected and the walls were built using hand-hewn wooden planks which interlocked together giving great strength. The huge planks were used vertically while on the great long ships they were used horizontally. For added strength, cross beams were installed and the roof was added in a series of steps so that the whole structure locked together like a giant cube. Each area of roof was surmounted by an ornately carved cross-beam ending in the shape of a dragon's head, or other mythical animal. The shingle clad roofs were very steep so that snow could not gather. In the later churches, the plank walls in their square timber frame were built on a stone foundation to prevent the wood rotting.

The first stave churches were small single-nave structures with a lower and smaller rectangular chancel. The columnar technique meant that the internal pillar construction went round the whole of the central nave, creating side naves or aisles on all four sides. The pillars were supported on a foundation of four cross beams, the ends of which projected to carry the external walls of the side naves. The buttressing of the pillar construction was achieved by using a series of struts extending to the external wall lintels and supported by arched 'knees' on both sides. It is exactly the same technique as the stone buttresses used in Gothic buildings. The roof framework consists of self-supporting pairs of scissor beams, a system widely used in stone churches in England and France during the same period.

The interior of the church was very dark because there were usually only very small openings high up in the walls. The church interiors, however, contained a mass of ornate carvings. The massive door posts and often the door itself, were heavily carved with animal and foliage motifs and pagan symbols. Initially the churches would have been plain inside with the altar as the only furniture. As the churches evolved, they were extended, pews were added and internal panelling was painted or carved.

In many of the oldest churches there was a covered passage running right round the church — where the men would leave their weapons — and there would have been two entrances, one for men and the other for women.

The following is a brief account of many of the remaining stave churches which can be viewed.

Borgund columnar church is the only one to remain that has not undergone significant renovation since it was built in the first half of the thirteenth century. It is the best preserved of the original Norwegian stave churches although the galleries, apses and ridge turrets were added during the Middle Ages. The bell tower also dates from this period. One of its finest features are

*Visitors to Oslo's folk
museum at Bygdøy will
see an example of
Norways magnificent
stave churches*

*The carved doorway to Heddal;
Norway's largest stave church*

the lavishly carved portals. The post-Reformation inventory was removed during the last century. Like most of the other stave churches, it is characterised by its huge carved dragons' heads.

Eidsborg in Dalen, Telemark is a single nave stave church built around 1300. It was restored in 1929 when a number of paintings and ornaments from the eighteenth century were discovered. The church contains a copy of a wooden statue of St Nikuls (St Nicholas).

Fantoft is a columnar stave church from Fortun in Sogn which was restored and moved to Fantoft in 1883. Problems arose in the reconstruction, however, and the present structure is almost certainly different in form from the original. The present buttresses between the pillars were not in the original church and the exterior has been reconstructed.

Fåvang church was built in the thirteenth century and rebuilt in cruciform style in the late eighteenth century. It was restored in 1951. The church has a pulpit and a fine Renaissance-style altar piece.

Flesberg stave church in the Numedal valley still contains the nave from an earlier columnar stave church although the pillars have been removed. There is a lavishly carved portal. **Nore** and **Uvdal** churches, also in Numedal, are single nave churches with a middle pillar and dating from the mid-thirteenth century. Both churches were rebuilt and added to later in the Middle Ages and then again in the seventeenth century, when both were also embellished with magnificent painted decorations.

The **Garmo** church in the Maihaugen folk museum near Lillehammer, contains many works of art rescued from other churches in the Gudbrandsdalen valley. It was built in Lom in Gudbrandsdalen about 1200 and was later expanded. At the beginning of the eighteenth century a new steeple and two log transepts were added which gave it the shape of a cross, the 'Crucifix' style which was very popular at the time. In 1882 the church had become so rotten that it had to be demolished and the timber was dispersed throughout the valley. Two locals Anders Sandvig and Trond Eklestuen salvaged what they could and the church was rebuilt at Maihaugen in 1921.

Gol church was built around 1250 at Gol in Hallingdal. It is a columnar stave church and when it was removed to Oslo on the orders of the king in 1885 its exterior had to be reconstructed because the original timbers were too badly damaged.

Grip stave church, in Møre og Romsdal, was built during the last half of the fifteenth century. Some of the furnishings pre-date the Reformation and the church was restored in 1621 when the interior was decorated with Biblical motifs and ornaments. It was restored again in 1933 and the tabernacle from 1500 was, together with a number of relics reinstated.

Hedal stave church, in Valdres, was built in the first part of the thirteenth century as a single nave church, although it was later rebuilt in cruciform style. It has an elaborately carved portal a number of interesting artefacts such as a statue of the Virgin Mary and a thirteenth-century reliquary.

Heddal stave church in Telemark is Norway's largest stave church, and the oldest part (the chancel) was consecrated on the Feast of St Crispianus, 25 October 1147. The chancel would originally have been the nave of the first church before it was extended. Almost a hundred years later in 1242 it was consecrated to the Holy Virgin and enlarged, and in about 1300 the interior was richly adorned with paintings. These were largely overpainted with rose paintings towards the end of the seventeenth century.

A chair in the chancel has carvings depicting an old Norwegian saga and probably predates the church, while the alter piece was installed in 1667. The church used to be known as Ryginar church after Rygi farm which still operates close by.

All the churches must have been expensive to build and reflect the country's prosperity during this period. Heddal stave church was built during the reign of King Håkon Håkonson and its size and furnishings reflect how rich Heddal must have been.

The square nave has four corner staves and there are a further eight massive wooden pillars, two at each corner of the building. The top of the pillars are all connected by brackets and crossbeams, while the foot of each pillar is jointed to fit into a wooden sill which runs around the structure. This sill rests on a stone foundation which acts as a barrier to prevent rising damp and stops the end of the pillars rotting. Tongue and grooved planks form the wall. These slot into the base sill and are held in place at the top by fitting into slots cut in cross beams.

Over the centuries Heddal church underwent many changes but it was restored to its medieval appearance in the 1950s thanks to the generosity of a local businessman. New paintings were carefully removed to reveal the medieval decorations and those added during the seventeenth century Renaissance. All the richly carved portals remain, and there is a row of highly stylized masks carved near the top of the interior pillars of the nave and chancel.

All the stave churches are different, both in structure and size and all are worth visiting. Many are now maintained by the local communities and most are in beautiful locations.

Hegge, Hurum and Lomen stave churches are all in Valdres. They are all columnar stave churches dating from the mid-thirteenth century. In each of the churches the walls of the nave were moved out last century to allow a new chancel to be built. The roofs and turrets are not original although it is not known when they were added. All have elaborately carved portals.

Lomen church in Ryfoss was built around 1250. The internal construction of the nave is very well preserved although the walls were moved in 1840 and a new chancel was added. There are many beautiful carvings, especially in the portals. There is a valuable altar piece and a carved baptismal font in the Romanesque style. The bell tower dates from about 1675.

Hurum was built around 1180 and rebuilt in the 1820s. It has elaborately carved portals and a cemetery portal which was originally the turret of the church. There is a bell tower and inside the church there are many runic inscriptions.

Holtålen church in Trøndelag, is a single nave church from the last half of the thirteenth century. It was moved and rebuilt at the open-air museum in Trondheim. The west portal comes from the neighbouring church in Ålen.

Hopperstad stave church in Vik was built around 1200 with a richly-carved western portal in 'dragon' style. The exterior was renovated in the last century. The altar canopy was painted in the fourteenth century while the trusses and cross buttressing between the pillars were a later addition from the Middle Ages.

Høyjord stave church in Andebu has a twelfth-century chancel while the rest of the church was built in the last half of the thirteenth century. The church was fully restored in 1953 and contains a number of paintings from the Middle Ages some of which have been restored while others have been repainted. The bronze weather vane on the church spire dates back to the Viking Age.

Kaupanger columnar church is the largest in Sognefjord and was built at the beginning of the thirteenth century. It has been thoroughly restored twice. At the beginning of the 1600s the church was given a new steeple and elaborate furnishings, and in 1864 it was again rebuilt which removed almost all its traditional character of a stave church. Fortunately it underwent major restoration in 1965-6 when it was restored to its seventeenth century appearance.

Kvernes stave church in Møre og Romsdal, was built in the fifteenth century and the pulpit with its carvings was added a century later. The paintings on the walls and ceilings are from the seventeenth century. There is a rebuilt tabernacle dating from the Middle Ages.

Lom church in Gudbrandsdal, with its famous dragons heads, has retained its original architectural form, despite some seventeenth-century reconstruction. It was built as a columnar stave church in the mid-twelfth century and is still used for worship today. The western extension was built of logs, and the transept and steeple, using stave techniques, were constructed in the seventeenth century. The interior furnishings date from the eighteenth century, and the paintings on the ceilings of the chancel are from the beginning of the seventeenth century. The pulpit dates from about 1790.

Øye stave church, on the shore of Lake Vangmjøsi, was originally built at the end of the twelfth century, and was carefully reconstructed from sections found beneath the present parish church which was built in 1747. It is a single nave church. The western portal is a copy from the original Øye church.

Reinli stave church in the Valdres is a single nave church built about 1300. It still has its original covered galleries.

Ringebu is a columnar church built at the end of the thirteenth century and extended in 1630 when the master craftsman Werner Olsen built a tower above the crossing — the area where the floor levels meet. Its fittings include a statue of St Laurentius (a deacon in Rome in AD258), crucifixes and a medieval twelfth-century font. There are a number of important runic inscriptions and an elaborately carved altar piece and pulpit. The church was restored in 1921.

Røldal church in Hordaland dates from the end of the thirteenth and beginning of the fourteenth centuries. It has a medieval crucifix while the inventory and the wall decorations are from the seventeenth century.

Rollag church is mentioned for the first time in 1425 but is almost certainly much older. It was rebuilt and expanded in 1697. The altar piece contains details and figures from a number of different styles and periods. The decorations are in Renaissance-style and the pulpit is Rococo.

Røvden in Møre og Romsdal was built around 1200, extended during the first half of the 1600s and restored between 1711 and 1712. The crucifix dates from about 1250, and the altar piece and the altar cloth are from the 1700s.

Torpo church, dating from the end of the twelfth century was badly damaged by fire in 1880. As a result the chancel was demolished and many of the more recent furnishings were removed. The impressively carved portals and thirteenth-century ceiling canopy paintings on the 'ship', the main body of the church, were saved.

Urnes columnar stave church is the oldest in Norway. Parts of the present structure date back to the early twelfth century and the wood used was taken from an even older single nave church, including the two portals which were incorporated in the north wall of the more recent church. Also salvaged from the first church were a carved corner post and carved sections of the gable — all with carvings and friezes of intertwined animals heads which has given rise to an art style known internationally as the Urnes-style. They date from around 1100.

The interior fittings such as benches and the wooden ceiling date from the Reformation in the sixteenth century, while the group around the Crucifixion and the chandelier all date from the Middle Ages. The paintings in the chancel date from 1601.

Vågå was built in the 1600s using materials salvaged from a single nave twelfth-century stave church. The carved west front and the main portal are from the original church. The soapstone baptismal font was made about 1150 and is thought to be the oldest in Norway. The large crucifix dates from about 1250, the pulpit from around 1630 and the altar piece from 1758. The church has a wooden bell tower and the old banner of the valley still hangs there.

Vang stave church in Ryfoss dates from the thirteenth century. In 1844 it was moved to Riesengebirge, now Brückenbergin in Polish Silesia.

Further details about most of the churches, their location and history are given in the various suggested tours.

2

IN AND AROUND OSLO

According to the old Icelandic chronicler Snorre, Oslo was founded in 1048 by King Harald Hårdråde (Harold the Hard) and he ordered the country's first stone church to be built. The foundations of the Gamle Aker church, dating from about 1100 can still be seen in Akersbakken. It is the oldest stone church in Scandinavia and is still used as a parish church.

Oslo became the country's capital during the reign of Håkon V (1280-1319). Bergen had been the capital, but in 1299 Håkon chose to be crowned in Oslo. He moved his court there and started to expand the city and increase its influence as a major port and trading centre. He also ordered work to start on Akershus Castle in about 1300.

In the mid-fourteenth century the Black Death hit Norway and the population of Oslo was decimated by the plague. More than a third of the country's population died from the plague although the mortality rate was very much higher in the urban areas.

Over the centuries the city has been ravaged by fire many times. After the Great Fire of 1624, the Danish King Christian IV ordered the city to be rebuilt in stone around the castle of Akershus and renamed *Christiania*. The 'new' city was built on classical lines with straight roads running parallel or at right angles to each other. The size of *Christiania* can still be seen by looking at an Oslo street map. The rectangular area bordered in the north by Kristian IV Gate and running south and east of Akershus was roughly the site of the rebuilt city although almost all the old buildings were pulled down long ago to make way for modern developments. A permanent exhibition showing how *Christiania* looked in 1838 is housed at Akershus.

During its union with Denmark, Norway lost many of its rights which were taken over by the Hanseatic League, and as a result the trading importance of Oslo declined considerably, although it continued as the spiritual and educational heart of the country. In 1694 work started on the cathedral and in 1811 the university was opened.

It was during the nineteenth century that Oslo started to flourish again. After being united with Sweden in 1814, the Swedish King Carl Johan XIV ordered a royal palace to be built in the centre of Oslo. It still dominates the city, and there are marvellous views from the royal park down the broad Karl Johans gate.

The city reverted to its original name of Oslo in 1924. The municipality of Oslo covers an area of 454sq km making it one of the largest capital cities in the world, although much of it occupies wooded hills. Its geographical centre is

Høgåsen, a hill to the north-east of Lake Sognsvann in the Nordmarka forest and the highest point is Kykjeberget, also in Nordmarka, which is about 580m above sea level.

The suburbs of Oslo now stretch upwards into the pine-clad hills and outwards along the shores of Oslofjord. There are few real skyscrapers in Oslo because so far there has been enough room to allow people to spread out rather than up, and it is this atmosphere of space and freedom which gives the city much of its charm.

While a car or public transport is needed to explore the outer limits of the city, you can walk around the centre although you will still need several days if you want to see everything of interest.

Ironically, for a city surrounded by sea breezes and pine forests, the centre of Oslo has had a major pollution problem because of the sheer weight of motor traffic. Efforts are now in hand to reduce the number of private vehicles coming into the centre of Oslo by using tolls.

Oslo makes a natural base for any tour of Norway and in fact, you could spend the whole of your holiday just visiting places around the capital. Oslo nestles at the head of Oslofjord, and if you take the ferry from Harwich to Oslo you can enjoy several hours steaming up the fjord with the capital getting ever close. There are more than 50 museums in Oslo, castles and parks. You can follow the trails of the Vikings, learn about Norway's famous Arctic explorers, discover the origins of skiing, and walk back into history in the open-air museum at Bygdøy. There are beaches to laze on, lakes to swim in, boat on or fish, wooded walks to follow, and parks to picnic in.

There are more than 2,200km of ski trails around Oslo and more than 50 of them are floodlit. There are also many good down hill slopes serviced by ski and chair lifts. During the day for the less active there are art galleries and statue-filled gardens to explore, and at night there is the cultural life of the theatres, cinema, opera and ballet and concert hall.

Hotels and hostels, boarding houses and campsites to suit all tastes and all pockets are in and around Oslo. There are internationally renowned restaurants, coffee shops and burger bars, and first-class shopping districts where you can buy your gifts and souvenirs.

The unmistakable twin-towered City Hall should be one of your first ports of call because it also houses the capital's tourist office. It is right down by the water's edge, and there is parking opposite along the pier. The tourist office will supply detailed information about accommodation, organised tours, where to go and what is on.

Organised city coach tours start from outside City Hall. The morning tour usually covers the Cathedral, Munch Museum, Frogner Park and views from the summit of Holmenkollen, while the afternoon tour takes in the harbour, Folk Museum and maritime museums containing Viking ships, *Fram* and *Kon-Tiki*. Both tours last for about 3 hours.

The Grand Tour, lasting about $7^1/_2$ hours, combines the best of the above with a boat trip across the harbour. There are, of course, many other organised tours, including forest safaris, walks, canoeing and fishing in the summer, and cross country and downhill skiing in the winter, and boat trips which usually start from the City Hall pier. Professional guides are available for individuals or groups.

If you plan to spend some time in Oslo, you should consider buying the Oslo Card from tourist offices, hotels or bus and train station. You can buy a one, two or three day card (which is less than double the cost of the one day card). They all give free travel on tram, bus, train or ferries, free parking in all municipal car parks, free admission to most museums and other attractions, half price on bus and boat sightseeing tours and special discounts to cinemas.

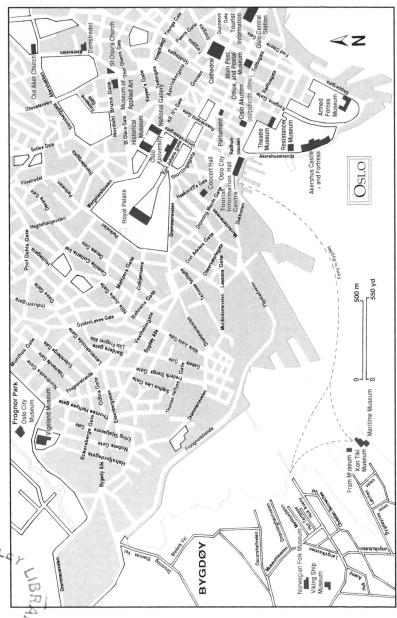

If you buy the card outside Oslo you also get reduced train fares to and from the capital. Children under 16 years old pay half price. If you intend travelling around by public transport and visiting as many museums and galleries as possible, the Oslo Card will save you a small fortune.

Planning a walking tour round central Oslo, can incorporate a visit to the maritime museums and folk museum on Bygdøy by taking the ferry across, and enjoying a boat trip into the bargain.

Oslo's imposing 'red brick' City Hall, as seen from the harbour

One of the colourful works of art in the city hall depicting Oslo's history

City Hall, Rådhusplassen, was started in 1933 but work was interrupted by World War II. It was finally completed in 1950 in time for the celebrations of Oslo's 900th anniversary. While not the most elegant of buildings, it is held in high regard by Norwegians, and is very important because of the works of arts it contains.

The huge red brick structure is dominated by the twin 60m high towers and was designed by Arnstein Arneberg and Manus Poulsson. It was agreed from the start that leading Norwegian artists and sculptors would assist in its completion, and its lavish decorations are its major attraction. The building is surrounded by sculptures and contains Europe's largest painting, Henrik Sørensen's *People at Work and Play*, which measures 26m by 13m. It is painted in oil on wood. Other artists involved included Per Krogh, Anne Grimdalen who created the statue of King Harald Hårdråde on the west wall, and Emil Lie, whose bronze and granite statues are displayed in front of the building. Many of the paintings show typical Norwegian scenes or illustrate folklore, but some of the later editions depicted scenes of German wartime occupation.

The clock on the east tower measures $8^1/_2$m across, and there is a peal from the 38 bells every hour. There is also a fascinating astronomical clock in the inner courtyard which not only gives details of time and date, but also the earth's position in relation to the stars, sun and moon.

Akershus Castle, founded by King Håkon V in 1300, is reached by a pleasant walk along the water front from City Hall. The main entrance is from Kirkegaten. It was built as a fortified royal residence on a hill overlooking Oslofjord, and although sieged many times, it was never taken. The last siege was in 1716. It was largely rebuilt by the Danish King Kristian IV after being extensively damaged by fire in the mid-1620s. The fortifications and ramparts were extended, and a Renaissance-style palace built in the centre. During the eighteenth century it was used as one of the country's main prisons, but it fell into disrepair in the nineteenth century. During the last war it was used as a political prison and has since been fully restored. The ramparts are open all year, concerts are often held in the chapel on Sundays, and guided tours are available. The castle's State Apartments are now used for official functions. The Royal Mausoleum lies in the crypt beneath the castle's church.

The castle also houses the Norwegian **Armed Forces Museum** and the **Resistance Museum**. The former, in what used to be a military arsenal, was opened in 1978 and traces the history of Norway's fighting forces from about 1500 to 1950. The exhibits are arranged in chronological order and there are fascinating insights into military life at the time of the Nordic Wars in the seventeenth and eighteenth centuries, and the struggle for independence in the nineteenth century. Exhibits include a Spitfire plane. The museum has a café, the only one in the area. Take a look at the *Christiania* model exhibition.

The Resistance Museum, in a seventeenth century building, has been designed to present a true picture of events in Norway during the German occupation between 1940 and 1945, through the use of exhibits, posters, photographs, working models and tape recordings.

Oslo **Cathedral**, Stortorvet, was designed by the German architect Chateaneuf and built between 1694 and 1699. It was restored between 1849 and 1850 and again between 1939 and 1950 when it acquired its present interior and new ceiling. The tempera ceiling and monumental decorations depicting scenes from the Old and New Testament are by Hugo Lous Mohr. The Dutch altar piece and pulpit date from 1699, and the massive organ façade was created by a Dutch artist in 1727. The new organ, with more than 6,000 pipes, was built by Ludwigsburg and installed in 1930.

Emanual Vigeland designed and installed the stained glass windows between 1910 and 1916, and the massive bronze doors, showing the Sermon on the Mount, were created by Dagfin Werenskiold, and installed in 1938.

Basarhallene, which is next to the Cathedral, was built between 1841 and 1858 and used to be the city's main food retail area. It is now a centre for arts and handicrafts.

Oslo University, Karl Johans gate, was founded in 1811 by King Friedrik VI and is Norway's oldest institute of higher education. It was designed by Grosch and completed in collaboration with the famous German architect Schinkel. It underwent extensive restoration at the beginning of this century in readiness for its centenary celebrations, and the Great Hall contains a number of murals by Edvard Munch.

The **National Gallery**, Universitets-gata, houses Norway's largest collec- tion of paintings and sculptures. Norwegian art from about 1810 is depicted with the period of National Romanticism represented by Tidemand and Gude. There are also exhibits from leading European artists such as Rembrandt, Goya and Picasso. Among the many Norwegian artists represented are Christian Dahl, Per and Christian Krohg, Harriet Backer and Jakob Weidemann. Edvard Munch has a separate room devoted to his works.

There is an excellent collection of French Masters including Delacroix, Manet, Degas, Cezanne, Van Gogh, Renoir and Gauguin, together with sculptures from Rodin and Maillol. The gallery also houses exhibitions of Danish and Swedish art and a priceless collection of Russian icons.

The **Historical Museum**, Frederiksgt, houses three collections: the Univer- sity Collection of Antiquities including the 'Treasury' where the most valuable gold and silver items are kept, and medieval ecclesiastical art; the Ethnographic Museum depicting how people live in different parts of the world, especially Indonesia, the Congo and Eskimo settlements, and coins and medals, which includes many of the decorations awarded to polar explorers Amundsen and Nansen. The Viking Hall tells the story behind the Viking ships now displayed at Bygdøy.

The **Parliament** in Karl Johans gate, was built between 1861 and 1866 although it has been extensively extended since. The interior has been richly decorated by contemporary Norwegian artists, and a huge wall painting by Wergeland hangs behind the Speaker's Chair, depicting the 1814 signing of the Norwegian Constitution at Eidsvoll.

The **Royal Palace** stands in its own park at the top of Karl Johans gate. It was built by the Swedish King Carl Christian Johan XIV between 1825 and 1848. The palace is not open to the public but the park is. The Palace Guard changes at 1.30pm each day, and when the King is in residence, the Band of the Royal Guard accompanies the ceremony.

There are many other interesting museums, galleries and special sites to visit in the centre of Oslo.

The **Museum of Applied Art** in St Olavs Gate traces the history of applied art in Norway and elsewhere from the Middle Ages to the present. It contains the twelfth-century *Baldishol Tapestry* and royal costumes. The background music changes to suit the period being viewed. In Josefinesgt the Museum of Architecture changes its exhibition regularly. The museum stands in Homansbyen, a residential area dating back to the 1850s, and Oslo's first garden suburb.

Others are the National Museum of Contemporary Art in Bankplassen, the Postal Museum in Tollbugata (first floor), which shows the development of communications in Norway over the last 300 years, and the Theatre Museum in Nedre Slotts Gate, housed in the Old Town Hall. It traces the history of Norwegian theatre since the beginning of the nineteenth century.

Sites of special interest include the Cemetery of Our Saviour (Vår Freslers Gravlund) where Munch and Ibsen are buried, and the nearby **Old Aker Church,** the oldest building in Oslo and the oldest stone church in Scandinavia, dating back to the twelfth century. It is still a parish church.

Damstredet in Bergfjerdingen is worth a visit. It is a delightful area of timber houses dating back to the beginning of the nineteenth century and famous for its narrow streets.

Also of interest is the island of **Hovedøya**, a short ferry trip from

The thought-provoking 20m high granite monolith in Frogner Park

Vippetangen, at the end of the Akershus promintory. The island was inhabited by Cistercian monks who arrived from England in May 1147. The remains of their monastery can still be seen.

Around Oslo

West Oslo

Frogner Park in the north-western suburbs of Oslo is home to one of the ❋ world's largest outdoor collections of statues and sculptures by Gustav

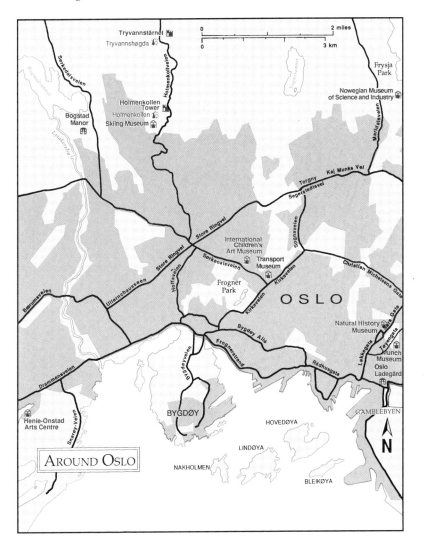

Vigeland (1869-1943). He started out as a wood carver but quickly switched to sculpting in marble, bronze, granite and iron. His collection started when he was commissioned by the City of Oslo to build a fountain. The result was hailed a masterpiece and a special site created for it in the royal park. Vigeland was commissioned by the city to produce more statues. Over the next 30 years he produced more than 191 pieces containing more than 600 sculptures. He quickly outgrew the palace park site and a new home for his works was found in Frogner Park. You enter the park through his massive wrought iron gates, with their carved animal designs, and the statues stretch out before you in an avenue leading to the spectacular fountain and 20m high monolith, a granite column carrying 121 figures struggling to climb higher. The column is surrounded by 36 groups of statues carved in granite, known as The *Wheel of Life*.

The park is open throughout the year and admission is free. In the summer it makes a charming picnic spot, although it has open-air restaurants a swimming pool, tennis courts and children's play area.

The **Vigeland Museum**, is south of Frogner Park in Nobels Gate. It used to be the sculptor's workshop and was built specially for him by the city as part of a unique contract under which they funded his work and received everything he produced. Apart from the works exhibited in the park, Vigeland produced another 1,650 sculptures, more than 3,700 wood carvings, 423 plates for woodcuts and and almost 11,000 drawings and sketches. There are concerts in the courtyard during the summer.

The **Skating Museum** is housed in Frogner Stadium, and tells the history of skating and displays medals and trophies won by Norwegian champions such as Oscar Mathiesen and Ivar Ballangrud and many others.

The **Oslo City Museum** is housed in Frogner Manor which was built about 1790, on the site of a manor which dates back to Viking times. The house contains furnishings from different periods and depicts life in Oslo over the centuries. In the new wing there are also models and prints of what the city used to look like and showing how it has grown. It has a café.

The **International Children's Art Museum** in Lille Frøensveien, has more than 70,000 examples of children's art from more than 130 countries and there is a children's workshop where they can do drawing, painting, music and dancing. Just over 11km west of Oslo, at Høvikodden is the **Henie-Onstad Arts Centre** (Henie-Onstad Kunstsenter). Opened in 1968 it is a museum of modern art built as the bequest of Sonja Henie, the world's top figure skater, who won three Olympic Gold medals and ten world championships, and her husband Niels Onstad, an international rower. Its spectacular setting beside a lake is an ideal venue for concerts, ballet and exhibitions. The museum has a large collection of art from the twentieth century featuring artists such as Braque, Picasso, Paul Klee and Hans Hartung. It also does an enormous amount to encourage art among Norwegian's youth. Sonja Henie's medals are displayed at the museum. There is a restaurant.

North-West Oslo

Holmenkollen, a short drive out of the city, is Oslo's highest hill and home of the world-famous ski-jump and Skiing Museum. There are spectacular views of the capital and Oslofjord from the top of the jump which is about 370m above sea level. You can drive to the ski jump along a well signposted route, or take the train from the National Theatre in the centre of town to Holmenkollen station.

Staring up at the jump is daunting enough but you need to go to the top to see how courageous the skiers are who take part. There is a lift for most of the way, but the last few metres have to be climbed on foot. The steepness of the slope seems even more daunting from the top. The Holmenkollen International Ski-Jumping Contest takes place every March and attracts enormous crowds who come to watch the world-class field. Jumps of more than 90m are possible and the event is regarded as one of the most prestigious in the international ski jumping programme.

The Skiing Museum is entered at the foot of the ski jump tower and the galleries housing the exhibits have been excavated into the rock. It is the oldest skiing museum in the world. Opened in 1923 it traces the history and development of skiing. Exhibits illustrate the world's oldest record of skis painted on rocks at least 4,000 years old, and include the equipment used by Nansen and Amundsen on their polar expeditions.

Bogstad Manor at Sørkedalen, is 10km north-west of the city centre, and is regarded as one of the most beautiful houses in Norway. You can drive there by taking the Sørkedalsveien road which runs to the north of Frogner Park, or by taking a bus. The lakeside house was built between 1760 and 1785 and extended in 1854 and the interior has been well-preserved. It has a marvellous art collection and was the first home in Norway to have a landscaped garden which contains many plants and trees.

An interesting excursion is to drive or take the 30 minute train ride on the Holmenkollen line from the National Theatre to its terminus at Voksenkollen to visit **Tryvannshøgda** a hill capped by the **Tryvannstårnet**, Norway's tallest tower, thus making it the highest point in the Oslo area. Although the hill is only 530m above sea level, compared with the 580m on the summit of Kyrkjeberget, the tower gives it the edge. The television and telecommunications tower, about 15 minutes walk from the station, from its 60m high observation platform affords a panorama covering about 30,000sq km. Fortunately there is a lift to help you get to the top.

The **Transport Museum** is close to the station of Majorstuen and the main entrance is in Gardeveien. It seems fitting that you travel there by train which you can catch at the station by the National Theatre. The museum contains Norway's only collection of old trams and buses, as well as a comprehensive collection of pictures and transport artefacts.

North Oslo

The **Norwegian Museum of Science and Industry** is next to Frysja Park and Crafts Centre in Kjelsåveien. It is the country's national museum of science and technology with a comprehensive collection from the birth of the industrial revolution to the space age, courtesy of NASA, the US space agency and the Soviet Union. There is a reconstruction of Norway's first industrial exhibition staged in 1883, and many working models. It also contains Norway's first Science Centre, and a hands-on telecommunications exhibition where you can try out the latest gadgets. There is a café, a large picnic area.

East Oslo

The **Munch Museum** in Tøyengata opened in 1963 and contains all the works bequeathed by the artist Edvard Munch (1863-1944) to the City of Oslo in 1940. The collection contained paintings, drawing, watercolours, lithographs and sculptures. Lectures and concerts are held there. There is a restaurant.

The **Natural History Museum** is in Sars gate in Tøyen. The museum consists of a number of buildings all housed in the botanical gardens which you can either bus, train or drive to. The various buildings house the mineral and geological museum, the paleontological museum, zoological museum and botanical museum. The zoological collection shows all Norway's native animals in their natural habitats, and often in both winter and summer coats. The paleontological collection covers Norway's prehistoric animals and plants. The extensive gardens concentrate on the flora of Scandinavia although there are specimens from more southerly countries.

Oslo Ladegård in Oslo Gate, is the restored medieval bishop's palace, and together with St Hallvard's Church, used to be the ecclesiastical centre of old Oslo in the thirteenth century. In the seventeenth century the palace was converted into a Baroque mansion and became the official residence of the mayor, and was later even used as a bordello for a short time. Between 1957 and 1968 it was carefully restored by the city, and the palace rooms and Middle Age vaults are fascinating.

The old city area is known as **Gamlebyen** and is around the Oslo Gate and Bispegata junction. Little of the medieval city remains but the area has been excavated since the beginning of the century and the finds are now preserved in a series of small parks. These are foundations of ecclesiastical buildings, including St Hallvard's church, where King Håkon V was crowned.

Bygdøy

The first thing that has to be said is that you should make as much time as possible available to explore everything that is on offer here.

The **Norwegian Folk Museum** is a magnificent collection of more than 170 old buildings from all parts of Norway. The homesteads and farms, ancient store barns and town houses from the eighteenth and nineteenth centuries are spaced out well among the trees, and looking down on them from the top of the hill is a twelfth-century stave church. In 1885 King Oscar II bought the church from the people of Gol in Hallingdal and had it erected near his summer palace on Bygdøy, on a site which is now the heart of the folk museum. The church contains many fine carvings.

The folk museum graphically portrays Norwegian life through the centuries. Many of the homes have the furnishings and utensils of their period, while others have become workshops where artisans, dressed in traditional costume, practise their crafts of weaving, carving and so on. One building houses Henrik Ibsen's study.

A restaurant is open during the summer. Folk dancers and musicians are often invited to perform in the museum which also houses the Norwegian Pharmaceutical Museum.

The **Maritime Museum** has a rich collection of boats housed indoors and also anchored in the bay just outside. The exhibits chart Norway's maritime history over the centuries. There is also an exhibition of fishing equipment used over the years. Nearby is the Sailor's War Memorial.

Outside the museum stands the *Gjøa*, the ship used by Roald Amundsen on his polar expedition when he discovered the North-West Passage. There are

A wide range of different vessels jostle for position below Oslo's castle

Log cabins in the folk museum at Bygdøy, whose grass roofs act as insulation

many scale models of ships and the Norwegian ports they used to sail from, and a number of slide shows to amplify notable episodes in the country's maritime history. The museum has a restaurant and café.

   The **Kon Tiki Museum** is across the road from the Maritime Museum, and houses the famous *Kon Tiki* raft built in 1947 on which Thor Heyerdahl and his crew sailed to show that the Polynesians were more likely to be descended from South American Indians than from Asian tribes. The balsa wood raft was copied from the sort of boats used by the Peruvian Indians in 500. The *Kon Tiki* sailed the 8,000 km from Callao in Peru to the island of Raroia in Polynesia in 101 days. You can walk round the exhibit which has been built in such a way that you can also get a wide view.

Exhibited with it is the 14m long papyrus reed boat *Ra II* used in 1970 by Thor and his eight nation crew for his successful crossing of the Atlantic, and a collection of artefacts from the Polynesian islands, including several huge carved standing stones from Easter Island.

   The **Fram Museum** is next to the Maritime Museum and contains the polar exploration vessel *Fram*, built by Colin Archer between 1892 and 1893 and used by Fridtjof Nansen, Otto Sverdrup and Roald Amundsen on their expeditions to the North and South Poles. No other vessel has ever been so far north or south.

   The **Viking Ship Museum** is the most spectacular of Bygdøy's treasures, not just because of the wonderfully preserved exhibits, but because of the magic they conjure up. The building was specially designed in the shape of a right-angled cross so that the three Viking ships on display can each be seen to best advantage. The three ships were all discovered in Oslofjord and the finds not only confirmed the remarkable boatbuilding skills of the Vikings, but gave enormous insight into their culture. The three ships *Oseberg*, *Gokstad* and *Tune* all date from between AD800 and AD900 and were used as burial vessels. Only royalty and the nobility were buried in such fine ships, and the vessels were laden with all the objects of everyday life which would be needed in *Valhalla*.

Oscarshall Castle, overlooking the fjord near the Folk Museum, was built in English Gothic style 1847 and 1852 as the summer palace of King Oscar I. The walls are decorated by Norwegian romantic painters, and the royal stables are opposite.

Additional Information

Places of Interest

OSLO

Akershus Castle
Oslo 1
☎ (02) 41 25 21
Ramparts open: all year. Castle open: May to mid-September, Monday to Saturday 10am-4pm. Sunday 12.20-4pm. Rest of year castle only open Sunday 12.30-4pm.

Museum of Applied Art
(Kunstindustrimuseet)
St Olavs gate, Oslo 1
☎ (02) 20 35 78
Open: all year, Tuesday to Friday 11am-3pm; weekends 12noon-4pm.

Armed Forces Museum
(Forsvarsmuseet)
Akershus Fortress
Oslo 1
☎ (02) 40 35 82

Open: all year, Monday to Friday 10am-
3pm; weekends 11am-4pm.

Basarhallene
Next to Oslo Cathedral
Open: all year (outdoors).

Bogstad Manor
Sørkedalen, Oslo 7
Open: May to mid-September, Sundays
only 12noon-5pm.

Cathedral (Domkirken)
Stortorvet
Oslo 1
Open: January to end May and September to end December, Monday to Friday
10am-1pm, June to end August, Monday to Friday 10am-3pm, Saturday
10am-1pm.

City Hall (Rådhuset)
Open: October to end March, Monday to
Saturday 11am-2pm, Sunday 12noon-
3pm, April to end September, Monday
to Saturday 10am-3pm, Sunday 12noon-
3pm.

Oslo City Museum (Oslo Bymuseum)
Frognerveien
Oslo 2
☎ (02) 43 06 45
Open: all year, June to end-August,
Tuesday to Friday 10am-6pm, weekends
10am-5pm; rest of year Tuesday to
Friday 10am-4pm, weekends 11am-4pm.

Christiania Town
Høymagasinet Building
Akershus Fortress
Model of the old city.
Open: June to mid-September, Tuesday
to Sunday 11am-5pm. Audiovisual
programmes every half hour.

Damstredet
Open: all year (outdoors).

Ethnographic Museum
(Etnografisk Museum)
Frederiks gate 2
Oslo 1
☎ (02) 41 63 00
Open: mid-September to mid-May,
Tuesday to Sunday 12noon-3pm; mid-
May to mid-September, Tuesday to
Sunday 11am-3pm.

Frogner Park
North-west suburb of Oslo
Open: all year.

Gamlebyen
Open: throughout the summer (outdoors).

Henie-Onstad Arts Centre
(Henie-Onstad Kunstsenter)
1311 Høvikodden
West of Oslo
☎ (02) 54 30 50
Open: all year Mondays 11am-5pm,
Tuesday to Friday 9am-9pm, weekends
11am-5pm (11am-7pm June to end
August).

Historical Museum
Frederiks gate 2
Oslo 1
☎ (02) 41 63 00
Open: mid-September to mid-May,
Tuesday to Sunday 12noon-3pm; mid-
May to mid-September, Tuesday to
Sunday 11am-3pm. Closed 1 January, 1
and 17 May, Christmas and Easter
holidays.

International Children's Art Museum
(Barnekunst Museum)
Lille Frøensveien 4
Oslo 3
☎ (02) 46 85 73
Open: all year, during school term,
Tuesday to Thursday 9.30am-2pm,
Sunday 12noon-5pm; end June to end
August, Tuesday to Friday 11am-5pm,
Sunday 12noon-5pm.

Oslo Ladegård
Oslo gaten
Guided tours May to end-September,
Wednesdays 6pm and Sundays 1pm.

Munch Museum
Tøyengata 53
Oslo 6
☎ (02) 63 37 41
Open: May to end September, Monday
to Saturday 10am-8pm, Sunday 12noon-
8pm, mid-November to end April,
Tuesday, Thursday and Saturday 10am-
8pm, Wednesday and Friday 10am-
4pm, Sunday 12noon-8pm.

National Gallery (Nasjonalgalleriet)
Universitetsgata 13
Oslo 1
☎ (02) 20 04 04
Open: all year Monday, Wednesday,
Friday and Saturday 10am-4pm, Thurs-
day 10am-8pm, Sunday 11am-3pm.

Natural History Museum
Sars gate 1
Oslo 5
☎ (02) 68 69 60
Botanical gardens May to mid-August,
Monday to Friday 7am-8pm, weekends
10am-8pm, mid-August to end Septem-
ber, Monday to Friday 7am-7pm,
weekends 10am-7pm, October to end
March, Monday to Friday 7am-5pm,
weekends 10am-5pm, April, Monday to
Friday 7am-6pm, weekends 10am-6pm.

Old Aker Church (Gamle Aker Kirke)
Geitemyrsvn
Open: all year Monday to Thursday
12noon-2pm.

Parliament Building (Stortinget)
Karl Johans gate 22
Oslo 1
Open: July to end August, Monday to
Friday 11am-2pm.

Postal Museum (Postmuseet)
Tollbugata 17
First Floor
Oslo 1
☎ (02) 40 80 59
Open: all year Monday to Friday 10am-
3pm.

Resistance Museum
(Hjemmefrontmuseet)
Akershus Fortress
Oslo 1
☎ (02) 40 31 38
Open: October to mid-April, Monday to
Saturday 10am-3pm, Sunday 11am-
4pm, mid-April to end September,
Monday to Saturday 10am-4pm, Sunday
11am-4pm.

Royal Palace (Slottet)
Drammenssveien
Public access to park only. Changing of
Guard daily at 1pm. When the king is in
residence, the band of the Royal Guard
plays Monday to Friday.

**Norwegian Museum of Science
and Technology**
Kjelsfveien 143
Oslo 4
☎ (02) 22 25 50
National museum of science and technology, many working models.
Open: mid-June to end August, Tuesday
to Sunday 10am-7pm, September to

mid-June, Tuesday 10am-9pm, Wednesday to Saturday 10am-4pm, Sunday
10am-5pm.

Skating Museum (Skøytemuseet)
Frogner Stadion, Oslo 3
☎ (02) 61 11 10
Open: all year by appointment.

Skiing Museum/Holmenkollen Tower
Kongeveien 5
Oslo 3
☎ (02) 14 16 90
Open: January to beginning April and
October to end December, Monday to
Friday 10am-3pm, weekends 11am-4pm,
May and September all week 10am-
5pm, June all week 10am-7pm, July all
week 9am-10pm. August all week 9am-
8pm.

Theatre Museum (Teatermuseet)
Nedre Slotts Gate 1
Oslo 1
☎ (02) 53 63 17
Open: all year Wednesday 11am-3pm,
Sunday 12noon-4pm.

Transport Museum (Sporveismuseet)
Gardeveien 15
Oslo 3
☎ (02) 34 49 71
Open: May to end September, weekends
12noon-3pm, October to end April,
Sunday only 12noon-3pm.

Tryvannstårnet Observation Tower
Tryvannstårnet
Open: January to end April and October
to end December, Monday to Friday
10am-3pm, weekends 11am-4pm. May
and September every day 10am-5pm,
June every day 10am-7pm, July every
day 9am-10pm, August every day 9am-
8pm.

Oslo University (Aula)
Karl Johans gate 47
Oslo 1
☎ (02) 42 90 91
Open: July, Monday to Friday 12noon-
2pm.

Vigeland Museum
Nobels Gate 32
Oslo 2
☎ (02) 44 23 06
Open: November to end-April, Tuesday
to Sunday 1-7pm, May to end-October
12noon-7pm.

BYGDØY

Fram Museum
Bygdøynes
Oslo 2
☎ (02) 12 36 50
Open: all year, April and November
11am-2.45pm, 1-15 May and September
11am-4.45pm, mid-May to end August
10am-5.45pm; November weekends
only 11am-2.45pm.

Kon Tiki Museum
Bygdøynesveien 36
Oslo 2
☎ (02) 43 80 50
Open: November to end March all week
10.30am-4pm, April to mid-May and
September to end October all week
10.30am-5pm, mid-May to end August
all week 10am-6pm.

Maritime Museum
(Norsk Sjøfartsmuseum)
Bygdøynesveien 37
Oslo 2
☎ (02) 43 82 40
Open: January to end April and November to 23 December, Monday, Wednesday, Friday, Saturday 10.30am-4pm,
Tuesday and Thursday 10.30am-7pm,
Sunday 10.30-5pm, May to end September all week 10am-8pm.

Norwegian Folk Museum
(Folkemuseet)
Museumsveien 10
Oslo 2
☎ (02) 43 70 20 170
Open: all year, January to May, Monday
to Saturday 11am-4pm, Sunday 12noon-3pm, mid-May to end August, Monday
to Saturday 10am-6pm, Sunday 11am-6pm, September, Monday to Saturday
11am-4pm, Sunday 12noon-5pm,
November to end December, Monday to
Saturday 11am-4pm, Sunday 12noon-3pm.

Oscarshall Castle
Oscarshallveien
Open: mid-May to end September,
Sundays only 11am-4pm.

Viking Ship Museum
Huk Aveny 35
Oslo 2
☎ (02) 43 83 79
Open: November to end March all week
11am-3pm, April all week 11am-4pm,
May to end August all week 10am-6pm,
September all week 11am-5pm, October
all week 11am-4pm.

Concerts

Oslo Concert Hall
Konserthuset)
Munkedamsvn 14
0115 Oslo 1
☎ (02) 83 32 00

Ticket Box Office:
☎ (02) 83 45 10

Rockefeller
Torggt 16, 0181 Oslo 1
☎ (02) 20 32 32 Rock and pop concerts.

Opera and Ballet

Den Norske Opera
Storgt 23, 0184 Oslo 1
☎ (02) 42 94 75 / 42 77 24
Open: 10am-6pm

Emergencies

Emergency telephones
Police: 002 or 66 90 50
Fire: 001 or 11 44 55
Accident / Ambulance: 003 or 20 10 90
Falken (car rescue): 23 20 85

Police
Police Headquarters
Oslo Politikammer
Grønlandsleiret 44
0190 Oslo 1
☎ switchboard: (02) 66 90 50
Duty Officer (24hr service) (02) 66 99 66
Aliens Office (02) 66 90 50

Emergency Medical Services
Oslo Kommunale Legevakt
Storgaten 40
Oslo 1 (24hr service)
Accidents, ambulance,
hospital admission.
☎ (02) 20 10 90

Oslo Akutten
Nedre Vollgt 8
0158 Oslo 1
☎ (02) 41 24 40
Open: Monday to Friday 8am-10pm,
Saturday 9am-3pm, Sunday closed.

Emergency Dental Services
Oslo Kommunale, Tannlegevakt
Tøyen Senter, Kolstadgata 18
0652 Oslo 6
☎ (02) 67 48 46
Weekdays 10-11pm, Saturday, Sunday
and holidays 11am-2pm and 10-11pm.

Car Breakdown Services
Falken Bil- og Froskemannsavdelin
☎ (02) 23 25 85

NAF Alarmsentral
24hr service.
☎ (02) 42 94 00

Viking Redningstjeneste
24hr service.
☎ (02) 60 60 90

Lost Property
Lost Property Office
(Hittegodskontoret)
Grønlandsleiret 44
Oslo 1
☎ (02) 66 98 65/66 90 50
Open: Monday to Friday 8.15am-
3.15pm, Saturday and Sunday closed.
Mid-June to mid-September, Monday to
Friday 8.15am-4.25pm.

Central Station
Oslo S Hittegodskontor
☎ (02) 36 80 47
Open: Monday to Saturday 9am-4pm,
Sunday closed.

Chemist-Pharmacy
Jernbanetorgets Apotek
Jernbanetorget 4 B
Oslo 1
☎ (02) 41 24 82
Open: 24 hr.

Shopping

Markets
In Oslo there are three large markets for
retail trade in fruit, vegetables and
flowers. Same opening hours for all:
Monday to Saturday 7am-2pm. During
the period 15 March to 14 October and
17-23 December, Monday to Friday
7am-3pm, Saturday 7am-2pm.

Youngstorget
Vegetables, flowers and fruit.

Stortorvet
Garden and hothouse flowers.

Travel

Airports
Air traffic to and from Oslo uses two
airports:

Oslo Airport Fornebu, is situated at
Snarøya, about 9km from the city centre
and is the country's most important
airport both for domestic and international traffic.

Oslo Airport, Gardermoen
Gardermoen, is situated approximately
50km from Oslo. Mainly international
charter traffic and US Flights.
(Airport bus, see below.)

Airport buses/'Flybussen'
Airport buses to **Fornebu** leave several
times per hour from: Airport bus
terminal (Galleri Oslo), Wessels plass,
National Theatre, Skøyen and Lysaker.
Travelling time: 20-25 mins.

The airport bus to **Gardermoen** leaves
Oslo city 2 hours before regular charter
flight departure.
Travelling time: 50 mins.

The Airport Bus Terminal is the main
terminal for airport buses to and from
Fornebu and Gardermoen.
The terminal is situated at Vaterland at
the ground floor of Galleri Oslo
☎ (02) 56 62 20
Open: daily 5am-midnight.

Timetables are available from travel
agents, tourist offices and hotels.
Further information about bus departures
☎ (02) 42 49 91.

Boat Connections
From Oslo there are regular passenger
car ferry departures.
To **Copenhagen**: daily (DFDS) at 5pm.

Also several days a week to
Fredrikshavn (Da-No and Stena) and
Hirtshals (Fred Olsen Line).
To **Newcastle**: once a week (Fred Olsen
Lines).

Train
All trains depart and arrive at Oslo
Station.
For timetable information
☎ (02) 17 14 00

Public Transport in Oslo

The public transport system in Oslo is well developed, comprising subways, trams and buses, ferries and local trains.

Subway

There are 8 subway lines, converging at Stortinget station. From here there are 4 westbound lines running through Majorstuen station and 4 eastbound lines running through Tøyen station.

Trams

There are 5 tram lines running through the city from east to west. Oslo M at Vaterland has become the city's new bus junction.

Bus

There are 20 bus routes operating within the city limits. These buses carry 2-digit numbers. The converging point for all the bus routes is Jernbanetorget. There is a single fare system within the city limits. Enquire at the ticket-offices for rates, maps and time tables.

Ferries

There is a ferry connection to Hovedøya and the other islands in the harbour from Vippetangen all year round. From Rådhusbrygge 3 (City Hall pier 3) there is a ferry connection to the Bygdøy peninsula from April to September. The summer sightseeing boats leave from pier 3. From the Aker Brygge pier there is a ferry connection to Nesodden all year, and to Håøya island by Drøbak in the south on summer week-ends.

Information

Questions regarding public transport should be directed to the information center, **Trafikanten**, at Jernbanetorget. Open: Monday to Friday 7am-10pm, Saturday and Sunday 8am-6pm.
☎ (02) 17 70 30

Taxis

Call Oslo Taxicentral
☎ (02) 38 80 90
Advance booking: ☎ (02) 38 80 80 (at least 1 hour in advance).
Administration: ☎ (02) 38 80 00
Taxis free for hire have a lit-up sign on the roof.

Parking in Oslo

The City of Oslo has usual traffic problems and in order to deal with these has introduced special parking regulations and a toll to enter the city. The rules are sensible, but can be very confusing at first.

1. *Parking discs:* These are colour-coded according to the length of time one is allowed to park. Yellow means maximum 1 hour, grey means 2 hours and brown means 3 hours. One can also buy special discs which allow parking for longer periods.

2. *Parking zones:* Parking is controlled during working hours (Monday to Friday 8am-5pm, Saturday 8am-2pm) and cars must obey parking signs. After 5pm weekdays (2pm Saturdays) and all day Sunday, parking is free everywhere.

3. *Parking at night:* There is an important regulation governing cars parked at the kerb overnight (midnight-7am). On odd days of the month, cars may only be parked on the side of the road next to the odd-numbered houses and correspondingly on even days. This is so that the streets can be cleaned overnight.

More exact information can be found in a leaflet entitled *Parking in Oslo* which is available from tourist information offices and petrol stations.

Useful Addresses

Airlines

British Airways
Karl Johansgt 16B
4th floor
0154 Oslo 1
☎ (02) 33 16 00

Embassies and Consulates

Australian Information Office
Jernbanetorget 2
3rd floor
☎ (02) 41 44 33

Britain
Thomas Heftyesgt 8
Oslo 2
☎ (02) 55 24 00

USA
Drammensvn 18
Oslo 2
☎ (02) 44 85 50

Motoring
KNA (Kongelig Norsk Automobilklub)
Royal Norwegian Automobile Club
Drammensvn 20
0255 Oslo 2
☎ (02) 56 19 00

Car Hire
Avis Rent a Car
Billingstadsletta 14
1312 Slependen
☎ (02) 84 90 60
Booking: (02) 84 78 80
Fornebu Airport
☎ (02) 53 05 57
Munkedamsvn 27
☎ (02) 83 58 00

Oslo Central Post Office
Dronningensgt 15
Oslo 1
Open: Monday to Friday 8am-10pm,
Saturday 9am-3pm, Sundays and
holidays closed.
☎ (02) 40 78 20

Tourist Information Office
Rådhuset, N-0037 Oslo 1
Norway
☎ (02) 33 43 86
Open: Monday to Friday 8.30am-4pm,
Saturday and Sunday closed.

Ascension Day 8.30am-2.30pm
Whitsun 9am-4pm
Christmas Eve 8.30am-12noon
New Year's Eve 8.30am-12noon
Closed:
New Year's Day
Good Friday
Easter Day
International Labour Day
Constitution Day
Christmas Day
Boxing Day

Tourist Office
Oslo City Hall
Rådmannsgfrden
Rådhusgt 19
0158 Oslo 1
☎ (02) 42 71 70

Tourist Information Oslo Station
(Central Station)
Oslo Sentralstasjon
Oslo 1
☎ 42 44 60
Open: All year, daily 8am-11pm.
Closed: Same as Tourist Information,
City Hall.

Youth Information
USE IT
Oslo KFUM
Møllergata 1
0179 Oslo 1
☎ 41 10 39

3

SOUTH TO THE SWEDISH BORDER

After exploring Oslo it is time to visit some of the areas around the capital and the journey south to the Swedish border provides a scenic and interesting day's drive.

Because greater Oslo now has almost a quarter of the country's population, the suburbs sprawl out for many miles in all directions. This area around Oslo covering more than 4,900sq km, is known as Akershus and consists of a collection of communities such as Asker and Bærum in the west and Follo, Nedre Romerike and Øvre Romerike in the east. There is no identifiable centre to this region which is now a mixture of traditional timber homes, modern dwellings and industrial and business complexes. The houses nestle on the hillsides among the trees while boats of all sorts bob at the water's edge, a reflection of the Norwegians love of sailing. During the summer there are regular trips down Oslofjord, but the drive along the eastern shore is lovely. You pass through rich farm land, massive forests, an impressive hill, ancient towns with castles and a spectacular bridge until you reach the Swedish border at Svinesund. For much of the route there are wonderful views of the massive fjord stretching away into the distance. You can stop off and swim on some of the sandy beaches or bathe in the many lakes. There are charming little harbours and ports like Son and Drøbak. In the forests you can hike, pick berries and mushrooms while nature lovers and bird watchers can explore the Nordre Øyeren nature reserve, at the northern end of Lake Øyeren.

For excitement, Norway's largest amusement park Tusenfryd has been opened in Follo. If you do not want to drive, take a canoe trip on the Halden canal which runs from the fjord to the Swedish border through the forests. If you do not feel like paddling, a steamer plies the route.

The area is rich in history and was the very part of Norway to be settled by roving Germanic tribes coming up from the south more than 10,000 years ago. There are many burial mounds, rock carvings, medieval churches, ancient farms and museums to explore, and castles which indicate that the border with Sweden has not always been so peaceful.

The area along the eastern shore of Oslofjord is called Østfold. It is about 115km from Oslo to the Swedish border and the round trip will take about 4 hours plus the time for stops. The immediate impression of the area is how green and how relatively flat it is, especially when compared with other regions of the country, which makes it excellent for cycle touring country. More than half the land is wooded, and over 20 per cent used for agriculture, making it one of Norway's most important farming regions. Forestry is also important and a number of towns and ports along the route depend on timber for their primary industry.

The roads are good throughout this region because it is the main crossing point into Sweden but there is no need to rush, and if you want to avoid the lorries on the highways, turn off and follow one of the smaller roads.

From Oslo take the E6 south. It is well signposted from the city and the ferry terminal. A short way out of town is a turn off for Ingierstrand, one of Oslo's most popular beaches. The E6 has replaced the old road which runs round Lake Gjersjøen and takes you close to **Svartskog**, the home of Roald Amundsen.

Follow the E6 to **Vinterbru** with its amusement park, where it divides into the E6 and E18. Remain on the E6 which runs south parallel with the fjord. The E18 runs inland to the Swedish border via Askim and Mysen, both of which have local museums, and Ørje. It is the best route for Stockholm, travelling through generally flat agricultural land and forests.

Continue on the E6 until the Korsegården crossroads with the 152 minor road. The left hand turning takes you to **Ås**, Norway's agricultural college which opened in 1893, while the right hand turning will take you to the charming town of **Drøbak** which has become increasingly popular with artists, and there are many galleries. The town was originally one of the ports servicing Oslo, but today it is a flourishing little resort with winding streets and old timbered houses. The church, built in 1776, has a rich Rococo interior. There are bathing and recreation areas and a car ferry which takes 10 minutes to cross over to Storsand on the west bank. There is a museum with a collection of old implements, tools and furniture, while the now ruined fort of Seiersten overlooks the town. A short distance from Drøbak, and in about 100m of water lies the German cruiser *Blücher*, which was sunk by the Norwegians on 9 April 1940 as it sailed up the fjord for Oslo. You can either return to the E6 or drive along the coast, past a number of beaches to the resort of Hvitsten.

The E6 takes you through **Hølen**, once a port but now land locked, with its eighteenth-century market place, to **Moss**, the provincial capital of Østfold. The town has a large number of industries, from glass blowing to ship building, and has been the home of craftsmen since the Middle Ages. The town is an ideal base for exploring **Vansjø** to the east, the area's largest lake with scores of island. It is a fisherman's paradise. To the east is the Jeløya peninsula with fine beaches, holiday homes and opportunities for water sports of all kinds. The Alby mansion is found here with its famous art collection.

You should also visit the Konventionsgården, built in the eighteenth century and the former headquarters of the Moss Iron Works. It was here in 1814 that the treaty uniting Norway and Sweden was signed but which allowed Norway to have its own Constitution. Verksgaten is the oldest street in town and has some wonderful old buildings. Moss has a number of hotels, youth hostel and campsite.

You can take a ferry from Moss across the fjord to Horten allowing you to return to Oslo along the west bank on the E18. Just up the coast from Moss is **Son,** another delightful fjord resort with seventeenth-century buildings.

Continuing south along the E6 you drive through some of the most attractive farm land in Norway with immaculately kept farm buildings, past the

Rygge military airfield, with its low-flying jets, to **Sarpsborg**. Turnings off to the right lead to beaches and small resorts such as Larkollen, and the area has a number of hotels and campsites. **Rygge**, just under 1km outside the town has a medieval stone church, and so does **Råde**, a few kilometres further south, although it was rebuilt in 1862. Detour off on highway 118 to visit them. The area is rich in archaeological remains, and there are 2,000 year old Bronze Age burial mounds at Råde.

There are many spectacular views along the route worth stopping for and taking photographs, including a view of the Visterflo, the broad lake into which one of the arms of the River Glomma flows. The best view is from just after the junction where highway 112 joins the E6.

Further on, there is a left turning to **Kalnes** noted for its 3,000 year old Bronze Age rock drawings of animals and boats. Nearby is the secondary school Østfold jordbruksskole, formerly an agricultural college.

The town of **Tune** has a summer youth hostel and beside the lake, the Tunevatn, there are more ancient burial sites. The E6 then runs into **Sarpsborg**, on the banks of Norway's longest river, the Glomma. The town is heavily reliant on its timber industry although new enterprises have now been developed. The town was founded, according to the sagas, in 1016 by King Olav Haraldsson (St Olav) and is famous for its waterfall, the Sarpsfossen which plunges more than 21m. The waterfall has been harnessed to provide power for the massive Borregaard wood mill, which has Norway's tallest chimney, 160m high.

Of interest is the Borgarsyssel Museum (check opening times locally), built around the remains of the twelfth-century Church of St Nicholas. It has exhibits tracing the history of the area from the Bronze Age, and the grounds contain a medieval medicinal herb garden and a number of old houses dating back to the seventeenth century.

The town has retained its commercial importance because the Glomma provides access between the harbour and fjord. On the southern outskirts of town in the suburb of Hafslund, is the **Hafslund**, a manor house built in the 1760s. It is well signposted and open to the public but check the visiting times with the local tourist office as they vary.

Fredrikstad is a major industrial centre and port. It was founded by King Frederik II in 1567 and its numbers swelled by the citizens of Sarpsborg. Gamlebyen, the old fortified garrison town, is still well preserved with houses dating back to the seventeenth century. Some are now used as studios by artists and craftsmen. Worth visiting are the impressive sixteenth-century fortifications of Fort Kongsten (open daily) with its network of underground passages and rooms, and the old working water mill on the river as you leave the town to make your way back to the E6 along highway 110. It is at Isegran, which was until 1680 Norway's main naval base. The 40m high bridge over the Glomma with a span of almost 900m is also spectacular, as is the view from it.

Vestre Fredrikstad church, restored in 1954, has stained glass windows by Emanuel Vigeland, and an altar piece by Alex Revold. Østsiden church in the old town was built in 1779. The town has plenty of hotels, motels and camping sites, and the royal family has a summer home on the coast. There are many islands just off shore.

The stretch of road between Fredrikstad and Skjeberg along highway 110,

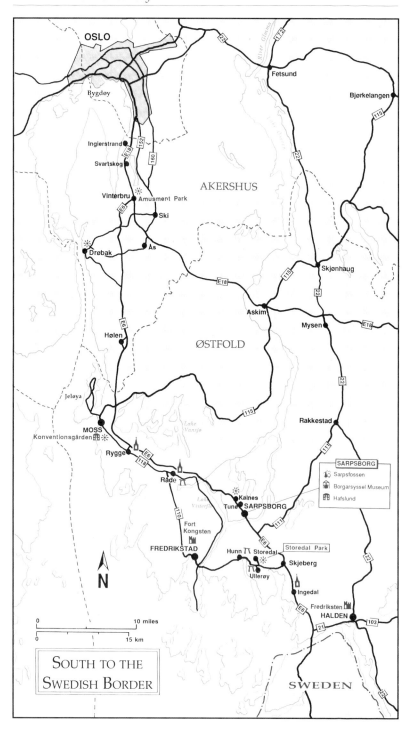

SOUTH TO THE
SWEDISH BORDER

is known as the 'Road of the Ancients' and is mentioned in the sagas. There are countless archaeological remains in the area, and many examples of rock drawings (*hellerisninger*) which are between 2,000 and 3,000 years old. One of the best spots to see these is at the Begby crossroads, just outside Fredrikstad. There are also rock carvings at Solberg and Hornnes, and both sites are well sign posted. At **Ullerøy** there is a 1,500 year-old burial ground, although the largest collection of antiquities is to be found at **Hunn** where there are around 100 burial mounds, stone circles and standing stones which date from around the birth of Christ to AD1000. You can walk the Oldtidsveien, a 2,000 year old bridle path that crossed Østfold, and climb to the top of the Ravneberget hill where there are the remains of a stone fort dating from around AD300.

Storedal Park with its open-air amphitheatre is also between Fredrikstad and Skjeberg on highway 110. It has been specially adapted so that blind people can use it, and a play about Magnus the Blind is performed there annually. It is open to the public daily but contact the local tourist office (Fredrikstad ☎ (09) 32 03 30) for further details.

The 'Road of the Ancients' ends at Skjeberg and here rejoin the E6 driving through **Ingedal** with its medieval stone church, down towards the Swedish border which is beyond the 60m tall, 420m long Svinesund bridge over Iddefjord. Customs controls are not very strict and you can drive across into Sweden if you wish, but it is more interesting to take highways 104 or 21 a couple of kilometres or so before the border and head for Halden.

Halden is still a major industrial centre, dominated by the massive fortress of Fredriksten which overlooks the town and guards the sea approaches. From the castle battlements you can look down over the town and far out to

Halden's fortress stands guard over the town

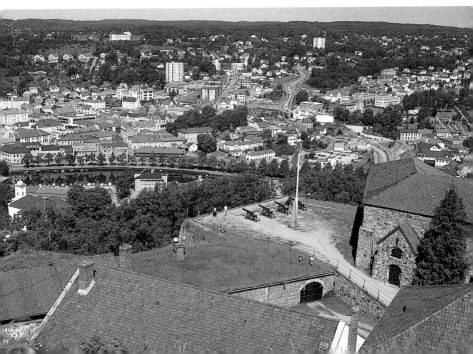

sea. It is well-signposted and open daily. Around the harbour are the huge timber yards and rail head which delivers the wood.

Halden was granted its town charter in 1665 after successfully repelling Swedish attacks 3 years running. It was called *Fredrikshald* and was not known as Halden until 1928. When work on the castle started in 1644, the Norwegian border was further south at Båhuslen. This fortress had the task of protecting the frontier, but repeated Swedish attacks persuaded the Norwegians of the need to strengthen the defences of Fredriksten. The town was destroyed several times by fire and although the castle was attacked and laid siege to on many occasions it was never taken.

You could spend hours wandering round the castle, which also houses the town museum. The views from the ramparts are spectacular. Although many of the original fortifications have disappeared, their position is marked by a series of stone tablets so it is easy to visualise what it must have looked like. The cannon and their emplacements built to protect the town are still there. If you look inland you will see a number of very old buildings which used to be command posts. Other things to see include the eighteenth century Rød Manor, about 1km west of the town, with its weapons collection, Immanuel's church, one of the few Empire style churches in Norway, and the medieval Berg church, about 4km west of the town.

After visiting Halden you can return to Oslo via highway 104 and the E6 (the fastest route) or detour via Rakkestad and Askim for different scenery.

Additional Information

Useful Addresses

Regional Tourist Board
Akershus Tourist Board
PO Box 6888
St Olavs Plass
N-0130 Oslo 1
☎ (02) 36 58 22

Local Tourist Offices
Halden Reiselivslag
Boks 167
N-1751 Halden
☎ (09) 18 24 87

Moss Turistinformasjon
Chrystiesgt 3
N-1500 Moss
☎ (09) 25 54 51

Østfold Reiselivsråd
By post:
Fylkeshuset
N-1700 Sarpsborg

'Phone/personal enquiries:
Turistinformsjonen SveNo
E6 Svinesund
N-1760 Berg i Østfold
☎ (09) 19 51 52

Sarpsborg Turistinformasjon
Jernbanegt 10
N-1700 Sarpsborg
☎ (09) 15 36 29

Drøbak ☎ (09) 935087
(not staffed the year round)
Fredrikstad ☎ (09) 320330
Moss ☎ (09) 252212

4

THE SOUTH COAST RIVIERA

The 600km coastal route between Oslo and Stavanger follows the E18 most of the way from the capital, and it is necessary to make a number of detours if you want to see all the things of interest along the way. The south coast is famous for its beaches and resort towns and the roads can be busy in the summer. The road runs through the regions of Buskerud, Vestfold, Telemark, Aust and Vest Agder and Rogaland and all have something different to offer. For much of the way the road cuts inland to avoid the hundreds of bays and inlets along the coast, and between Kvinesdal and Moi there is some spectacular fjord scenery. The train journey to Stavanger is equally rewarding.

If you are driving to Stavanger to catch the ferry home, do not leave it until the last minute. It is a long haul and it is much better to take it slowly with an overnight stop or two, so that you do not miss anything.

The fastest way to get out of Oslo is to take the westbound E18, which is clearly signposted to Drammen. It is a toll road but it helps you get out of the Oslo suburbs quickly and is worth the small charge. The toll is paid just outside Drammen. South-west of Oslo you drive through Bærum and its administrative centre Sandvika.

Not far from Skaugum, the road passes the residence of the crown prince, and there are many turn offs to the lakes and fjord inlets. These are very popular boating areas but there are also beaches and Hvalstrand is very popular with Oslo residents.

The E18 by passes Asker and leads you into Drammen, 40km from Oslo. It is the capital of the Buskerud region, and Norway's sixth largest town. **Drammen** is really made up of two towns Stromsø and Bragernes which were officially united in 1811, although historians know from rock carvings found that the area has been settled for at least 5,000 years. The huge bridge over the River Drammenselva splits the town in half although it has flourished in recent years, especially the harbour. There is a regional museum, housed in the eighteenth-century Marienlyst Mansion, and an open-air folk museum with many old buildings. Stromsø church was built in 1667 but totally rebuilt in Empire style in the 1840s. The town hall in the town centre, built in 1872, won an international award in 1986 because of the 'exemplary restoration work'.

If you do not plan to come this way again it is worth making a detour out of Drammen on the E76 to the **Drammen Spiralen**, a 1.6 km long road tunnel with almost corkscrew twists climbing up through the Bragernesåsen mountain. There is a restaurant at the top and breathtaking views. The tunnel, which is open year round and consists of six spirals, came about when it was decided to stop quarrying for stone in 1953 in order to protect the countryside.

Art lovers are recommended to take a trip to **Hurum** nestling betweeen the fjords, and home of Holmsbu Gallery including Henrik Sørensen's collection.

From Drammen the E18 runs through the hills to Sande at the head of Sandebukta, a finger of the Oslofjord, and then along the coast to the charming market town of Holmestrand.

You are now in the region of **Vestfold** which covers an area of 2,216sq km making it the smallest of Norway's nineteen districts. It is a region of huge forests, hidden lakes and long ridges. There is walking, excellent fishing, water sports of all description and some wonderful beaches. The sheltered harbours have been the home of sailors and shipbuilders for centuries. It was from this coast that the Vikings sailed to Ireland where they founded Dublin.

✳   **Holmestrand** has been a market town since the eighteenth century and it has retained many of its fine old buildings and narrow twisting streets. The town's church dates from 1674 has a rare Y-shaped plan and its museum depicts the town's history and records many of the famous artists who have lived there, including painter Harriet Backer, her sister-composer Agathe Backer Grøndlah, and the author Nils Kjær. Water still provides the main leisure action and has also been harnessed to power the expanding aluminium industry. The town has some pleasant beaches.

The E18 continues through **Horten**, a former naval base because of its natural harbour. The Karl Johansvern base is now the Naval Museum (open daily) and is separated from the town by the charming Horten canal. The town also has a veteran vehicle museum.

About $2^1/_2$km south of Horten and just off the E18 is **Borre** with a medieval church, just north of which is Norway's oldest national park containing the largest number of royal burial mounds in Europe. You can take a ferry from Horten for the 30 minute crossing to Moss on the eastern shore of Oslofjorden.

Because this area is so popular with tourists there is no shortage of accommodation with hotels, youth hostels, huts and camping sites, although obviously it is advisable to book well ahead for peak periods.

Next is **Asgårdstrand**, regarded by the locals as Norway's Paris. Edvard Munch was just one of the many radical artists who lived here, and his home, Lykkehuset is now a museum in his honour. Check with the local tourist office at Tønsberg for opening times.

The next town **Tønsberg** is Norway's oldest as well as being the regional capital of Vestfold. Snorre the chronicler recorded that the town existed before the battle of Hafrsfjor which took place in AD872. Its history can be traced back to the ninth century. Because of its harbour's sheltered location at the head of a fjord inlet, it was for almost 200 years Norway's most important trading centre, but its importance declined because of the proximity of Oslo when it was made the country's capital. During the eighteenth and nineteenth centuries it was an important shipping centre and the base for Norway's whaling fleet. The Vestfold County Museum in the town contains collections on the area's whaling and maritime history, and the open air section contains a number of fine old buildings. The museum opens daily during the summer while the open air section can be visited throughout the year.

Other sights to see include Møllebrakken, an old courtyard just to the south of the city centre, and Slottsfjellet with the ruins of the thirteenth-century Tunsberghus Castle built by King Håkon Håkonsson. There are excellent views from the top of the hill. There are the ruins of the Church of St Mikael built in 1150, and King Magnus Lagabøter's castle. Sem Church just to the north of the town, is the oldest in the county and was built in 1100 in Romanesque style.

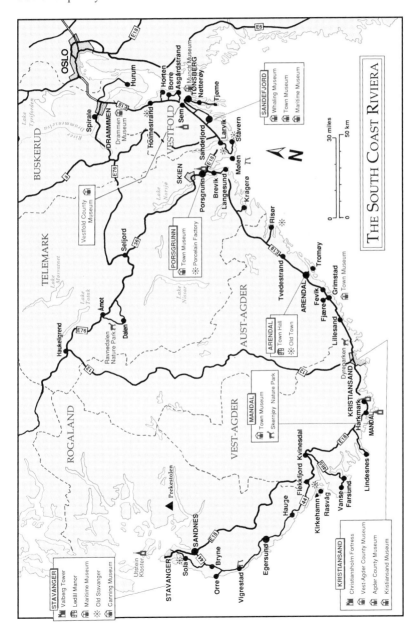

76 *Visitor's Guide: Norway*

Many Viking burial mounds have been found nearby, and one excavated in 1917 was the grave of King Bjørn Farmann who was killed by his brother Eirik Blodøks at the Sem Royal Court in AD933. Also close to the town, just to the north-east, is Oseberg which gave its name to the Viking burial ship found there, now displayed in the viking museum at Bygdøy.

A worthwhile detour, especially if it is hot, is to take the road south out of Tønsberg which crosses the islands of Nøtterøy and Tjøme, all connected by bridges, which jut out into Oslofjord. **Nøtterøy** church was built at the end of the eleventh century, while Tjøme church was built in 1866 on the site of the medieval church which had been demolished. The new church contains many of the furnishings from the old including the wonderfully carved seventeenth-century altar piece and pulpit, the sixteenth-century gallery paintings, and a thirteenth-century crucifix. There are also many beaches and campsites. Return to the E18 and follow it south for about 15km before turning off left to Sandefjord, the next town to explore.

Sandefjord is a bustling modern town although it has retained much of its provincial charm. The large naturally protected port used to be the world's top whaling centre, and the town has the only Whaling Museum in Europe. Apart from the town's impressive whaling statue and fountain, the museum has a 21m model of a blue whale. The first factory ship sailed to the Antarctic waters to hunt whale in 1905. Today the port exports mainly timber while the major industries are ship building and repairs and light industry.

There are two other museums: the Town Museum, in a house dating from the 1790s, tells the story of Sandefjord, while the Maritime Museum has a fine collection of model ships, pictures and artefacts. It was in the northern suburb of Gokstad that the second of the Viking burial ships on display at Bygdøy was found. Sandar church, built in classical style, dates from 1792. The town and neighbouring area has many beach and recreation areas.

Return to the E18 turn left and head for **Larvik**. As you enter the town there is a turning off to the right, highway 8 which goes to Kongsberg. Larvik is a charming seaside resort and lies between Lake Farris (famous for its mineral water) and Larvikfjord as it starts to open out into the Skagerak.

The Larvik ferry leaves here to cross to Frederikshavn in Denmark — there are still many important links with Denmark. The Herregaarden, built in 1673-4, was the official residence of the Danish governor of Norway, and today it is a museum. Larvik developed as a whaling station and ship building centre — Nansen's vessel *Fram* was built here — but timber and timber exporting are now the major industries. There is a maritime museum in the Old Custom's Shed, dating from 1740. Exhibits include models of Thor Heyerdahl's famous vessels, *Kon Tiki* and *Ra*.

Other things to see include Larvik Old Church, with its painting in the choir by the German artist Lucas Cranach (1472-1553), and the war memorial created by Vigeland standing in front of the new church. There are a number of medieval churches around Larvik at Tanum, 6km to the south-west, Tjølling, 6km to the east, and Hedrum, 8km to the north. Also to the north lies Norway's largest beech forest (Naturpark Bøkeskogen).

Although the E18 now heads inland along Langangfjorden, it is worth the short detour south to the tip of the **Mølen** peninsula with its lovely beaches, including the famous Oddane Sands, and the nearby Bronze Age burial mounds. There are many campsites and huts in the area. Another interesting detour is to **Stavern**, a picturesque seaside resort which used to be one of the country's main naval bases (Fredriksvern, built between 1750-56), and still has its eighteenth-century sea defences. There is a Rococo church and a war memorial to sailors killed during the Great War. There are many small, attractive seaside resorts along this stretch of coast including Helgeroa and Nevlunghavn.

From Larvik follow the E18 along Langangfjorden to **Porsgrunn**. The town has long been one of Norways leading ports, and is also now noted as the base for Norway's only China industry, and the home of the multi-national Norsk Hydro company, whose nitrate factory is at Herøya. Just up the road is Skien, Ibsen's birthplace, and a little further on at Venstop is the Ibsen museum.

The porcelain factory is open to visitors daily. The two churches Østre Porsgrunn, built in 1760, and Vestre Porsgrunn, built in 1758, both have Rococo interiors. The town museum is in an old rectory and the open-air section contains many old buildings with their original interiors. It is open daily but check the times with the local tourist office.

An interesting, but consuming trip, is to take the ferry through the Telemark Canal to Dalen. You can make your way back by bus, but it is better if one member of your party goes ahead in the car to meet you.

From Porsgrunn the E18 heads south again, through **Brevik** with its quaint fishermen's cottages, narrow streets and eighteenth-century town hall. Brevik has been a trading centre since the sixteenth century. Both the town hall and the old customs house are worth visiting. The road leaves town over the 45m high, 677m long bridge spanning the Brevikstrømmen, through the small port of Stathelle on the west bank, and into the district of Sørlandet, noted for its many seaside resorts and charming coastal towns.

The E18 is the fastest way to travel through the region but there are so many detours that can be made to visit the seaside towns and resorts, that you may prefer to follow the smaller coast roads which usually run parallel with it.

A mini detour to **Langesund** is worthwhile. It dates back to 1765 and is an old fishing town although now a popular resort because of its beaches, campsites, fishing and boating. The church, built in 1755 has a Rococo interior and the town hall dates from 1758. Just outside the town on the E18 is Bamble with the thirteenth-century ruins of St Olav's Church.

Next is **Kragerø**, one of a cluster of communities known as the 'white towns'. Kragerø is now a very fashionable resort with its old timbered houses and narrow, winding streets. The town museum is at Berg 4km away surrounded by marvellous gardens.

Visit the batteries at Gundersholmen, used to repel English warships during the Napoleonic wars. There are many small offshore islands to visit, and boats can be hired, or you can take one of the many organised trips. Just off the main road is Sannidal with a church dating back to 1771 but incorporating the porch from a medieval stave church.

Risør is another delightful resort with its well-preserved wooden houses nestling around the harbour. The town is one of the oldest on the south coast, and has been a port since 1630. The Church of the Holy Ghost dates from 1646 and is a fine example of Baroque cruciform style with ornate carvings and paintings. Søndeled church, originally built in stone about 1150 has a fine old tapestry. The Kastellet Citadel by the harbour was built at the beginning of the nineteenth century, and the Risørflekken is one of the oldest navigation aids along the south coast and can be seen from more than 19km out to sea.

Risør is famous for its beaches, the many small offshore islands to explore, and the summer regattas which culminate in the Wooden Boat Festival. An art exhibition is held in the town centre all year round, and the town has its own 'watchman' whose job is to patrol the older parts of the town and offer information to visitors. Risør also boasts the largest porthole in northern Europe measuring 6m across and 5m deep.

Tvedestrand, although a popular summer resort, earns some of its income from making Christmas decorations, and there are a number of cottage industries producing dried flowers. Strykejernet (the iron) in Tvedestrand is thought to be Norway's narrowest house. The town is built round the old iron works (Nes Verk) where some of the oldest workmen's homes in Norway are to be found dating back to 1738. The large wooden town hall by the harbour, is now an art gallery and you can watch craftsmen at work there, including glassblowers. The former defensive outer harbour can be seen running from island to island offshore. Tvedestrand has some marvellous fish restaurants. A short distance west of the town is Holt with its medieval church which was enlarged to a cruciform church in 1753.

Arendal was granted its charter in 1610 and was a major shipping centre in the late Middle Ages because of its large, well protected harbour, and last century more than 100 sailing ships were registered in the port, and hundreds more used to use it. Today the boats do not go quite so far afield but there are many sightseeing trips organised around the numerous offshore islands. The old town (Tyholmen) is delightful and very well preserved with its old brightly painted wooden houses. It used to be the Venice of the north because canals used to link many parts of the old town but these were drained and became streets.

The town hall is one of Norway's tallest wooden buildings, built in Empire style around 1812-14, and Trinity Church built in 1888 and the largest in the county, has an almost 90m tall musical tower, which plays choral works during festivals. The old battery overlooks the harbour, and the museum is on the nearby island of Merdøy, and has been arranged to resemble an old sea captain's home.

Other things to see include the medieval church at **Tromøy**, and the Aust-Agder Museum at **Langsæ** which records the history of the region (check visiting times with local tourist office). There is lots of accommodation in the area, from hotels and huts to camping sites, and boats can be rented. There are some marvellous fish restaurants.

Just beyond **Fevik**, with its excellent beaches and nearby Bronze Age burial mounds, is a turn off to **Fjære** with its medieval church famed for the carved headstone over the south porch, and springs (St Olav's Springs) outside.

Grimstad has been a port since 1791 and is now famous for its fruit preserving and fruit wine industries. It is the region's major cultural centre. The art centre stages exhibitions, plays, films and concerts during the year. The many offshore islands used to afford protection to the sailing ships in the nineteenth century which is why the port became so popular. Many of the houses today were owned by seafarers, and retain their original charm.

Things to see include the Town Museum. It used to be a chemist's shop and  was Henrik Ibsen's home for a time. The museum has the world's largest collection of Ibsen manuscripts, as well as a large collection of maritime exhibits. Ibsen also lived in what is now the art gallery between 1844 and 1850 and is open all year. During June and July special exhibitions are held. Just outside the town is the eleventhth-century Fjære stone church where Terje Vigen of Ibsen's famous poem is buried.

At **Nørholmen**, you can visit the home of author Knut Hamsun bought with his Nobel Prize money in 1918. The town hosts an annual film festival.

The road then arrives at **Lillesand**, a small town with a long trading history and a wide variety of architectural styles reflecting its international character. During the eighteenth and nineteenth centuries its traders visited England, Scotland and France and the styles of these countries can be found among the old houses around the harbour. One of the finest examples is the estate of merchant Carl Knudsen, built in Empire style in 1827 and now the home of the town and maritime museums.

The town hall, dating from 1734, won an international award for its resto-

An example of the varied architecture to be found in Kristiansand's shopping centre

ration in 1984. The medieval stone Vestre Moland church was extended to a wooden cruciform in 1797. If you have time take one of the many boat trips.

Continue along the E18 to **Sørlandsparken**, with its zoo, trotting course and amusement park, and then on to Kristiansand.

Kristiansand

Kristiansand is the capital of south Norway, and the country's most important ferry port linking it with Hanstholm and Hirtshals in Denmark and Amsterdam. There are several sailings daily. It is a flourishing town with a growing population and an ideal base for touring both the south coast and the spectacular hinterland. It is serviced by the airport at Kjevik, just to the north of the town.

Apart from its bustling harbour, the first thing that strikes you as you explore the town centre is its chessboard lay-out, a legacy of Denmark's King Christian IV who planned it in 1641 and gave it its name. This oldest part of town is known as Kvadraturen and is famous for its interlocking right angled streets, highly characteristic of the rectangularity of the Renaissance. The streets were built deliberately wide to reduce the risk from fire, but the timber buildings were very vulnerable, and the centre of town was destroyed on a number of occasions by fires raging out of control. Unfortunately many of the old timber buildings have been replaced by stone and brick. Some of the survivors can be seen in Elvegaten, and around the market and town hall.

Kristiansand, now Norway's fifth largest town, has always been an important centre because of its sea links and road connections along the coast and inland. The town flourished in the nineteenth century both as a port handling the ocean-going sailing ships and windjammers, and as a shipbuilding centre, but the real growth has been this century because of industrial development. Although now the 'holiday capital' of Sørlandet, at the heart of the Norwegian riviera, Kristiansand is an important industrial town with its harbour and factories.

There are many things to see and do. The Christiansholm Fortress, dating from 1674-9, stands beside the eastern harbour and today houses an arts and cultural centre, and a delightful restaurant. The walls of the rotunda are 5m thick.

There are also interesting art collections in the Billedgalleriet, the Vest-Agder County Museum, an open-air museum with more than thirty fine old buildings, as well as church fixtures and town and country furniture and costumes; and the Arne Vigeland Museum, with its bronze and plaster sculptures, on the nearby island of Lagmannsholmen. The Kistiansand Museum, Gimle gård (open daily except Monday), shows the cultural history and natural history of the area and is set in beautiful parkland. The Monte Carlo Bilmuseum next to the zoo, has a collection of old and luxury cars.

The Gothic cathedral with its 70m high tower, Norway's third largest, was built in 1885 and can seat 1,800 people. The previous cathedral was destroyed in a fire. The Oddernes church, built about 1040, has a Baroque pulpit dating from 1704, and an interesting rune stone outside. The rose painted interior of the wooden Søgne church is also worth inspecting.

To the north of the town is Grovane where railway enthusiasts have re-opened a section of the old Setedal line and now run the restored steam locomotives along it while the history of the narrow gauge railway can be traced at the Setesdal Railway Museum.

The biggest attraction in the area is the **Dyreparken**, Norway's only zoo, 12km out of town just off the E18, and reached by crossing the 600m long Varrord Bridge, one of the longest in Scandinavia. The 40 hectares (100 acre) zoo, funfair and activity park have more visitors than any other attraction in Norway.

Also worth visiting is the Ravnedalen Nature Park, established more than 100 years ago to protect the special flora and fauna in the area. There are spectacular views from the summit of the rocks which you can scale using the 200 steps hand hewn a century ago.

There is another nature reserve at the northern end of Kvadraturen with marked nature trails and a number of small lakes where you can bathe.There are many beaches in the area, islands to explore and boat trips to take.

The town has many interesting shops, restaurants and cafés. You can visit the harbour and marinas and stroll round the fish market, which divides the eastern and western harbours, or really stretch your legs on one of many marked trails in the hills north of Kristiansand.

Close to Kristiansand is the Falconbridge nickel factory, just off the E18, with its 120m high chimney, the second tallest in Norway.

For those with plenty of time to spare and who want to explore the area thoroughly, the local tourist office suggests two 5 day car tours with maps — one to the west and the other to the east. Both start in Kristiansand.

Kristiansand to Stavanger

The main route from Kristiansand to Stavanger is the E18 which swings quite deeply inland to skirt the many fjords along the coastline. There are, however, scores of attractive little coastal towns and resorts to explore and frequent detours can be made. Smaller coastal roads link many of these places if you are not in a hurry, although travelling to resorts only a few kilometres apart might take a long time and you will need to consult a good map. Two resorts may be just across the water from each other but you might have to drive right round the head of the fjord to get from one to the other.

Another interesting way to get to Stavanger is to take the train which cuts through the mountains, while an alternative car route, although less interesting, is to travel north on the E12 to Evje, west along the E9 to Tonstad, and then down Gyadalen to rejoin the E18 for Stavanger.

If you take the E18 from Kristiansand, you pass the Falconbridge nickle factory and the town of Søgn before arriving in Mandal. As you approach the town, a section of the old road running alongside the E18, has been preserved and is now used as a picnic area. It is known as the Knuden.

Mandal is Norway's most southerly town and one if its most picturesque. It is the oldest of the towns along the south coast and the old town, with its white painted wooden houses, has retained all its charm. The town sprawls on either side of the estuary of the Mandal river, and the oldest quarter is built round the market place and the finest of the old houses are found in Store Elvegaten. The parish church, built in Empire style in 1821 and capable of seating 1,800 people is Norway's largest wooden church. The Skrivergården was built in 1776 in the style of a Scottish country house, and is now the town hall. The town museum and art gallery is housed in Andorsengården, which was built in 1801. The gallery has a large collection of pictures of early sailing ships, and there is a statue by Gustav Vigeland, who was born in the town.

Other interesting buildings include the Hald Summerpension which was built in 1795 and 'moved' to Mandal on board the sailing vessel *Caledonia* in 1899, and Risøbank, the old summer residence of Lord Salvesen. It was built in 1901 and the house, now a museum, is preserved in its own parkland. The open-air folk museum has a beautiful rose painted storehouse and is open 10 June to 10 August.

Three hundred years ago Mandal salmon was considered a great delicacy and the importance of the fish to the town's early economy is witnessed by its inclusion in the municipal coat of arms, where it is depicted as the *glade laks* (merry salmon). Salmon is still fished locally and in season can be eaten fresh in many of the town's restaurants.

There is a charming 100 hectare (250 acre) nature park (skernjøy, open daily) with maple walks running down to a 2km stretch of coves and beaches, the Sjøsanden.

At **Harmark**, 12km to the east of Mandal, there is a timber church built in 1613. An old sawmill and smithy have also been faithfully restored here.

After leaving Mandal, a detour to **Lindesnes** is almost obligatory. You turn left off the E18 at Vigeland onto highway 460. Norway's most southerly point

A spare berth in Kristiansand's extensive yachting harbour

is 27km from the turn off, and well worth the trip both for the hills and moors you cross on the way, and the sea views at the cape. Sometimes in the summer, however, it is easy to get the impression that almost every other tourist in Norway is there as well. The crowds can sometimes get so large they even obscure the lighthouse down on the point. Beside the lighthouse stands the beacon built in 1822 which burned charcoal. From Lindesnes, Norway's south cape to the north cape is 2,518km. Retrace your steps to the E18 and turn right for Lyngal, a centre of trade and tourism, with two of the finest beaches in southern Norway at Rosfjord and Kvaviksanden.

A detour along highway 43 takes you to **Farsund**, famous as the base of the privateers which operated during the 1807-14 war with the English. Although still important as a shipping centre, its influence has declined considerably. It used to be one of the largest shipping towns of the world in relation to size of population.

Things to see include **Loshamn**, the port built 5km out of town with the money the privateers 'liberated' at sea, the museum at **Spindsodden** which depicts a sea captain's home, and the Lista Museum, 6km away at **Vanse**, where there is also an interesting church, part of which dates back to the Middle Ages.

There are many excellent beaches along this stretch of coastline, and lots of archaeological remains and burial mounds, especially near Listalandet. It is

The shopping centre at Mandal, Norway's most southerly town

an ideal place for windsurfing, and there are boats for hire for sea fishing, or touring the coastline.

You can return to E18 on either highway 43 or 465 which will take you into **Kvinesdal**, a town nestling at the head of Fedafjord. The E18 crosses Kvinesheia which is 350m above sea level at its highest point, and from the summit there are wonderful views down on the town. Kvinesdale is famous for its week-long Evangelical rally held every summer, which attracts tens of thousands of Christians who gather in Sarons Del (valley).

The Utsikten hotel also houses the local museum, and is a good vantage spot for viewing the fjord. Just outside the town is Øye with its metal works. The next town is **Flekkefjord**, an attractive settlement almost surrounded by hills and with a well protected harbour. The town straddles the river and is sandwiched between the hills and Flekkefjord to the south-east and Grisefjord to the north-west.

The old part of the town is still known as Hollenderbyen (Dutch Town) because its principal trade in the 1820s and 1830s was shipping timber to Holland, although fishing was also important. Today the major industries are fishing, tanning and furniture making. Some of the oldest houses were even built in Dutch style and you can wander round the narrow, twisting lanes and view them and the boat houses fronting the water. The town's octagonal wooden church was built in 1833, and the museum is housed in a local dignitory's home built around 1720.

Just offshore lies the island of Hidra which has two charming villages, **Kirkehamn** and **Rasvåg**. The Ancestor's Memorial Museum (check locally for opening times) has a fascinating and unique collection of exhibits recalling the history of the island.

Egersund is the next destination and you can reach it by either following the E18, and turning off left on the E9, or by taking the coastal highway 44. Both routes offer spectacular, although very different scenery. The coastal route cuts its way through tunnels and past beaches and more charming little resorts, such as the fishing village of Åna Sira.

You can take a detour up the twisting road to the summit of the ridge overlooking Jøssingfjorden, scene of an heroic rescue during the World War II. On 16 February 1940, boarding parties from the British Royal Navy destroyer *Cossack* stormed the anchored Altmark, a German merchantman, being used to hold 300 British Seamen prisoners of war. There is a monument recording the action on the summit, which affords splendid views. The road is very steep in places with a number of hair-pin bends, and it returns to rejoin highway 44 at Hauge.

At **Hauge**, noted for its Sogndalstrand beach, there is a fishing museum (check locally for opening times) and Sokndal is noted for its church built in 1803, one of the few Louis XVI style churches in the country. There are lovely beaches along this stretch of coast, such as Sokndalstrand and Rekefjord.

Egersund is a market town whose prosperity was built on its herring fishing and processing industry last century, and fishing is still its mainstay. It was the home of the fleet fishing the Fladen Banks. There are many lovely old wooden homes, especially along Strandgaten, and during the summer there are direct ferry links with Hirtshals and Hanstholm in Denmark. Egersund church was built in 1605 and rebuilt in cruciform style during the eighteenth century. The

altar piece dates from the beginning of the seventeenth century. Also visit the
Dalane open-air folk museum in the northern suburb of Slettebo. Take the E9
out of town to find it. The museum has a number of fine old eighteenth- and
nineteenth-century buildings with period furnishings. You can also take a
side trip down to the lighthouse at Eigerøy, and the safe bathing beaches at
Eigerøya.

If you continue along the coastal highway 44 you travel through the very
rich agricultural lands of the Jæren district. The area grows mostly cereals and
vegetables, and has many livestock farms. There are many small coves and
bays to explore, and at **Ogna**, which has a small medieval church, there are
huts and camping facilities alongside the beach. Close by there is **Brusand**
which still has some of the invasion defences built during World War II which
you can inspect from the long beaches. There are many ancient monuments
along the coast, such as the 1500 year old burial mounds around Kvassheim,
and the Iron Age and Bronze Age burial mounds, and prehistoric farm at
Kåsen, near Bryne.

For a while the road runs alongside the North Sea, and this stretch of
highway is known as Nordsjøveien. Stop and visit the ancient Evestad burial
ground at **Vigrestad**, and then on through Bryne, home of the national dairy
college, to Sandnes and the E18 for the short drive north to Stavanger.

If you want to explore around **Bryne**, there are some wonderful beaches,
especially those on Jærens Reef which are also popular with bird watchers
because of their rich wildlife. The coast road which bypasses Bryne is highway
507 which turns off from highway 44 at Søyland. At Bore it connects with
highway 510 which runs into Stavanger. The 507 passes through **Orre**, with its
fifteenth-century church, and many good beaches. The 510 skirts Hafrsfjord,
where in about AD900, Harald Hårfagre defeated the tribal kings to become
the undisputed king of a united Norway.

Sandnes is an industrial town at the northern end of the Jæren Plains,
although it is also an important tourist destination. It is surrounded by scores
of sheltered, sandy beaches, about ten or fifteen minutes away by car, and it
is in each reach of the mountains inland, which provide skiing into early
summer. Sandnes is the second largest town in Rogaland, and is known as the
bicycle town, because the famous DBS bikes are made there. Close to the town
is the popular Kongeparken amusement park.

Stavanger

Stavanger is an oil boom town, has grown enormously in the last few years
and is now the fourth largest town in Norway. As the population has grown,
so the town has spread and its suburbs extend a long way south. The southern
approach to the town now consists of a long drive through industrial and
residential areas.

The sea has always played an important part in the town's 850 year-old
history. It was a trading centre in the eighth century, but its fortunes blos-
somed in 1125 when work started on the cathedral.

Since the twelfth century it has been an important trading and shipping
centre although its population did not expand until the nineteenth century.

Today it is a bustling, growing town although still a charming combination of old and new. Canning is important again, but all industries are overshadowed by oil. The large North Sea ferries are dwarfed as they sail past the massive oil rigs under construction or repair in the harbour, and many of the town's newest and most modern buildings have been built by the oil companies and the industries servicing them.

Despite the rapid changes of the last two decades, the essential character of old Stavanger has hardly changed at all.

Although you should plan to spend several hours exploring Stavanger, you can still get a feel of the town by just walking through the old quarter. The tourist centre is next to the railway station. It has literature about the town and area, details about sightseeing tours, and can arrange guides.

The Stavanger Card is useful if you plan to spend some time in the town. You can buy it when registering at your hotel, guesthouse or campsite, or in advance, through Stavanger Tourist Office. It gives 50 per cent off museum entry, railway and bus travel, concerts and some sports facilities, and smaller but still significant discounts off boat trips, cinema and theatres and so on.

Stavanger Cathedral is across the road from the market square and between Haakon VII's Gate and the Breiavatnet lake, was built on the orders of King Sigurd the Crusader, when he made the town a Bishopric in 1125. Bishop Reinald from Winchester was in charge of the building work, and many English craftsmen were recruited. The cathedral is dedicated to St Svithun, and was originally built in Anglo-Norman style. After being damaged by fire in 1272, the chancel was rebuilt in Gothic style and completed in 1300. It is the only medieval cathedral in Norway to have retained its original style.

Kongsgården, beside the cathedral, was originally the Bishop's Palace and built in the thirteenth century. The Mauke Chapel was subsequently added. The palace was taken over as one of the Danish-Norwegian Royal residences and then became the home of the district governor. For the last 150 years it has been used as a cathedral school for further education. To the north of the market square is the Valberg Tower, a former watch tower, which now gives visitors an excellent view of the town, fjord and mountains.

Ledål Manor is a mansion built in 1800 for the wealthy Kielland family and restored with furnishings of that period. It is the official royal residence when the king or members of the royal family visit the area.

The **Maritime Museum** in Nedre Strandgate, has exhibits showing the town's maritime development over the last 200 years from sail to oil. There is a ship owner's office suite and a small sail makers loft dating back to the last century and includes a trade museum with a turn of the century shop.

Old Stavanger around Øvre Strandgate, is the best preserved old quarter of wooden houses in northern Europe. The 150 or so houses are all in a conservation zone and are inhabited. The houses all date from the end of the seventeenth and beginning of the eighteenth centuries, and are remarkably well maintained.

The **Canning Museum** in Øvre Strandgate, is a reconstructed sardine canning factory dating its heyday between 1890 and 1920. Breidablikk in Eiganesveiein, is a mansion built by the architect Henrik Nissen in 1880 for the

(opposite) The Valberg Tower rising above the rooftops of Stavanger

merchant and shipping magnate Lars Berentsen. The villa is furnished as it would have been at the end of the last century.

Stavanger Museum in Muségt, contains cultural and zoological exhibits. It shows Rogaland's flora and fauna from the sea to the mountains, as well as the region's arts and crafts. There is also an archaeological exhibit containing finds discovered locally since the Iron Age, including Stone Age finds from the Viste Cave and the oldest skeleton found in Norway.

Vestlandske Skolemuseum in Hillevåg is in the old Kvaleberg school, and has a collection of old and new educational equipment, and a large library of educational books which can be borrowed. Other things to see include the Mission Museum in Misjonsveien; prehistoric settlement at Svarthola, Viste and the aviation museum showing Stavanger Airport's history at Sola Sjø.

There is an exhibition of ceramics, jewellery, textiles and glass at the Brukkskunstsenteret in Valbergtårnet; an Iron Age farm reconstruction, and the Stavanger Botanical Garden at Ullandhaug. Stavanger has a rich cultural life with many galleries, theatres and concert halls. The **Stavanger Art Gallery** has a fine collection of paintings by Norwegian artists, including Stavanger's most famous artist Lars Hertervig. The Stavanger Concert Hall at Bjergsted is home of the Stavanger Symphony Orchestra.

Utstein Kloster (check the opening times with the local tourist office), on the island of Mosterøy is Norway's best preserved abbey and cloisters from the Middle Ages. It has also been a royal residence and a manor house. It has been restored and furnished and although open to the public is now used for seminars and conferences. There is a boat between Fisskepiren and Askje on Mosterøy with a bus connection taking visitors to the monastery.

Other trips include Mosvanns Park with its rich wild bird life, the telecommunications tower at Ullandhaug for its spectacular panoramic views, and a day tour along Lysefjord to the **Prekestolen** (Pulpit Rock). You can ferry and bus, or drive close to the rock, but the ascent has to be on foot. It is quite a difficult climb to the top of the huge slab of rock with its sheer cliff sides. The top is 600m above sea level. You must wear tough shoes or boots, allow about 4 hours if you are fit for the round walking trip, and take a picnic to enjoy at the top because the views are stunning.

There are many beaches in the area but the nearest is at **Sola**, famous for its white sand. There are opportunities for deep sea fishing and all types of water sports. Accommodation abounds from hotels and hostels, to cabins and campsites, but reservations are advisable during the high season.

Additional Information

Places of Interest

Drammen
Drammen Museum
Konnerudgata
Open: summer only Tuesday 12noon-8pm, Wednesday to Friday 12noon-6pm, weekends 12noon-4pm.

Grimstad
Town Museum
Open: daily, 1 June to 1 September 10am-3pm.

Lillesand
Town and Maritime Museum
Carl Kmudsen Gården
Open: 25 June to 15 August 11am-1pm.

Mandal
Town Museum
Open: 1 July to 15 August, Monday to
Friday 12noon-6pm, Saturday closed.
Sunday open 2-6pm.

Sandefjord
Whaling Museum (Hvalfangstmuseet)
Museumsgt 39

Maritime Museum (Sjøfartmuseet)
Prinsensgt 18

Town Museum (Bymuseeum)
Hystadveien 21
Opening times for all three museums,
May to September, Monday to Saturday
11am-4pm, Sunday 11am, October to
April, Sundays only 12noon-4pm.

Kristiansand

Agder County Museum
Vigevn 22b
Open: 20 May to 19 June and 21 August
to 9 September.

Dyreparken
On E18, 11km east of town
Open: 17 September to 18 May 10am-
3pm, 23 June to 12 August 9am-7pm, 19
May to 22 June and 13 August to 16
September 10am-6pm.

Kristiansand Zoo
☎ (042) 46200, Open: daily 10am-4pm.

Monte Carlo Bilmuseum
Open: 2 May to 15 September 11am-
7pm, 1 December to 30 April. Weekends
11am-4pm.

*Vest Agder County Museum
  (Vest-Agder Fylkemuseum)*
Vige, ☎ (042) 90228
Open: Monday to Saturday 10am-6pm,
Sunday 12noon-6pm.

British Consulate
Rigetjønnveien 51, ☎ (042) 24452

Police
Tinghuset
Rådhusgaten 34
4614 Kristiansand
☎ (042) 29500

Post Office
Kirkegt 11
Open: Monday to Friday 8am-4pm,
Saturday 9am-1pm.

Tourist Office
Kristiansand Turistkontor
Henrik Wergelandsgata 17
Postboks 592
N-4601 Kristiansand S
☎ (042) 26 065
Open: weekdays 8am-4pm, Saturday
10am-6pm, Sunday 1-6pm.

Youth Hostel
Kongsgård Allé 33
☎ (042) 95 369
2km from the railway station
Open: mid-June to mid-August,
closed 10am-4pm.
Campsite
☎ (042) 94 759

Stavanger

Stavanger Art Gallery
Madlaveien
☎ (04) 52 04 63
Open: September to May, Monday to
Friday 9am-2pm and 6-8pm, Saturday
12noon-3pm, Sunday 12noon-5pm.

Canning Museum
Øvre Strandgate
Open: mid-June to mid-August, Tuesday
to Sunday 11am-3pm, rest of year Sunday 11am-4pm.

Iron Age Farm
Ullandhaug
☎ (04) 53 41 40
Open: May to September, Sunday
12noon-3pm, June to August daily 11am-
3pm plus Tuesday and Wednesday 6-
8pm.

Ledål Manor
Eiganesveien 45
☎ (04) 52 60 35
Open: June to August, Monday to
Saturday 11am-1pm, Sunday all year
except December and January 11am-2pm.

Maritime Museum
Nedre Strandgate 17
Open: mid-June to mid-August, Tuesday
to Sunday 11am-3pm, rest of year Sunday 11am-4pm.

Preserved timber buildings in Old Stavanger

Lake Breiavatnet in the centre of Stavanger

Stavanger Museum
Musegt
☎ (04) 52 60 35
Open: June to August daily except
Monday 11am-3pm, rest of year, Satur-
day 10am-1pm, Sunday 11am-3pm.

British Consulate
Great Britain, Kongsgt 10
☎ (04) 525801

Opening Hours

Shops
Monday to Wednesday 9am-4pm
Thursday to Friday 9am-7pm
Saturday 9am-2pm.

Post Office
Stavanger Post Office is open 1 June to
31 August Monday to Friday 8am-4pm,
Saturdays 9am-12.30pm. Rest of the
year: Monday to Friday 8am-5pm,
Saturdays 9am-1pm. Foreign exchange,
American Express.

Banks
15 May to 31 August Monday to Friday
8.30am-3pm, Thursday to 5.30pm.
Closed Saturday. Stavanger Airport,
Sola open: Monday to Saturday 7.45am-
4.30pm. Sundays 11am-4.30pm.

Telephone — Telegraph
Nygaten 15. Opening hours: Monday to
Wednesday and Friday 8.30am-4pm,
Thursdays 8.30am-7pm, Saturdays
8.30am-2pm.

Ticket Desk
Stavanger Cultural Center ☎ (04) 507030.
Tickets for cinemas, theatre and con-
certs. Open: weekdays 11am-9.30pm.

Dispensing Chemists
After normal opening hours call
☎ (04) 520 128.

Car Rental
Avis Bilutleie A/S, Kongsgaten 50
☎ (04) 528565
Europcar, Lagårdsveien 125
☎ (04) 522133
Hertz Bilutleie, Hillevågsveien 33
☎ (04) 581700
Interrent, Hillevågsvn 21-23
☎ (04) 589702
Stavanger Bilutleie, Kong Karlsgt 71
☎ (04) 520352/523469

Travel

Information Service (Ruteservice)
On scheduled buses, ferries and trains:
☎ 522600. Monday to Friday 8am-7pm,
Saturday 9am-2pm, Sunday 3-7pm.

Taxi
The Taxi Central ☎ (04) 526040

Airlines
Braathens SAFE
Strandkaien 2, ☎ (04) 536070
British Airways, Sola ☎ (04) 651533
Dan Air, Strandkaien 2 ☎ (04) 536070
KLM, Sola ☎ (04) 651022/651070
SAS, Rosenkildetorget 1
☎ (04) 521566

Bus Timetable
Bus to Airport: From the Atlantic Hotel
every 30 mins
Morning bus to Airport — from hotels,
see hotel reception
City buses, SOT — Stavanger and
Omegn Trafikkselskap ☎ (04) 532120
'Ekspressen', Express bus Stavanger-
Kristiansand, twice daily ☎ (04) 525868

Tour Buses
Sola Ruten ☎ (04) 650099
SOT Reiser ☎ (04) 555088
Haga Bilruter ☎ (04) 68 95 55

Breakdown Service
NAF, Langflåtveien 3 ☎ (04) 582500
Falken, Auglendsdalen 1 ☎ (04) 586020

Car Ferries
DSD, Det Stavangerske
Dampskibsselskap ☎ (04) 520020
Fred Olsen Lines, Strandkaien
☎ (04) 530149/530291
Norway Line, Strandkaien ☎ (04) 524545
Kystveien, A/S Team Askøy-Bergen
☎ (05) 141100

Trains
Stavanger-Oslo. Information regarding
schedules, ☎ 520103/536137

Left Luggage
Stavanger Express boat terminal,
open: 7.15am-9pm
Railway station, open: 7am-10pm
Opening Hours

Tourist Office
Stavanger Reiselivslag
Postboks 11, N-4001 Stavanger
☎ (04) 53 51 00

Useful Addresses

Regional Tourist Boards

Aust-Agder Fylkeskommune
Fylkeshuset
N-4800 Arendal
☎ (041) 17 300

Buskerus Tourist Board
Storgt 4
N-3500 Hønefoss
☎ (067) 23 655

Rogaland Tourist Board
Øvre Holmegt 24
N-4006 Stavanger
☎ (04) 53 48 34

Telemark Tourist Board
Postboks 743 - Hjellen
N-3701 Skien
☎ (03) 52 92 05

Vest-Agder Tourist Board
Postboks 770
N-4601 Kristiansand S
☎ (042) 74 500

Vestfold Tourist Board
Storgt 55
N-3100 Tønsberg
☎ (033) 10 220

Local Tourist Offices

**Drammen Kommunale
  Turistinformasjonen**
Radhuset
N-3000 Drammen
☎ (03) 83 40 94

Farsund Turistinformasjon
Torvet
N-4550 Farsund
☎ (043) 90 839

**Flekkefjords
  Turistinformasjonskiosk**
Brogt, N-4400 Flekkefjord
☎ (043) 24 254

Staffed during the summer only.

Haugesund:
Reisetrafikkforeningen for Haugesund
N-5500 Haugesund
☎ (04) 72 52 55

Holmestrand:
Kulturkontoret
Tordenskjoldsgt 5
N-3080 Holmestrand
☎ (033) 51 590

Kragerø Reiselivslag
Postboks 176
N-3771 Kragerø
☎ (03) 98 23 30

Kvinesdal:
Vestre Vest-Agder Reiselivslag
N-4480 Kninesdal
☎ (043) 50 042

Larvik Reiselivsforening
Storgt 20
N-3250 Larvik
☎ (034) 82 623

Mandal:
Mandalsregionens Reiselivslag
Postboks 278
N-3401 Mandal
☎ (043) 60 820

Porsgrunn Turistkontor
Østre Brygge
N-3900 Porsgrunn
☎ (03) 55 43 27

Sandefjord Turistkontor
N-3201 Sandefjord
☎ (034) 65 300

Tønsberg Summer Information
Honnørbryggen
N-3100 Tønsberg
☎ (033) 10 211

Tourist offices shown in bold type in the list below are staffed the year round.

Arendal ☎ (041) 22193

Egersund ☎ (04) 490819

Grimstad ☎ (041) 44041

Horten ☎ (033) 43390

Lillesand ☎ (041) 71449

Risør ☎ (041) 52200

Sandnes ☎ (04) 625240

Sola ☎ (04) 651575

Tvedestrand ☎ (041) 61101

Tønsberg ☎ (033) 14819

5

TOURING TELEMARK, ROGALAND AND HORDALAND

Telemark

The area of Telemark is one of the most famous and most beautiful in Norway. It has something for everyone from skiing to swimming and fishing to walking. There is breathtaking scenery, wonderful old buildings, and a peace and calm that quickly helps you unwind and relax. Although many people know about Telemark because of its skiing, it is a very popular summer holiday area.

Telemark covers about 15,300sq km and although forested and hilly inland, has a number of towns and villages, each of which makes an ideal base for touring the area. There are also many camping sites and cabins for those who want the freedom to move around. It is quite easy to spend your whole holiday wandering through Telemark, and there is no reason why you should not because it has a wealth of accommodation.

Telemark starts at the sea with its rocky island, coves and white sandy beaches, runs inland through forests, long, deeply etched valleys, and then climbs above the timber line into a wilderness country of lakes and high mountains.

The tour of Telemark is a round trip of about 375km and starts in the charming fishing town and resort of Kragerø, follows the coast west for a short distance before heading inland to Lake Nisser, one of Norway's largest inland lakes. It takes in the magnificent Heddal stave church, the best preserved in the country, Notodden, Bø and Skien before returning to Kragerø via Porsgrunn.

Telemark is one of the most historic parts of Norway and there are more buildings from the Middle Ages in this district than anywhere in Norway. The finest examples are the stave churches at Heddal and Eidsborg, but almost everywhere it seems are centuries old farmsteads and marvellous store barns, some of which are almost 1,000 years old.

The special architectural style developed in Telemark is preserved in many of the open-air folk museums with their rich collections of restored buildings. You should try to visit the folk museums at Rjukan and Vrådal. The fashion of *rosmaling* is also more popular in Telemark than anywhere else in the country, and there are many wonderful examples of it throughout the district.

Further evidence of Telemark's rich cultural heritage can also be seen in the number of folk groups still dancing and playing the music that has been passed down from generation to generation for centuries. It does not matter where you are in Telemark as there is always something to do if you enjoy being out of doors and active. Along the coast you can take part in water sports of every kind, or just enjoy swimming and lazing on the beach. Inland there are almost endless trails to follow through the woods and hills, you can cycle, walk or canoe and there is excellent fishing.

Kragerø makes a convenient starting point as you can take in the circular Telemark tour before continuing along the E18 towards Stavanger as part of a more general tour of the south. Apart from the beaches for swimming, there is good fishing along the coast and the local tourist office in Kragerø can help you arrange windsurfing and waterskiing, sailing, riding and organised hiking.

Enjoy the coastline down to Risør using the twisty sea hugging highway 351 rather than the E18, and then follow highway 411 to Tvedestrand, where you start to drive inland into the heart of Telemark. Follow highway 415 to Ámli and then turn right on to highway 39 to Treungen at the foot of Lake Nisser which covers 77sq km. This whole area is a walker's paradise in the summer and it does not really matter which road you take because you will find excellent, well marked trails to follow. You can swim, fish or boat in the lake or take a cruise on the Fram.

Follow highway 39 which hugs the eastern bank of the lake through Grimstveit and **Nissedal**, which claims to be the home of Father Christmas. It has a good bathing beach and boats can be hired. There is also a camping site here and at Steane, a few kilometres beyond. At Vrådal you can take a chair lift up into the mountains.

 Just before Tjønnefoss you can detour off on highway 355 which climbs over Våmurfjellet to **Fyresdal** and gives spectacular views across Fyresdalsvatn and the mountains beyond. The museum at Fyresdal has some fossilised trees. The road then continues to Skafsá, where you can either turn left to visit Dalen at the head of the Telemark Canal, or turn left for Vrådal where you rejoin the tour.

The area around **Dalen** is an excellent place to spend some time exploring. You can camp out or hire a cabin and enjoy long, glorious walks through the woods or laze by the water. It really is worth the drive to the summit of Holte bru 994m beneath Lauvikfjell. Despite the hairpin bends the drive is worthwhile because the views both on the way up and at the top are fabulous.

Just north of Dalen on highway 45 is **Eidsborg** which has a charming open-air museum built on the hill with lovely views over the surrounding woodland and lake. The museum has a number of ancient farmsteads which are spaced well apart and blend in naturally with the scenery. The stave church (see section on stave churches p44) was built around 1300 and restored in 1929 when a number of important eighteenth-century paintings and ornaments were discovered. The church contains a wooden statue to St Nicholas and is next to a charming little museum with local costumes and exhibits telling of the life and folklore of the area. Highway 38 from Dalen Åmot is also worth exploring for its magnificent scenery. The narrow, twisting road passes to the east of Bessefjell (1,156m). There are marvellous detours left through the Rukkejuvet to Mo, and right along Ravnejuvet which connects with the E76 east of Åmot at Gøytil. The incredible cliffs in the Raven's Gorge create powerful updraughts. At Åmot the rivers Tokke and Vineå meet and used to

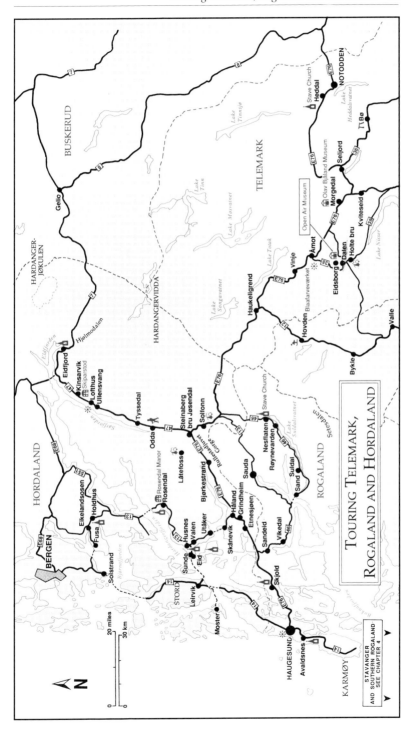

TOURING TELEMARK,
ROGALAND AND HORDALAND

form a massive waterfall but this has now been harnessed to power a hydro-electric plant.

A short detour from Åmot to **Blaafarveværket** is well worthwhile if you time. Take highway 287 to this beautifully preserved mining settlement which is open to the public during the summer. The settlement was founded by the Danish King Christian VII in 1772 to process cobalt from the Modum mines into cobalt blue which was used as a colouring by many of the world's leading ceramic, porcelain and glass industries. Cobalt blue from the mine was exported to Wedgwood, Meissen, Sevres, Limoges, Japan and China. Today the museum and mines are run as a small national park. There is a restaurant and large picnic area beside a lake. Other things to see are the Haugfossen, a short walk away and Buskerud's highest waterfall, and the farm with its traditional Norwegian cattle and horses. There is also an annual exhibition of Norwegian painters.

From Åmot you can head west on E76 for Haugggesund or Bergen, picking up route 4b at Jøsendal. From Haukeligrend you drive along the Haukeli road which crosses Haukelifjell. This road was built at the end of the last century to link east and west and until quite recently was impassable in winter because the many passes were usually blocked by snow drifts. Tunnels now avoid many of the most exposed areas and the road is open year round.

This is a very popular summer walking area and there are many places offering accommodation along the highway, such as Vågslid, Prestegård, Haukeliseter and Røldal with its stave church (see section on stave churches p47), and Seljestad. This is a high altitude road, much of it over 1,000m and the highest point is 1,148m on the old road which skirts the Dyrskard tunnel, one of the many that you encounter. The old roads are still open for summer driving although they are usually very steep, very narrow and full of hairpin bends. Snow often lies in sheltered areas by the road all the year round, and the surrounding mountains almost always have snow caps.

Back in Dalen the tour continues by taking highway 38 to the south of the lake and then swinging north round its eastern end to cross over a ridge of land into **Kviteseid** which has an open-air museum and a fine stone church dating from the Middle Ages. Built about 1150 it has some fine interior carvings. The road then joins the E76. If you detour left for about 20km you arrive in **Morgedal**, a very popular winter sports resort, known as 'The Cradle of Skiing'. There are two museums: the Olav Bjåland Museum has a collection of skiing equipment, including some used on polar expeditions, and Øvrebø, the cottage home of Sondre Nordheim, 'the father of modern skiing.' Both are open daily but hours vary so check with the local tourist office.

If you turn right at Brunkeberg on to the E76 you reach **Seljord**, with its medieval church and beautiful lake. You then drive to Heddal either along the E76, or the much more picturesque and quieter route, along highway 36 to Gvarv, and then north on highway 360 to Notodden, just a few kilometres east of Heddal. This second route follows two of Telemark's prettiest lakes, Seljordvatnet and Heddalsvatnet.

Heddal stave church is a must. It is the largest stave church in Norway, and all the more amazing when you think that parts of this timber structure have stood for almost 850 years. The chancel is the oldest part of the building and was consecrated on 25 October 1147, the feast of St Crispianus. A century later the church was enlarged and its appearance today is little changed. Although Heddal is now little more than a village, it must have been a very rich and much larger community during the Middle Ages, both because of the size of the church, and the richness of its furnishings. The structure of the church is dealt with in detail in the special section for stave churches on page 45.

There is a charming open-air folk museum at Heddal, a short distance away from the church, with a fine collection of old buildings. Head back for Notodden, the main town of eastern Telemark. It is an industrial town established last century, and overlooking Lake Heddal.

On the outskirts of the town turn right and south on to highway 360 for Gvarv and then on to **Bø**. Here there is a remarkable grocer's shop, exactly as it was 100 years ago, and Telemark Sommarland, a huge water park with a very high slide for those brave enough to try it.

Follow highway 36 along the banks of Lake Norsjø to **Skien**, the birthplace of Henrik Ibsen. There are many memorials to him, including a park and Venstøp, the house he grew up in which is now a museum. It is open to the public but check the local tourist office for the opening times. There is also a museum tracing the history of the area in Brekkeparken. Skien is also important because it is the start of the Telemark Canal which connects the Skagerak with the small town of Dalen more than 105km away, deep in Telemark.

Work on the canal, five locks, eighteen lock basins and eight sluices, all took place last century and represents a tremendous building and engineering feat. Ferries ply the route daily and although the journey takes 10 hours, it is a fascinating trip through spectacular scenery.

The canal really consists of two water systems which have been ingeniously linked. The Skien-Norsjø canal was finished in 1861 and links the Skienfjorden which runs into the Skagerak, with the inland lake of Norsjø. The connecting Norsjø-Bandak canal was opened in 1892. All the huge stone blocks used to build the lock basins were cut by hand, and the lock gates still have to be cranked by hand. From Skien you drive through Porsgrunn to rejoin the E18 which runs round the coast back to Kragerø.

Note: If you plan to spend some time in Telemark, buy the Telemark Card. Telemark was the first district in Norway to introduce a discount card which gives reductions on admission to museums, sightseeing trips, hotels, restaurants, and even gifts. The local tourist offices will give further information.

Rogaland and Hordaland

Rogaland is quite a small area, covering only 9,100sq km with Stavanger and Sandnes, as its two chief towns. Because Stavanger is an important ferry port, people tend to be rushing to catch their boat, or anxious to get under way at the start of their holiday, so Rogaland is not always given the attention it deserves. For detailed information on Stavanger see chapter 4 .

Apart from its importance because of the battle of Hafrsfjord which led to the unification of Norway, Rogaland has many other famous links with the past. It was from its coast that the Vikings set out to discover North America, and more recently it was from the port of Stavanger that many of the giant oil

Intricate carving around a doorway of Heddal church shows the skill of the craftsmen

Heddal stave church (opposite)

Scouting the Telemark Canal

platforms were towed out into the North Sea to play their part in Norway's post war economic boom.

In the south-west corner of Rogaland is the county of Jæren, with its flat fertile fields of cereals, vegetables and rich grasslands, and long stretches of white sandy beaches. To the east where south Rogaland meets Sørlandet, the coast is rough and rocky, with hundreds of small, sheltered valleys. To the north and the east, the landscape starts to rise, from rolling hills to high mountains.

The western coast of Rogaland is characterised by long narrow fjords pushing deep inland through the forests and stopping only at the high mountains where the rivers tumble over the rock cliffs in spectacular waterfalls.

Hordaland is a marvellous region to explore because nowhere in Norway is there such a wide range of different scenery. The region covers an area of 15,634sq km. It covers hundreds of small islands, fertile plains, spectacular fjords, secluded bays, crashing waterfalls and imposing mountains and glaciers. In the east you climb up into the rugged Hardangervidda National Park and the beauty of the countryside the south — fruit trees laden with blossom with a backdrop of snow-capped mountains — was the inspiration of much of Edward Grieg's music. It is also a region rich in history with many fine old buildings and the remains of earlier settlements dating back to the Stone Age.

One of Norway's most impressive views in Rogaland is offered from Prekestolen which towers 600m above Lysefjorden. The rock walls plunge almost vertically into the water, but the top is large and flat with tremendous views on clear days. A little caution needs to be exercised from the summit of Prekestolen because it can be quite windy at the top.

Getting to Prekestolen can also be exciting because the new road at the end of the fjord, Lysefjordveien has twenty-seven hairpin bends rising from sea level to 900m. Nervous passengers should keep their eyes shut on the way up and down, but if you choose to peep, the views, and the drop, are incredible.

The coastal strip in the north of Rogaland is a mixture of grassland and marsh. There is a galaxy of islands to explore, especially Karmøy which can be reached by ferry from Stavanger, or by island hopping, from Sand for example.

Karmøy, like many of the islands, has a rich past and many ancient sites. It has many Viking monuments, the medieval Olav church, and Norway's first royal farm. At the southern tip of the island is the charming fishing port of **Skudeneshavn**, with its lovely wooden houses, while the northern tip looks across to the port of Haugesund, on the outskirts of which is the national monument Haraldshaugen, commemorating the battle. It does not matter where you choose to explore as you will find plenty to do. You can fish inland or offshore, and the Suldalslågen is the longest salmon river in fjord country. You can get up into the mountains and hike for days on end. The Stavanger Mountain Association (Muségt 8 ☎ 04 527566) maintains twenty-six modern mountain huts while the Haugesund branch operate a further seven.

The waters between the island provide excellent sailing and boating, and for the experienced, it is ideal for canoeing. It is also a great place for diving, while many of the islands are a birdwatcher's paradise, especially Utsira, beyond Karmøy, which is one of the country's remotest settlements.

Fishing possibilities are almost endless either at sea, or in lakes, rivers or fjords. All salt water fishing is free, and some of the best spots are at Karmøy, north of Haugesund, and along the Jæren coast south of Sirevåg. You can fish year round in the fjords while the lakes can offer trout, arctic char and eel. A licence is usually required to fish lakes, although a day permit usually costs only a few kroner.

Salmon and trout fishing in the rivers is more expensive. The best rivers are Bjerkreimselva, Ognaelva, Håelva, Figgjo, Frafjord, Dirdal, Helle, Jørpelandselva, Vorma in Tøtlandsvik, Ulla, Hålandselva and Suldalslågen.

The best hill walking and climbing in the region is in the area which stretches from Etne, Sauda and the Hardanger plateau in the north, to the Ryfylke mountains and Setesdal mountains down to Sirdal. There are many long distance routes through the mountains but the mountain cabin network, where food is available, means you do not have to carry everything you need.

Rogaland also enjoys a very pleasant climate thanks to the warming influence of the Gulf Stream. The outer fjords record Norway's highest average yearly temperatures. Winters are mild with most fjord districts generally ice-free although there is snow inland and on the mountains.

Getting around Rogaland poses no problems despite all the fjords because of the ferries. Some routes can be very busy at peak times, such as the Randaberg to Skudeneshavn on Friday afternoons, and vice versa on Sunday evenings. If you are planning a lengthy stay on the Ryfylke islands, it is a good idea to take bicycles with you, or hire them if you can, because they are certainly the best way of getting around.

It is possible to spend your whole holiday touring in Rogaland and still not see everything the area has to offer. It is easiest if you split the county up into areas and tackle these one at a time.

Southern Rogaland
The main places of interest here, apart from the spectacular coastline, are **Egersund** church and museum and the Dalane Folk Museum, on highway 9 north-east of Egersund. Formerly a judge's home, the museum now houses a fine collection of old crafts and agricultural implements. For detailed information see chapter 4.

Also worth visiting are Egersund harbour, Eiherøy Fyr (lighthouse), Gloppedals scree which has boulders the size of houses, Klogetveittunet, the Ørsdalen old boat and Old Sogndals beach. The pulpit in Sokndal church was made by Andrew smith in 1654. **Jøssingfjord** is famous for the Altmark Affair when men from the British destroyer *Cossack* raided the German troopship and rescued 300 British seamen being held prisoner. Also take a trip to the Sira-Kvina hydro-electric power station with its impressive dams, Helleren and the River Bjerkreimselva.

Activities in the area include riding, freshwater and seafishing, diving, hiking, and swimming, while there is accommodation to suit all tastes from hotels, motels, cabins, apartments to camping grounds.

Things to see in Jæren
Places to visit include the Kongeparken theme park (open daily), Månafoss which is Norway's seventh largest waterfall, and the seventeenth-century restored vicarage at Hå (Gamle Prestegård). **Grødaland** local museum is

housed in an old farm and is open on Sunday afternoons in the summer, and on Wednesday afternoons in July.

Varhaug Gamle churchyard (kirkegård) dates back 800 years and contains many graves of the crew of a ship which foundered in a violent storm in 1842. Gaborgheimen and Knudaheio were, at different times the home of writer Arne Garborg, and Tinhaug was where the ancient Jæren parliament used to meet and is also noted as an area of Bronze Age burial mounds.

Also worth visiting are **Varden** Lifeboat Museum, Time Agricultural Museum and **Time** Technical Museum housed in the disused power station. **Høyland** Rural Museum at Austrått has a fine collection of agricultural equipment and vehicles and Høyland church, built in 1841 is the best preserved Empire church in the county and noted for its medieval soapstone font. Kvernelands smithy, which grew into the world's largest plough manufacturer, is open daily by appointment (☎ 42 39 00). **Klepp** Rural Museum has almost 1,000 exhibits (check variable visiting times locally) and check out the beaches at Jæren and the old church ruins at Sola and Ytraberget.

Activities available include riding, fresh water and sea fishing, swimming, cycling, hiking, tennis, squash, skiing, golf, archery, windsurfing, canoeing, boating, and the Jær Pearls treasure trail, an orienteering car rally designed for the whole family. There is also plenty of accommodation ranging from hotels, motels, guest houses and apartments to cabins and camping.

Ryfylke

You must make time to see Lysefjorden and Prekestolen with its famous hairpin bends road. Other things to see are the old monastery at **Utstein** (Utstein Kloster), the Suldalslågen salmon river with an observation post beside the salmon steps and the churches at Kvitsøy, Rennesøy, Talgje, Finnøy, Sternarøyene, Jelsa and Årdal, as well as Rødal stave church in Hordaland.

There are museums at **Kolbeinstveit** with one of Norway's oldest wooden houses dating from about 1250 (open Sundays during the summer), **Vigatunet** (open Sundays during the summer), **Røynevarden** (for opening times ☎ 97 377), **Lidtunet** (the owner farmer lives on site), **Tveittunet** (open afternoons during July), **Finnvik**, Rennesøy ☎ 51 33 26 for opening times), **Hjelmeland** (open Sunday 2-4pm during the summer), and the Erfjord Rural Museums (viewing by appointment ☎ 97 377).

Jelsa School Museum (viewing by appointment ☎ 97 377), the Industrial Workers' Museum at **Sauda** (open July 2-5pm), sculpture collection at Sauda (open daily 8am-9pm except July), the old wharf warehouse (Sjøhuset) at Sand and the painted building (*rosebua*) at Løland, are all worth visiting.

There are also historical sites at **Solbakk**, noted for its rock carvings, **Forsandmoen**, the scene of several large excavations, and **Ritland** where there are a number of burial mounds.

Activities include boating, sea, river and lake fishing, swimming, cycling, hiking and diving. The range of accommodation includes hotels, motels, guest houses, cabins and camping sites.

Northern Rogaland

Places to see should include the old sailing ship town of **Skudeneshavn**, the old harbour at **Utsira**, and Olavs church at **Avaldsnes**, built in the second half of the thirteenth century and fully restored in the 1920s. Close to the northern side of the church is a $6^1/_2$m tall monument known as *Jomfru Marias synål* — the Virgin Mary's sewing needle. Legend has it that when it falls against the church wall, the Day of Judgement will begin.

Other things to see include the copper mines museum at **Gruvemuseet**

Prekestolen offers awe-inspiring views

where the copper for the Statue of Liberty came from and the **Haraldshaugen** national monument built in 1872 to celebrate Norway's 1,000th anniversary. It is just to the north of Haugesund which has a charming town centre. **Karmsund** Rural Museum is worth a call, and you should stop to see the Five Foolish Virgins (De fem Dårlige Jomfruer) at Karmsund bridge. The exact age of the five monoliths is not known but they are thought to go back to the time when the first Germanic tribesman made their way north. There is a Quaker Cemetery at **Tysvær**, and it was from the port that the Norwegian emigration to the USA started in 1825 when the first Norwegian Quakers sailed aboard the *Restoration*.

There are rural museums at **Bokn** (open Sunday afternoons in the summer), **Vikedal** (open Tuesday afternoons in the summer), and **Nedstrand** (☎ 78 253 for opening times). The lock at **Skjoldastraumen** is very impressive, built in 1908 to let ships enter the fjord previously very difficult because of the strong currents. Some of the world's largest oil platforms have been assembled in the docks at Vat. Outdoor activities include sea, river, fjord and lake fishing, diving and hiking, and there is accommodation of all types to choose from.

The Setesdal Trail

One of the greatest attractions of Norway is that almost any route you choose will offer spectacular scenery, and on only a short visit it is important to take in the very best. The route from Kristiansand north to Haukeligrend (about 250km) is not only very scenic but provides a major artery inland. The route travels through Setesdalen, a charming valley rich in culture, folklore and centuries-old crafts.

For passengers entering the country via Kristiansand and planning to tour the north of Norway, it is the most direct route. For those exploring the south of the country, the route can be incorporated into any one of a number of circular tours starting from Oslo, Kristainsand, Stavanger, Bergen, or anywhere else you choose. The network of E roads (76, 18, 9 and 12) that cover the south of the country makes it easy to plan your own tours, although there is no reason, of course, to stick to these main highways, and detours on smaller roads along valleys or up into the mountains, almost always pay dividends.

Take the E12 out of Kristiansand. Because of the grid network of roads in the western part of town, follow any road westwards and you should hit Vestre Strandgate. Turn right and follow the road until it joins Setesdalsveien, which becomes the highway out of town. The route through the town takes you past the Fred Olsen Lines terminal, which links Kristiansand to Harwich via Hirtshals in the summer, and then past the bus and railway stations, also on your left.

At the small industrial town of Mosby, you can make a small detour on road 405 to see the Otra Rapids and Hunsfoss. Either retrace your route or continue until you come to highway 454, turn right and this will take you back to the E12.

There is a very attractive octagonal church at **Hægeland**, built in 1830, and the road then runs alongside the west bank of the River Otra which frequently widens out to form large lakes. Just before Hornnes there is a left turn on to the

E9 for Tonstad and Egersund, while the eastern section of the E9 for Arendal is taken just before Evje, a few kilometres to the north.

Hornnes also has a very attractive octagonal church, built in 1828. It is a flourishing little tourist town on the banks of the Breiflå, one of the larger of the lakes formed by the Otra, Norway's sixth longest river. There is very good camping in the area, safe bathing in the lake and lots of fishing. Boats can be hired.

Just off the main road at Hornnes is the largest go-cart track in northern Europe, and you can try your hand at racing one of the highly tuned machines.

At Evje the E12 crosses over the Otra and follows the eastern banks of the river as it runs through Byglandsfjorden. The town also marks the start proper of the beautiful Setesdal.

Evje is another small town which relies heavily on tourism. Jewellery is the ❄ main local craft and the valley is famous for its craftsmen, who work in silver and precious and semi-precious stones. You cannot miss their elaborate signs as you drive along. The mines in and around the town are a magnet for amateur geologists and prospectors, and there are many outcrops of rock containing different minerals and semi-precious stones. Many of the original mine workings have been re-opened because the interest in stone-collecting has grown so much in the last few years.

There are a number of specially marked 'mineral' trails where, if you are lucky, you might find a precious stone. The tourist industry built up around the mineral finds is so geared up, that you can actually have any stone you find, cut, polished and mounted while you wait.

About 5km south of Evje there is the **Setesdal Mineral Park** with exhibi- ❄ tions and displays of mining equipment housed in galleries cut into the side of the mountain. The park also contains a number of old wooden huts which act as studios for local craftsmen. An interesting side tour is to take the Eikild road out of Evje along Dåsvassdalen up into the mountains where there are scores of trails to walk. The paths are open all year. There is a charge to visit the galleries which open daily. Check the local tourist office for opening times.

Setesdal has been nick-named the 'Valley of Adventure' by the local tourist office, and with good cause. The valley stretches for more than 150km between Evje and Bykle with magnificent scenery as the Otra twists and curves round the steep rock faces of the valley sides, or moves more leisurely through rich, lush farmland. The E12 makes travel through the valley easy nowadays, but for centuries many parts of Setesdal were isolated from the rest of the world which is why it has retained such a rich cultural heritage. Centuries old farmsteads and store barns lie in lush meadows, which in the summer are bursting with wild flowers. The people who live in the valley are fiercely proud of their heritage and ancient customs and traditions are nurtured.

Apart from their own style of architecture, the people of Setesdal speak their own dialect, have their own folk music, their own version of the national costume, and still practise many of the ancient crafts on which the valley's prosperity was founded, such as working in silver. It is an area rich in *rosmaling* and examples can be found of this on buildings throughout the valley, as well as on the embroidered costumes worn on special occasions.

The best time to see the folk culture and hear the folk music of Setesdalen is at the beginning of August when the annual 3 day festival is held. The event of folk dancing and folk singing brings together all the best performers from the south of the country.

Apart from its cultural charms, Setesdal is an ideal base for an activity holiday. There are endless walking, backpacking and climbing opportunities, excellent fishing and boating, and scores of little roads to explore which will take you up into the mountains where you might spot a herd of wild reindeer.

Autumn doesn't last long in Setesdal but it is a time of glorious colours as the leaves change from green to orange and gold. It is also the time to be out picking the wild mushrooms and wealth of wild berries, especially the blueberries, cranberries and cloudberries.

Winter arrives early in the valley and the mountain tops are usually covered with snow by mid-October, but it still a time to be enjoyed. The flat plateaux afford marvellous cross country skiing along well marked trails, while there are enough slopes to keep even the most ardent downhill skier busy. There is a wealth of accommodation through the valley from first class hotels to campsites, from motels to mountain huts.

At the Fennefoss Museum, 2km south of Evje, there is the mineral collection amassed by Theodor Gautestad. Equipment used by Madame Curie can also be seen as she was a frequent visitor to this part of the valley to collect radio active rock samples. It is open daily from June to August. The local tourist office will give specific details.

 Byglandsfjorden offers an enormous range of outdoor activities. There are many beaches, some sandy and others made up of huge, flat smooth stones which absorb the sun's heat during the day and make very comfortable sunbathing spots. There is water skiing, wind surfing and scuba diving, horse riding or fishing, and if you want, you can shoot the rapids in canoes or aboard rafts. For the more leisurely, there are cruises along the 50km long fjord.

The fjord is also noted for its fishing such as trout and char, but especially the whiting a much sought after member of the salmon family, only found in these waters. Fishing permits are needed.

Both sides of Setesdalen rise up on to vast mountainous plains where you can walk undisturbed for days on end. The local tourist office, however, does arrange guided tours for those preferring company.

 Just to the north of Birkeland is the Syrtveitfoss, and at **Årdal** there is an octagonal church dating from 1827 with an interesting runic stone in the churchyard and an old pulpit above the altar. Close to the church stands an oak known as Landeeiki which is reputed to be 900 years old. For a touch of nostalgia visit the closed railway station at Byglandfjord. It was the last stop on the narrow gauge Setesdal line which operated from 1896 until 1962.

As you travel along the E12 approaching Fånefjell, you can see how the route developed along the valley. Originally all goods were carried by mules following a trail which crossed the mountain, then a lower level track for mule and horse drawn carts was developed, then a road for heavy traffic which went round the mountain, and finally the modern road for modern day traffic which was built using all the latest engineering skills and which goes straight through in a 600m long tunnel. **Bygland** has a number of interesting old houses in its folk museum which is open 15 June to 15 August; check with the local tourist office for opening times. The church dates from 1638. There is the state forestry school just outside Bygland which you can visit.

*Norway's
rivers provide
excellent sport
for fishermen*

Things to see in the area include the Løyland log cabin at Grendi, the medieval collection of wooden buildings known as the Bygland bygdetun, and the equally old timber building at Haugen in Åraksbø.

Just before Ose with its old coach station, you drive past Reiårsfossen, which plunges almost 300m. It is named after Reiar, an outlaw, who was promised his freedom if he could ride over the falls. He died in the attempt.

Ose is an old traffic junction in Setesdal and was the final port of call for the old fjord steamer Bjoren. The Ose Cultural Workshop stages folk music concerts, exhibitions and workshops for budding fiddlers and weavers. Visit the county magistrate's house built around 1650.

The surrounding mountains are rich in archaeological remains and near the signposted Neset camping ground are the Tjuv excavations of a 4,000 year old Stone Age camp. The area used to be a favoured hiding place for robbers and fugitives. There is a marked path to the site.

Another reminder of the lawlessness of the region in distant days is the pillory which still remains at Austad, and between Austad and Sordal is Steglefloti, the old place of execution. Sordal also has some ancient sacred trees.

While this area is very popular in the summer, it can be packed during the winter because of the excellent skiing. There are many ski lifts in the area and these carry you 1,200m up into the mountains where the views over Setesdal and Byglandsfjord are stunning. The Byglandsfjord Ski Centre has a restaurant at the top, and both it and the ski lift operate during the summer. On the huge plateau there are many kilometres of cross country trail, and a fishing through the ice, snow surfing and dog sleigh rides. There are also a number of mountain cabins on the plateau for walkers to use during the summer.

As you drive between Ose and Valle you will see many old store barns, some of them around 800 years old. It is the area where centuries old customs and traditions have survived unchanged. The coat of arms for Valle county has give golden St Andrew's crosses on a red background, and this symbol is found repeatedly on buildings, especially churches, and in the embroidery of the famous Setesdal jacket.

Helle and the hamlet of Rysstad, across the road from Hylestad stave church, are two of the main centres of the silversmith craft in the valley. The old stave church at **Hylestad** used to stand at Bjørgum, and is noted for its wood carvings on the door and portals, which tell the story of the saga of Sigurd Fåvnesbane. At Rysstad there is also the modern Brokke power station which turns the liquid silver of the Otra into electricity. The area is now heavily wooded and the mountains on either side of the road rise up to more than 1,000m above sea level.

Valle seems to attract craftsmen and today's silversmiths, rosmaling and woodcarvers are still using the techniques practised hundreds of years ago. These artists have been joined by others and there are now potters, sculptures, weavers and embroiderers offering a wide range of hand made artwork. The artists advertise their presence and have no objection if you want to watch them at work, and there is no hard sell either. Silversmiths are recognised by their *sylvsmeder* sign.

During the summer, and as an added inducement to the tourists to stop, you can see folk dancing and listen to the sound of folk music being played on

elaborately carved fiddles. The people of Valle claim they produce the best
fiddlers in Norway. Valle church dates from 1844 and the altarpiece is a copy
of a painting by the Italian master Federigo Barocci, produced about 1650. The
mountain range to the left of the road opposite Valle is known as Valleheiene,
and the tallest peaks reach 1,377m above sea level.

A few kilometres north of Valle at **Flatelend**, visit the Rygnestadtunet, a
lovely old farm with outbuildings, where the saga hero Åsmund Rygnestad
lived in the 1500s. The logs used to build the farm have a diameter of about 1m.
The buildings are part of the Setesdal open-air folk museum.

From either Rotemo or Rygnestad you can take highway 45 over the
mountains to Dalen. The county is rich in old buildings and there are many
fine rural museums where you can see how these ancient homes were constructed, and how the people lived. The Tweitetunet, in its beautiful setting,
was built by the nobleman Knutsson Tveiten, who was a founder of the
Norwegian Constitution in 1814.

The next county is Bykle, which has as its coat of arms silver droplets of
electric power in the district. Despite its hilly, isolated position, the northern
end of Setesdal has always had settlements, and at Storhedder there are rock
drawings dating from the Iron and Bronze Ages showing hunting scenes.
Excavations of early Viking sites in the area have revealed charcoal kilns
showing that there was an iron industry producing weapons and tools.

In the old days the only way to reach Bykle from the south was to take the
mule track, the Byklestigen, which was in use until 1870. You can still walk
sections of this very steep path and the views make the effort worthwhile.

Bykle is a charming old village with many centuries-old houses, and one of
Norway's smallest churches, the oldest parts of which date back to the thirteenth century. The church clock bears the date 1660, and although originally
built in Renaissance style, the building was restored and extended by the
addition of two galleries and the steeple in 1804. In 1826 the whole of the
interior was rose-painted by the artist Aslak Vasshus which is why it is so
special today.

Huldreheimen is also worth a visit. It is a fine collection of old buildings
gathered from throughout Setesdal. There is a grinding mill from Nesland, a
herdsman's summer mountain cabin and many other well restored buildings,
the oldest of which dates back to the sixteenth century.

Morten Henriksen Junet, near Bykle church, is another collection of about
a dozen old buildings, all faithfully restored with their original contents.
Nearby is the Sarvfossen with its 48m drop. Between Bykle and Hovden are
the Vatnedal dams which are worth a detour. A road leads from the E12 up to
the 60m and 120m high dams.

This northern end of Setesdal is highland country and an area particularly
attractive to visitors, both winter and summer alike. Around the tourist centre
of Hovden, about 850m above sea level, there are many hotels, huts and cabins
and campsites. Facilities range from international standard skating rinks to
tennis courts, ski and alpine centres, horseriding, fishing, walking, swimming
and wildlife watching.

Hovden is one of southern Norway's best known winter sports resorts, and
its double chair lift, one of the largest in the country, goes to the top of mount
Nåsi, 1,250m above sea level. In the summer there are wonderful views from

the peak and many walks on which you might spot wild reindeer, elk, ptarmigan and hare. The lakes and rivers provide excellent fishing.

This is a vast playground area of mountains and hills, wide open spaces, clear tarns and sparkling rivers. It is an ideal area for hiking and backpacking as the air is clean, and the water pure. There are many marked routes and having found the perfect pitch, you can try and catch a fish supper. For the less energetic, there are even air taxis for hire, which will take you into the mountains from their base at Hegni.

The Hegni Nature Park (open all year, but check with the local tourist office for specific times), near Hartevann, also offers good fishing and walking along numerous well marked trails. If you have the time, try to visit the park in the evening when many of the trails are floodlit. The Lislevatn and Vidmyr nature reserves are both areas of marshy land popular with migrating birds. Vidmyr is considered a wildlife sight of international importance.

The whole area around Hovden is protected and details of this, as well as information about the 2 nature reserves, are given on the large open-air map on display in Hovden.

The road then continues over the mountains before descending in a series of hairpin bends to connect with the E76. The highest point along this stretch of road is at Sessvatn, 917m above sea level. The area is very exposed and in good weather the views are fantastic, but mist and cloud can quickly sweep in.

From the junction at Haukeligrend, you can either turn left for Haugesund or Bergen, or right if you want to go back to Oslo. This journey is described in chapter 8.

The Land of Kings

There are a number of motoring options open to those who want to continue their explorations from Stavanger. Rather than return to Oslo along the south coast or along the E9, you can head north for Bergen. From Stavanger you can ferry hop and see the western islands, or you can hug the coast using highways 13 and 46 or 520 until they join the E76. You follow the E76 for about 20km and then turn off right on highway 47 which heads north along the eastern shores of Sørfjorden as far as Kinsarvik where you catch the ferry across to Kvanndal on the E68. From here you drive westwards for about 140km into Bergen. It is possible to catch the coastal steamer direct from Stavanger to Bergen and beyond and this is dealt with in a later section.

Unless you have a strict time-table to follow, flexibility is the key for enjoying this part of the route. Decide each day what you want to see and do, and then determine how best this can be achieved. Coastal ferries are not a good idea if there is driving rain and fog because you are going to see very little, but if driving conditions inland are very bad the sea route might get you to your destination quicker.

There are so many routes and ferries in this part of Rogaland and Ryfylke to choose from that you can afford to be adaptable. There are many options for getting out of Stavanger. You can ferry to the island of Karmøy and then island hop, seeing Haugesund, Leirvik and Osöyro. You can catch a ferry through the islands of Ryfylke as far as Sand where you pick up highway 46 and then on past Suldalsvatnet to the E76. The other alternative is to drive south out of Stavanger to Sandnes and then pick up highway 13 to Lauvvik for the short ferry hop across to Oanes. This route takes you along the coast through Hjelmeland to the ferry across Jøsenfjorden to Sand.

Once you have got used to hopping on and off the ferries, you may feel like detouring from Sand to visit Haugesund and Kopervik or any one of the charming communities that can be discovered on the western islands.

The road hugs the coast because to the east the mountains climb rapidly and for most of the year are impenetrable. There are a number of small roads running inland but it is best to seek advice from the locals about whether your vehicle is suitable to use them.

Via Karmøy

The ferry from Randaberg takes about 65 minutes to cross over to Skudeneshavn, on the southern tip of the island of Karmøy, which used to be the seat of the Norwegian kings in the early Middle Ages. **Skudeneshavn** is ❈ one of the most picturesque harbour tours on the west coast and developed in the seventeenth century because of the rich lobster fishing in the area. More recently its prosperity depended on the herring fisheries.

Much of the old town has been preserved and there are some delightful walks through the narrow twisting lanes between well preserved houses from the beginning of the nineteenth century. The old part of town is known as the Empire Quarter because of the style of architecture which predominates. There is also an interesting park which has been planted with trees from around the world.

This area is very popular during the summer because of its pleasant climate and there are many camping sites and cabins for hire. There are also many good bathing beaches and boats for hire.

From Skudeneshavn you can drive either along the island's western coast on highway 14 which looks out across the North Sea, or along highway 511 which follows the more sheltered eastern coast looking out Boknafjorden.

There are a number of beaches along both coasts but the highway 14 route is more dramatic, taking you through the fishing village of Sandve and the beach complex with camping site and cabins for hire at Sandvesanden. There is also a youth hostel here. Åkrehamn is another fishing village but rather special because of its massive sea defences needed to protect it from the fury of North Sea storms.

Åkre church dates from 1821 and has a very old altar piece. This area is one Ⓗ of the most popular bathing spots and the beach Åkresanden stretches for more than 1km.

The road then crosses the island with highway 511 merging with it at Kopervik, a major pilot station. There is plenty of accommodation in the area from hotels and guesthouses to campsites and cabins.

Continue along highway 14 to Avaldsnes, famous for its church built in 1250 and the Virgin Mary's Needle which stands nearby. According to legend, the world will end on the day that the slightly tilting $6^1/_2$m tall stone touches the wall of the church.

There are many archaeological remains in the area as proof that this was one of the earliest parts of the country to be settled. At Bø there are Stone Age burial mounds, and at Rehaugene, a number of ancient monuments from the Bronze Age can be seen. You leave the island on the 690m long Karmsund Bridge which is 65m above the water, and affords magnificent views all round.

After crossing the bridge you will spot five standing stones, known as the Five Foolish Virgins. The reason for their name is not known, but the stones have been standing there since the Iron Age.

Highway 14 then runs into Haugesund, a very old settlement. Although it did not receive its town charter until 1854, the settlement has played a long and distinguished role in Norway's history.

About 2km to the north of the town centre is **Haraldshaugen**, the grave of Harald Hårfagre (Harold the Fairhair), one of the most famous of all the Viking kings, and responsible for uniting Norway into one country. In 1877, a 17m tall granite obelisk was erected on the site and is now a national monument, symbolising the unity of the country. The obelisk is surrounded by twenty-nine stones, one for each of Norway's different districts at the time of unification. Close to the south of the site is Krosshaugen, an early meeting place of the Thing (the Assembly for Lawmaking and Legal Judgements) with a stone cross dating back to AD1000.

Haugesund itself is now a modern fishing and shipping port, one of the largest in Norway. It is also internationally famous for its annual North Sea Festival, which attracts anglers from all over the world, and as the venue of the Norwegian Film Festival. The town hall is worth visiting and there is a very interesting museum. It is the place to be if you have ever wanted to try your hand at deep sea fishing. Every day during the summer there are boat trips organised by the local tourist office. There is a wealth of accommodation in the town and nearby, a local youth hostel and a campsite at Haraldshaugen.

From Haugesund you take the E76 or highway 14 to Valevåg if you want to continue island hopping. The ferry takes you to the island of Stord where you can break your journey for bathing or walking. There are a number of campsites on the island, many good beaches and some good hills to climb, including Midtfjell (498m), Kinno (568m), St Melen (500m), and Kattnekken (724m). **Leirvik** on the south-east coast of Stord, is a product of the oil boom. Although a long standing ship building centre, its fortune was transformed after the discovery of North Sea oil and most of its activities are now oil related. There is a large Bronze Age burial site at Fitjar on the north-west coast of the island.

From Sandvikvåg on the northern tip of Stord you can ferry across to either Tysnesøy, Huftarøy or direct to Halhjem on the mainland, about 26km south of Bergen on highway 14. An interesting detour from Stord is to take the ferry to the island of **Moster** and visit Norway's oldest stone church, built by Olav Tryggvason in 995. If you take the E76 from Haugesund the road climbs steadily and it is worth stopping on top of the hill to look back and take in the views.

At Skjold there is a church with a pulpit and altar piece dating from 1625, and about 5km up the road at Knapphus it is time to take another decision.

The quickest route is to stay on the E76 through Ølen and Etne until you reach highway 47. The final stretch of this journey is through marvellous mountainous terrain with many bridges and tunnels, and sheer drops. You should stop for Langfoss which crashes down almost 400m. The more interesting and scenic route however, is to turn left on to highway 46 and follow the route which follows the banks of Vindafjorden and Saudafjorden. This route takes in the villages of Sandeid and Vikedal, which have some charming guesthouses, and the small town of Sauda before rejoining the E76 at Horda. It is a mountain road but it affords spectacular views over the fjords and Lake Røldalsvatnet.

The area around Sauda provides excellent skiing and there are spectacular mountain views. The road climbs out of the industrial town of Sauda and the highest point at 900m above sea level, is about 5km beyond the Breiborg tourist hut.

The road passes Reinaskarnuten (1,242m) on the left just beyond Hellandsbygd, and Røldalssåta (1,442m), to the left of the pass. The tallest peak to the east is Skaulen (1,540m) which can be seen to best advantage as you drive towards Elverkryss.

Turn left when highway 520 meets the E76, and then right on to highway 47 at Jösendal. If you take the E76 the route takes you to Etnesjøen, at the head of Etnefjorden. It is an ancient settlement and is mentioned in the sagas. The nearby Gjerde church was built in 1675 and at Sæbøtunet, there is a typical old fjord farmstead. These farms became mini settlements because they gradually expanded as the children married and needed homes of their own.

There are many hotels, campsites and cabins for hire in the area. At Håfoss it is worth the small detour to **Grindheim** where there is a church dating from 1728 with an ancient runic stone in the churchyard. A small detour to the west of Håfoss leads to Stødle where there is a medieval church which was enlarged in the early 1600s.

Just north of Håland there is another alternative route along highway 13 to **Skånevik**, a lovely fjord village and now a popular tourist spot. There are lots of hotels and cabins, campsites and even houseboats for hire. There is a youth hostel and the ferry link with Utåker, a crossing of about 30 minutes. From Utåker take highway 13 through Valen to Sunde where you catch the ferry for the island of Halsnøy which has the ruins of an Augustinian monastery. Eid Church dates from 1824, and the island also houses the maritime section of Sunnhordland's Museum.

Return to Sunda and take highway 13 through **Husnes**, with its aluminium plant, along Hardangerfjorden to Rosendal. There are a number of guest houses, campsites and cabins for hire along the way.

Rosendal is another fishing and boat building centre nestling between the mountains and the fjord, but it is most famous for the Rosendal Manor, now owned by Oslo University. Built in the 1660s by Ludwig Rosenkranz, the buildings are a mixture of Baroque and Renaissance. The park has a wonderful rose garden which makes a fitting setting for the annual musical festival held each May. The Baronly Play is also performed there each July. The park is open to the public daily but house opening times vary so check with the local tourist office. Just to the north of the town is Kvinnherad church, built in Gothic style and dating from the Middle Ages.

Take the ferry from Løfallstrand to Gjermundshamm (about 30 minutes) and then follow highway 13 through Mundheim to **Holdhus**, noted for its chapel. Built in the early eighteenth century, the chapel has many fine painted decorations and an alabaster statue of the Virgin Mary.

The route continues past the Koldeldalsfoss falls to Eikelandsosen. Turn left on to highway 552 for Fusa where you catch the ferry across to Hattvik, 25km south of Bergen. If you take this route you will drive through Solstrand on your way to Bergen and it is worth a look around. The views over Bjørna-fjorden are spectacular as are those to the east over the Hardanger mountains.

If you decide to stay with the E76 at Håland there is a lovely drive alongside Stordalsvatnet up to Tjelmeland where it follows the eastern banks of Åkrafjorden. The road here was literally carved out of the steep rock face as it plunges into the fjord, and there are more than a score of bridges and a dozen tunnels. A few kilometres beyond Bjørkestrand is the famous Langfoss wa-terfall which has a drop of almost 500m. At the head of the fjord is the village of Fjæra which has a youth hostel, hotel and campsite. The road then plunges through the Rullestadjuvet Gorge which at Vassvatn is about 430m above sea level. At Jøsendal the road splits and you follow highway 47 for Bergen.

Via Sand

If the weather is fine the ferry trip from Stavanger through the fjords and islands can by idyllic. The views are truly spectacular and the pace is leisurely and relaxing so that you can take everything in.

Sand is a very popular village in the summer with lots of accommodation and a wide range of activities on offer. There are good beaches and some excellent salmon fishing, especially around the Sandfossen falls.

Take highway 46 out of Sand to Suldal. The road runs beside the Suldals-lågen, through a very lush valley. The river is fast flowing and there are many falls and rapids. Gradually the river opens out into Suldalsvatnet and beyond it to your right is Stråpkollen (433m), known locally as 'sugar top' mountain.

This is a fascinating area and can trace its routes back many centuries. At Suldal Bygdetun there is a marvellous collection of old houses, many 500 and 600 years old. Alongside the stream there is also a collection of old mills.

The mountains drop right down to the lake edge, and the road cuts through a series of tunnels — Hylstunnelen, Vågstunnelen and Lalidtunnelen — before arriving at Røynevarden, worth a stop because of its well restored crofter's farm. Follow highway 46 to Nesflaten, with its youth hostel, and then through the narrow, steep sided Brattlandsdal with its fast flowing river, to Røldalsvatnet and Horda where the road joins the E76.

Turn left and head for Jøsendal where the road divides and you need to turn right on to highway 47 for Bergen. This area of country leading down to the coast is **Kvinnherad**, and popular for winter and summer sports alike. There is excellent skiing and the mountains provide marvellous walking and climb-ing. Experienced walkers and climbers can tackle Folgefonna, Norway's third largest glacier, and there are plenty of opportunities for lake and river fishing.

The E76 starts the long, steep ascent up Hordabrekkene in a series of sixteen hairpin turns. To the left of the road and several hundred metres below are views of Røldalsvatnet. From the summit, the road, zig zags its way down through the Seljestadjuvet Gorge, with views of Folgefonna. There is a chair-lift at **Solfonn** which climbs to 900m and affords wonderful views.

Throughout this stretch of road there are many places to stop and eat, a sign of how popular it is during the winter with skiers. There are also a number of campsites and many cabins to hire.

At Jøsendal take route 47 north past Steinaberg bru to **Låtefoss** with its twin waterfalls which drop almost 180m. It is considered one of the most beautiful waterfalls in Norway. The road follows the eastern shore of Sandvinvatnet to Odda, an important industrial town. It is at the head of Sørfjorden which feeds into Hardangerfjorden, and has an aluminium smelting plant and zinc works.

Before the industry came to **Odda**, the town was the tourist centre of the region, and despite the works, its beautiful setting still has a lot to offer visitors. If you are interested in glacier walking, Odda makes a good base. An arm of the glacier which reaches out towards Odda is known as Buarbreen and there are walks to it from Buar which can be reached by a small road running off highway 47 on the southern outskirts of the town. All glaciers are dangerous and inexperienced people should not venture out alone. Guides are available for conducted tours.

There is a 1.6km tunnel between Odda and **Tyssedal**, another industrial town with an aluminium works. A worthwhile detour is to take the small road up to Ringdalsvatn with its 35m high dam. There is also a cable car to the summit of Mågelitoppen, about 930m above sea level.

As the road runs alongside Sørfjorden on your left, there are magnificent

A modern bridge spans the harbour at Haugesund

views of Hardangervidda on your right. This is desolate country on your right and much of it is protected as part of the Hardangervidda National Park but there is some wonderful walking and back packing country to be enjoyed.

 If you arrive in **Lofthus** in the late spring you are likely to see a sight that will stay with you for ever. This popular tourist spot is also the centre of the largest fruit growing district in Norway and the sight of acres of orchards in blossom with snow capped mountains as the backdrop is breathtaking and memorable. Lofthus is a good base for a car touring or walking holiday. There is ample accommodation to choose from and many boat trips.

Follow the fjord a few kilometres to Kinsarvik where you can catch a ferry which goes via Utne to Kvanndal. It is then about 140km to Bergen. **Kinsarvik** is a very busy ferry port so at peak times it pays to get there in good time. While you wait have a look at the medieval Romanesque church and the Skiparstod, the remains of a Viking boat house. There are a number of waterfalls in the area, the nearest is Tveitafossen, about 6km away. Take the Råi road. Other falls, which collectively are known as the Kinso Falls, include Nykkjesøyfossen and Søtefossen.

Alternatively, continue up to Brimnes and take the ferry across Eidfjorden to Bruravik which gives you a choice of routes into Bergen, either directly on the E68 (about 145km) or detouring through Voss and Dale (about 160km).

If you want to drive to the head of **Handangerfjorden** continue through Brimnes until you come to Eidfjord, an ideal base for exploring **Handangervidda**. This is a massive high plateau dominated by the Hardangerjøkulen whose highest peak is 1,862m above sea level. It is a wonderful area for mountain walking and climbing and fishing. You can camp out or hire one of the many huts and cabins in the area. If you follow highway 7 out of Eidfjord, you come to Sæbø where there is a road running off to the right to Vedalsfossen and Valurfossen. The last part has to be carried out on foot along a narrow path which runs over Hjølmodalen.

Take the Sima road north out of Eidfjord to the power station which is open to the public daily during the summer. Check times with the local tourist office. It is fed via the 1,166m long and 84m high Sysen dam. **Eidfjord** has a stave church dating from the end of the twelfth century.

Continue along highway 7 to Isdøla and there is another turn off, on the left, to Vøringfossen which plummets 182m down the mountain side. If you continue along highway 7 you come to Geilo where you have a choice of route if you want to return to Oslo using either highways 7 or 8.

Additional Information

Places of Interest

Blaafarveværket
Open: 1 June to 30 September 10am-8pm
☎ (03) 78 49 00

Ose
Ose Cultural Workshop
Open: daily, ☎ (082) 35 885

Dalane Folk Museum
Open: June to September 11am-5pm or by appointment.

Hå
Vicarage
Open: Saturday and Sunday 12noon-5pm and from 12noon-5pm daily throughout July.

Varden
Lifeboat Museum
Open: June to August, Sundays 12noon-5pm.

Time
Time Agricultural Museum
Open: Sunday 1-5pm, May to September

Time Technical Museum
Open: Sunday 1-5pm, May to September.

Austrått
Høyland Rural Museum
Open: first Sunday in every month 4-6pm.

Karmsund
Rural Museum
Open: Monday to Friday 10.30am-2pm.

Useful Addresses

Offices marked with an asterix* are staffed during the summer only.

Regional Tourist Boards

Hordaland and Bergen Tourist Board
Slottsgt 1
N-5033 Bergen
☎ (05) 31 66 00

Rogaland Tourist Board
Øvre Holmegt 24
N-4006 Stavanger
☎ (04) 53 48 34

Telemark Tourist Board
Postboks 743 — Hjellen
N-3701 Skien
☎ (03) 52 92 05

Local Tourist Offices

Bø Turistkontor*
Bø Sentrum
N-3800 Bø i Telemark
☎ (03) 95 18 80

Fyresdal Turisthotell
N-3870 Fyresdal
☎ (036) 41 255

Haugesund:
Reisetrafikkforeningen for Haugesund
Haugesund
N-5500 Haugesund
☎ (04) 72 52 55

Hovden Ferieservice A/S
N-4695 Hovden
☎ (043) 39 630

Husnes Turistinformasjon*
N-5460 Husnes

Karmøy Reiselivslag
Rådhuset
N-4250 Kopervik
☎ (04) 85 22 00

Kinsarvik Turistinformasjon
N-5780 Kinsarvik
☎ (054) 65 112

Kragerø Reiselivslag
Postboks 176
N-3771 Kragerø
☎ (03) 98 23 30

Kristiansand Turistkontor
Henrik Wergelands gt 17
Postboks 592
N-4601 Kristiansand S
☎ (042) 26 065

Kvinnherad Reiselivslag*
N-5100 Rosendal
☎ (054) 81 311

Kvitseid Reiselivslag
N-3848 Morgedal
☎ (036) 54 144

Notodden:
Øst-Telemark Reiselivslag
Storgt 39
N-3670 Notodden
☎ (036) 12 633

Odda Reiselivslag
v/Odda Reisebyrå
Postboks 147
N-5751 Odda
☎ (054) 42 622

Sauda Reiselivslag
N-4200 Sauda
☎ (04) 78 30 11

Skien Reiselivslag
Postboks 493
N-3701 Skien
☎ (03) 52 82 27

6

THE PILGRIMAGE ROAD

T his is not the fastest route to Bergen (550km) but it is certainly the most scenic, and if you do not plan to travel any further north, it gives a wide variety of scenery, including lovely drives through the mountains and the opportunity for a spectacular fjord crossing. For centuries pilgrims from all over northern Europe have followed this route as they journeyed to the ancient Norwegian capital of Trondheim.

The drive, which should not be hurried, takes you through Hønefoss, the beautiful Valdres valley and then into the mountains to Revsnes where you catch the ferry for the most incredible trip through Aurlandsfjorden and Narøyfjorden to Gudvangen. As you climb the mountains out of Gudvangen there are stunning views back over the fjord, and then it is through the mountains to Voss, and then on to Bergen. The route can easily be adapted as you wish, and it fits marvellously into a circular tour returning to Oslo via Bruravik and Stavanger and the south coast.

Within minutes of leaving Oslo you have wonderful lake views on one side and impressive mountains on the other. The road travels through rich farm-land with centuries-old farmsteads and even older storehouses. There are stave churches and folk museums, waterfalls and white water rivers, forest walks and mountain trails.

From Oslo drive west out of the city, past the Fornebu airport turn-off to Sandvika where you hit the E68. The left hand fork, the E18 runs south-west to Drammen, but you want to turn right and follow the signs for Hønefoss. On the city outskirts there are ski lifts up into the hills and the road follows the eastern bank of Tyrifjorden with spectacular views to the west and south. During the summer the lake is very popular at weekends and there are summer chalets along its banks, as well as a number of small resorts.

To the right there are views of Nordmarka, the hills north of the capital where the Osloites ski in the winter and walk in the summer. It is known locally as the 'Playground of Oslo'.

It is worth stopping in Sundvollen and exploring. The area has been famous since the Middle Ages because it was a major staging post for people travelling north. It was especially popular with people making the pilgrimage to Trondheim. In the old days the pilgrims used the Krokkleiva, an ancient trail linking Oslo with Sundvollen. The trail runs south-east to north-west through the forests and today is preserved and protected.

The trip to Kleivstua, about 4km to the south-east, is also worthwhile. There is a toll road to the top of Kleivstua which gives marvellous views over the surrounding countryside, but even more spectacular is the panorama from the summit of Kongens Utsikt 'the King's View', which is half an hour's walk away along a well marked path, or you can drive to the summit. A little further north on the E68 there are turn offs to the left which allow you to explore some of the charming lakeside villages. There is an eleventh-century church at

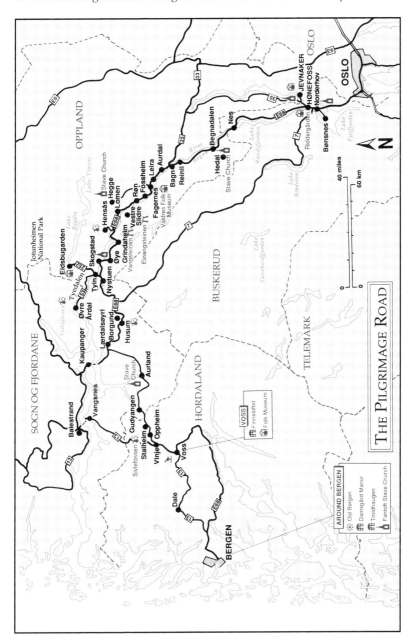

Bønsnes, and the small peninsula has a number of large immaculately kept farms. There are a number of places to stay along this stretch of road and boats can be hired both on Tyrifjorden and Steinsfjorden, to the right of the E68.

A little further north again is Norderhov which has an interesting medieval stone church and then you drive over the Hole Peninsula into Hønefoss. The district around Hønefoss is known as Ringerike and is really a miniature Norway offering virtually every landscape that you can see throughout the country except the far north.

Hønefoss is a thriving, growing community and a major communications centre. From Hønefoss there are roads radiating out in all directions and it is perhaps because of this that it became a military garrison. The station also provides rail links to Bergen, Jevnaker, Oslo and the south coast.

Today, it is the commercial centre and market town for the region, with wood processing as the major industry. Hønefoss is split by the rivers Begna and Randselva which converge to form a massive waterfall in the centre of the town. It was harnessed to provide the power needed by the local industries.

Also in the centre of the town is Riddergården, once the estate of nobleman and now a wonderful open-air folk museum. Some of the buildings are 600 years and many have had their interiors faithfully restored. Plenty of accommodation is available in and around the town and as well as the hotels and guesthouses, there is also a summer youth hostel, very good campsite and cabins for hire.

An interesting detour is to take highway 35 north-east out of Hønefoss to **Jevnaker**, where there is a glass blowing factory and museum open to the public during the summer. The town is at the southern tip of Randsfjorden which runs north as far as Dokka.

After returning to Hønefoss the route heads north on the E68. There is a faster route through the magnificent Hallingdal valley and via Geilo using highway 7 which is dealt with in the following section. The route follows the River Begna and then the Ådalselva through Ådalen until it runs into Lake Sperillen.

Nes lies at the top of the long, narrow Sperillen, and you must detour off on highway 243 to visit **Hedal**, famous for its stave church. Although built in the Middle Ages, the church was converted in 1536 although many of its original carvings and paintings have been preserved (see section on stave churches p44). This church should not be confused with the one at Heddal near the industrial town of Notodden, which is the largest surviving stave church. From Hedal you should take the small road which rejoins the E68 at Begnadalen. The road continues to follow the river and there are many places to stop and have a swim. There are a number of campsites in the area and some good spots for fishing. Boats can also be hired.

At **Bagn**, whose church was built in the 1730s, there is a turning off to the right to **Reinli** stave church, built in the early Middle Ages (see special section on stave churches p46). The small road then continues climbing up into the hills to Fjellstølen. There are a number of small roads running off the E68 around Bagn which give access to the hills and some wonderful walks.

At Bjørgo there is a right turning off the E68 on to highway 35 which runs to Dokka at the head of Randsfjorden, and on to Gjøvik on the western bank of Lake Mjøsa.

Continue north to **Aurdal**, for a time the home of Nobel prize winning author Knut Hamsun. He wrote the novel *Victoria* while staying here. The town also has a charming church built in 1735 with a rich interior.

About 15km up the road is the rural centre of **Leira** which has a number of secondary schools and colleges. Highway 49 runs south-west from the town over the hills to Gol in Hallingdal. It crosses through some spectacular country and there are mountain huts along the road that can be rented if you want to spend a few days walking in the area. The highest point of the road between Leira and Gol is 860m above sea level. A few kilometres from Leira on the E68 is Fagernes.

It is said that Valdres is where east and west Norway meet. It is an area rich in culture and history and the valley is proud of its centuries-old traditions. **Fagernes** has one of the country's largest folk museums, with more than 50 old buildings, as a reminder of its past. The Valdres Folk Museum (open daily) is also the venue of a number of folk festivals during the summer.

Fagernes is another ideal base for exploring this lovely valley and the mountains which surround it. It used to be an important railway terminus but the line is now closed. There are many small roads up into the mountains. There is excellent fishing, many beaches for bathing, and a wide choice of accommodation, as well as cabins and boats for hire. One of the most popular camping and bathing areas is Strand Hyttesenter, just to the west of Fagernes.

If you have time take a side tour from Fagernes using highway 51 which runs north into the high mountains of the majestic Jotunheimen National Park. Many of the peaks are above 2,000m. The medieval stave church at **Hegge** was rebuilt in the early 1800s with elaborately carved heads capping all the pillars (see section on stave churches p45).

The E68 from Fagernes follows the right hand bank of Slidrefjorden, a long, narrow lake which run through the valley of Vestre Slidre. Again there are lots of opportunities for bathing, camping, fishing and boating.

From **Ulnes**, with its medieval church and rose-painted interior, there is a toll road, known as the Panorama Road, which runs south-west across the mountains for about 48km to Hemsedal, in the lovely valley of the same name which runs into Hallingdal. Apart from the spectacular views along the route there are a number of famous trout waters, especially at Vaset and Nøsen. This is an area with many lakes and mountains, such as Skogshorn (1,728m) which is on your right as you approach Hemsedal.

A little further up the lake is **Fossheim**, named after the nearby spectacular falls. You then enter an area steeped in history as six of Norway's remaining stave churches are to be found in Valdres, and there are many ancient farms and storehouses.

At **Røn** there is an eighteenth-century church, while the stone church in Slidredomen is medieval. At **Vestre Slidre** you can see the Einangsteinen, the oldest runic stone in north Europe. It dates from the third century and is at the centre of more than 1,200 burial mounds. The stone church here, with its medieval paintings, dates from the mid-twelfth century, and the stave church at **Lomen**, was built around 1170 (see the section on stave churches p45). The road passes a number of campsites and at Ryfoss there is an impressive waterfall plunging about 35m. From Kvismo there is a small road heading inland a short distance to Høre stave church, built around 1200.

If you follow this minor road it takes you past some old mills at Kvie to **Hensås** with its hill-top chapel and fine views. The road then sweeps round to rejoin the E68 at Hemsing bru, at the eastern end of Lake Vangsmjøsa.

You have a choice at Hemsing Bridge because you can follow either side of the lake. The little road that runs along the northern shore has many places where you can stop and swim, or enjoy the views of the mountains to the north. If you take this road you can also explore the old mills at Vennes. If you follow the E68 south of the lake you arrive at Grindaheim which nestles on the lake with the towering Grindane, rising to 1,724m to the south.

Autumn reeds in the Valdres valley, where east and west Norway meet

Grindaheim is famous for the Vangsteinen, a runic stone dating from the eleventh century, which is found near the church. The mountains are very popular with skiers in the winter and there are a number of ski lifts and plenty of accommodation, including campsites and cabins for hire.

At **Øye** at the western end of the lake there is a stave church which has been rebuilt. The original church was built around the end of the twelfth century, and the present stave church was reconstructed from pieces of old timbers found under the present parish church which dates from 1747. See the section on stave churches p46.

This is wild and mountainous country, ideal for hiking and backpacking. There is a youth hostel at Skogstad and plenty of accommodation in and around the popular winter resorts of Hugostua and Tyinkrysset, an excellent base for walking holidays in Jotunheimen.

Highway 53 runs north from Tyinkrysset and then turns left round the southern end of Lake Tyin at Tyin. It then runs west through the mountain valley of Tyedalen to **Øvre Årdal** with its massive aluminium works and power station, and then to Årdalstangen, on Årdalsfjorden. The road is very steep in places and climbs to just over 1,000m before falling quickly through a number of tunnels to the fjord where you can catch the ferry for Kaupanger. A small detour from Øvre Årdal is to take the small road north to Hjelle, where you can park before walking through the Vettisgjelet Gorge to Vetti. The walk will take between $1^1/_2$ and 2 hours and then from Vetti it is about another 20 minutes to walk to Vettisfossen, where the waterfall plunges almost 300m, one of the biggest perpendicular drops in Europe.

Highway 252 branches off route 53 and runs north from Tyin to **Eidsbugarden**, with its fascinating mountain museum (open to the public, but check locally) at the western end of the Lake Bygdin.

If you stay on the E68 heading west you enter Fillefjell and areas of lakes and peaks. The road reaches its highest point just to the west of **Nystuen** where it is 1,004m above sea level. The settlement is dominated by the towering Mount Stugunøsi (1,900m) to the west with its almost sheer cliff faces.

There are many lakes in the area and some excellent fishing. The road passes St Thomas' Church, and Maristova, an old inn built in 1791 which is still offering hospitality to travellers making their way through the mountains. The road then drops down to Borlaug where it is joined by highway 52 from Gol. There is a youth hostel and campsite here.

At **Borgund** there is what many consider to be the best preserved and most typical stave church in Norway. Built around 1150 it has remained virtually unchanged since then. The roof carvings of dragons' heads are of particular interest, although the church has a wealth of other carvings and runic inscriptions.

The black pitched roof drops steeply in layers around the main body of the church and is the main reason why the timbers have been so well protected. The church has doors on three sides and all the portals are richly carved. There are carvings on the pillar heads inside, but the interior is so dark because of the lack of windows, that these are difficult to make out. At the western end of the church there is a runic inscription dating from the twelfth century. The belfry is isolated across the churchyard. See the section on stave churches p42.

Close by is Husum with its strange waterfalls which plunge into the Lærdal river. There is an old post trail called Vindhella which runs alongside a ravine with its fast flowing river and rapids before climbing up to Sjurhaugfoss where, if you are lucky, you can watch salmon trying to negotiate the specially installed salmon ladder.

Lærdalsøyri has a number of old houses similar in style to those found in Bergen, as well as hotels and a youth hostel (☎ 056 66 101 open May to September). The settlement is on Lærdalsfjorden, an arm of Sognefjorden, and the road follows the southern coast of the fjord until Revsnes. From here you can catch the ferry across to Kaupanger, or the one for Gudvangen which you need to get to Bergen.

The ferry cruises down Ardalsfjorden, one of the many branches of the Sognefjorden, Norway's longest and deepest fjord. It then swings into the narrow Aurlandsfjorden.

The ferry trip lasts for more than 2 hours and before the boat swings into the Nærøyfjorden it makes a mid-stream connection with the ferry plying between Aurland and Kaupanger. Passengers from Aurland who want to get to Gudvangen have to step from one ferry to the other as they bob about in the middle of the fjord.

The head of the fjord is less than 500m wide while the surrounding mountains which plunge down into the waters are almost 1,500m high. Because the fjord is so narrow and the mountains so high, the water is in shadow for many months of the year. During the summer, however, when the sun is at its highest, the water sparkles and stunning photographs can be taken. On a fine day the effect is breathtaking with hundreds of waterfalls crashing over the sheer rock faces. To the east Mount Stiganosi rises up to 1,761m and, in the waters below it, seals can often be watched at play.

Cruise ships still sail the fjord as far as Gudvangen, and it is an amazing sight to see a massive ocean liner lying anchored at the end of the fjord, dwarfed by the towering mountains.

Gudvangen is still an important ferry terminal and, in the height of summer, scores of cars use it. There is plenty of accommodation in and around the village with hotels, campsites and cabins for hire.

The road out of Gudvangen twists and turns as it climbs into the mountains and there are a number of stopping points which allow you to look back down the fjord. If there is a cruise ship off Gudvangen it is good to photograph it from one of these stopping points because you can then appreciate the sheer size of the mountains with what appears to be a little boat anchored below.

Leaving Gudvangen behind, the route follows the E68 for Voss. The Nærøydalen is famous for its excellent fishing and at the Hylland Bridge it is often possible to see leaping salmon and trout during July and August.

It is worth spending some time in **Stalheim** at the head of the pass which offers spectacular views. The water dropping over Stalheimfossen falls perpendicularly more than 125m into the canyon below. There are interesting views to be had on both sides of the ravine. On the far side of the canyon there is Stalheim Hotel which can be reached by car, but there are equally stunning views just off highway 68. This is a very popular tourist spot and there are lots of places to park and a number of well worn trails to the falls a short distance away. The ground is covered by large stones worn smooth over the years by rain and feet and they can be a little slippery after wet weather.

Stalheim is now approached by a road opened in the early 1980s which has a number of tunnels to by-pass the difficult terrain. In the old days the road was on the far side, passing close to the site of the hotel and hugging precariously to the side of the canyon. This road which takes you to the hotel, is known as Stalheimskleiva and has the distinction of being the steepest in Norway. Built more than 100 years ago it was a major feat of engineering with 13 hair pin bends in one $1^1/_2$km stretch. The gradient in places is 1:5. It is not a wide road and in parts is unmetalled.

Stalheim museum has many interesting exhibits depicting the history of the region. To the north of Stalheim is **Sivlefossen**, named after the poet Per Sivle, and from the falls there are very good views of Jordalsnuten 936m, known locally as the Sugar Loaf Mountain.

The road now enters one of Norway's most popular winter sports areas — although there is still plenty to do in the summer including some excellent walking and fishing. Around **Oppheim**, a popular winter resort, there are several chair lifts and cable cars. There are particularly fine views from Bergshovden.

At Vinje stay on highway 68 which runs south to Voss. Highway 13 which runs north goes to Vik and Vangsnes where you can catch the ferry for Balestrand, Hella and Dragsvik (see chapter 9).

Vinje is popular throughout the year. It affords plenty of opportunities for winter sports and there is marvellous fishing in the summer in the Strandeelva. There is also a beautifully decorated church.

Continue south on highway 68, past Tvindefossen and Lønahorgi (1,412m), on your right, to **Voss**, an ideal place to spend a holiday at any time of the year.

It is as popular with skiers as it is with summer hikers and apart from being easily accessible by car, it is on the Oslo-Bergen railway line. On Sunday afternoons during the winter months the station is packed with skiers waiting for the train back to Oslo. The public transport network is such that several minutes before the train arrives in Voss, buses arrive at the station ready to take passengers on to outlying destinations. It is the same at many other stations throughout the country and it makes travelling around Norway such a delight if you do not have a car or do not want to drive.

Apart from being a tourist centre with many hotels, pensions, youth hostels and campsites, Voss is also an educational centre with a number of schools catering for the children of surrounding districts, and it is at the centre of a rich agricultural region. Voss has also become something of a cultural centre and has a rich folk music and folk art tradition.

Things to see here include Voss church with its rich interior. Nearby is a memorial to Knut Rockne who emigrated to the USA and is responsible for modernising American football into the game today. A few hundred metres to the west of the railway station is the Finneloftet, Norway's oldest secular building and dating back to the Middle Ages — about mid-1200 — when it was used as a meeting place for the nobles of the district. The Folk Museum Mølstertunet is well signposted and contains a beautifully preserved old farm typical of the area, and many other fine old buildings.

Things to do include an almost obligatory trip by the Hangursbanen cable car. There are fantastic views as the cable car climbs towards the summit of Hangurstoppen. The journey covers almost 1,200m and the cable car climbs more than 750m to the restaurant almost at the top of mountain. There is then a chair lift to the summit which is about 815m above sea level. From here there are numerous walks radiating out in all directions. For those who do not want to walk to the summit, it is a good idea to take the cable car and then walk down at your own pace.

There are hundreds of kilometres of summer walking trails, all well way-marked and suitable for hikes lasting from a few hours to several days.

Close to the station is the impressive Fleischer's Hotel and opposite a motel run by the same management. The cabins are fully-equipped mini apartments and make an ideal base for touring the area. The area around Voss teems with lakes and streams which are great for fishing. The tourist centre in Voss will provide details about walking in the area. The free *Voss Guide* has listings and useful information and timetables.

From Voss you have a choice of routes to Bergen. You can take highway 13 to Dale 48km to the west. It is a spectacular drive and a shorter, although not quicker, route than following highway 60 south-east to Granvin and then heading west through Øystese and Tysse, and on to Bergen.

The first of the routes, on highway 13, takes you past Vangsvantnet on your left, and then the Hamlagrøvatnet Reservoir whose dam marks the highest point on the road between Voss and Dale at 625m. The road is narrow and in many places was literally blasted out of the mountain. It follows the contours of the mountain and is very windy and often only capable of carrying one lane of traffic. The mountain side towers above you and there are sheer drops down to the river on your left. There are frequent places to stop, however, if you do meet oncoming traffic. Generally it is a good idea to give way to local traffic. They obviously know the road better and travel at what seems a very fast pace. The road passes close by countless waterfalls, and goes through many tunnels. This route is not really suitable for caravans as the road is narrow and there is not much clearance in some of the tunnels. The road runs parallel with the river with its crashing rapids as it travels through Bergsdalen towards Dale.

At **Dale** with its timber mills and factories producing textiles and knitwear, you can detour off into Eksingedalen. If you have the time it is worth taking highway 569 north into this wild and beautiful country past the old church at Straume into a scenery of mountains and lakes. There are waterfalls at Eikemofoss and Gunhildsfoss and scores of lakes. You can detour off to Mo and then drive up to the slopes of Storefjell. The railway line to Bergen also goes through Dale, named after the Viking word *dal* which means valley.

From Dale highway 13 runs south parallel with the railway line, and through a number of tunnels to the mill town of Vaksdal. The road runs along the shores of Veafjorden and then swings west for Bergen via the increasingly built up areas of Indre Arna, Haukeland and Nesttun.

Bergen

Bergen, the fjord capital of Norway, is steeped in history and culture and is the country's second largest city. It is one of the most beautiful cities in the northern hemisphere surrounded by mountains and fjords. As rain can sweep

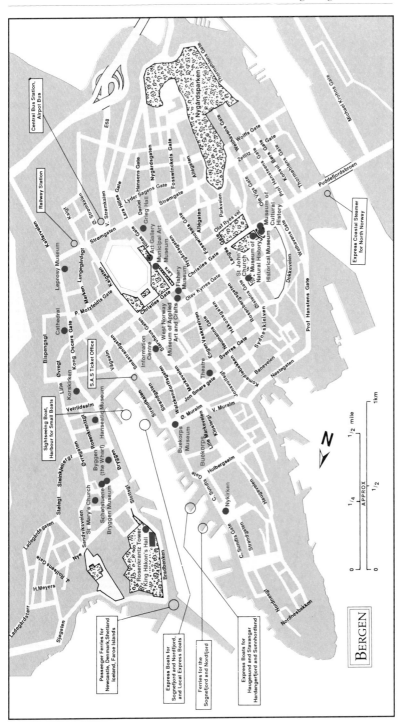

BERGEN

N

APPROX

0   1/4   1/2 mile

0   1/2   1km

Central Bus Station,
Airport Bus

Railway Station

Express Coastal Steamer
for North Norway

Sightseeing Boat,
Harbour for Small Boats

S.A.S Ticket Office

Passenger Ferries for
Newcastle, Denmark, Shetland
Iceland, Faroe Islands

Express Boats for
Sognefjord and Nordfjord,
and Local Express Boats

Ferries for the
Sognefjord and Nordfjord

Express Boats for
Haugesund and Stavanger
Hardangerfjord and Sunnhordland

in suddenly from the North Sea, Bergen is one of the wettest places in the country.

Bergen is famous for its music and drama and its annual international festivals. It has one of the world's oldest symphony orchestras and a fine theatre. There are old buildings, cobbled streets, markets and parks to explore.

One of the easiest ways to start your visit and to appreciate just how beautiful the city's setting is, is to take the funicular railway to the summit of Mount Fløien (320m), or Mount Ulriken (600m). From either you can see Bergen spread out beneath you, with its massive natural harbour on which its prosperity was built, and the fjord reaching through the mountains to the sea. Bergen's tourist offices have a wealth of information and there are daily guided tours of the city, as well as scores of other sightseeing trips available.

History

Bergen was officially declared a city during the reign of King Olav Kyrre (Olav the Peaceful 1066-93), although records show that it was the site of a much older trading post. Its large natural harbour meant it quickly grew as a fishing and trading port. In the twelfth and thirteenth centuries Bergen was Norway's first capital and it remained Scandinavia's largest port and trading centre throughout the Middle Ages. Hanseatic merchants had their houses along one side of the harbour and today, they provide a living museum, an elaborate network of tall dark buildings with pointed gables, narrow alleys and cobbled courtyards leading to the workshops and warehouses behind. In 1217 King Håkon signed a trading agreement with Britain, the start of a long association between the two countries.

Bergen is a significant education centre with its university and several colleges of further education, and the cultural heart of the region. The Bergen Philarmonic Orchestra was founded in 1765 and the country's first permanent theatre was built in 1850.

Above all, Bergen is a place to enjoy. There is plenty of accommodation, a marvellous city centre with its colonnades of shops, restaurants and cafés, and wonderful open-air markets where you can buy and eat some of the freshest fish you will ever have tasted.

The most important cultural event is the International Festival of Music, Drama and Folklore held annually at the end of May and beginning of June, and which is world famous.

Note: A road toll is levied for all vehicles driving into the city centre on weekdays between 6am and 10pm. The toll is to pay for the massive road rebuilding programme now taking place. If you plan to make frequent visits into the city centre buy a book of toll tickets which gives a 10 per cent reduction, or use public transport. You are not charged a toll for driving out of the city.

Touring the City Centre

The city has grown around the harbour and the easiest way to explore is on foot. If you get tired you can always stop and have a coffee or beer in one of the many cafés, and at lunchtime you can enjoy a famous Norwegian buffet which most of the hotels and restaurants offer. The choice is usually enormous but the prices are very reasonable. You can explore the Torget, the famous fish market, which stands at the head of the main harbour Vågen. The market not only sell fish, but a huge variety of fruit, vegetables and flowers. It is open daily, except Sunday 8am-3pm.

HISTORIC BUILDINGS

Bergenhus Fortress grounds contain some of Norway's most famous medieval buildings. Håkon's Hall was built by King Håkon Håkonsson between 1247 and 1261 as the largest and most imposing building in the Royal residence in Bergen. There are guided tours of the Great Hall where Norway's kings were crowned, and Rosenkrantz Tower. It is used as one of the spectacular venues for the International Festival.

Rosenkrantz Tower was built in the 1560s by Erik Rosenkrantz, the Governor of Bergen Castle, as a combined defence and residential tower. It incorporates two much older structures, King Magnus the Lawmender's keep from about 1260 and Jørgen Hannsøns outwork from about 1520. It was destroyed in an explosion during World War II but faithfully rebuilt in the early 1960s.

Bryggen is a wonderful collection of wooden buildings facing the harbour, and to the west of the Torget market. It gets its name from *tyskebryggen*, which means 'docks' or 'quays' in German, and was the the name given to the quarter when the Hanseatic merchants moved in. This unique collection of medieval Norwegian architecture has been recognised by UNESCO and is included in their World Heritage list as 'being one of the world's most significant cultural-historical reminiscences of medieval settlement'. The protected old homes now house artists studios and workshops where painters, weavers and other craftsmen work. Many of the studios are open to the public. The character of the area has been preserved even though it is now the home of a number of boutiques and restaurants.

St Mary's Church to the north of Bryggen, is the oldest building in Bergen and one of the outstanding Romanesque churches in Norway. It was built in the first half of the twelfth century and has the richest Baroque pulpit in Norway. Much of the finance for the church came from Hanseatic merchants which explains the large number of German inscriptions and motifs.

The oldest part of the **cathedral** dates from the late twelfth century while the choir and the lower part of the tower were built in thirteenth-century Gothic style. It has extended over the centuries which accounts for the different styles.

St John's Church, on Syndneshaugen, was built in 1894 and is one of the best preserved buildings from the neo-Gothic style in Norway.

Korskirken was first built in the mid-twelfth century but little of the original building remains. Today, it is mainly a church of Renaissance architecture dating from the seventeenth century.

Nykirken was built in the early eighteenth century, and was one of the many buildings destroyed during the war by an explosion in 1944. It has now been fully restored to its former glory.

MUSEUMS AND ART GALLERIES

For opening times and addresses of the following points of interest, please refer to the additional information section on p133.

Bryggen: a row of timber-fronted shops facing the harbour in Bergen

A cobbled street and eighteenth-century houses in Old Bergen

Bergen Fine Arts Museum, Rasmus Meyers Allé has alternating exhibitions of contemporary visual art.

Bryggens Museum, incorporates the Erling Dekke Næss Institute for Medieval Archaeology. It is a fascinating museum based on the extensive archaeological excavations of the Bryggen which took place between 1955 and 1972. There are remains from the oldest buildings in Bergen dating back to the twelfth century. Exhibits include early European ceramics, runic inscriptions and there are displays depicting commerce, shipping, handicrafts and daily life in the Middle Ages.

Buekorps Museum is a collection of pictures and other items showing the 135 year history of the Buekorpset, a brigade of boys noted for their marching displays, usually with crossbows.

The Fishery Museum tells the story of Norwegian fishermen and how the industry developed. It has won many prizes and has become a model for similar museums around the world.

The **Hanseatic Museum** is housed in one of the oldest and best preserved wooden buildings in Bergen and furnished in the style of the sixteenth century. It gives an insight into the life and home of a Hanseatic merchant.

The **Leprosy Museum** is home to the Bergen Collections of the History of Medicine housed on the site of a hospital for lepers founded in the Middle Ages. The present buildings date back to the beginning of eighteenth century, when they were rebuilt after a fire in 1702, and the exhibits pay tribute to the many Norwegian doctors and scientists who contributed to research in the fight against leprosy.

The **Museum of Cultural History** exhibits concentrate on the culture and history of western Norway. There are fine collections from prehistoric and medieval times to the present day, including unique pieces of religious art from the Middle Ages, and collection of tools, utensils, furniture and folk art from the region's urban and rural areas.

The **Municipal Art Museum** is a famous collection of Norwegian paintings spanning 150 years as well as other European works.

The **Museum of Natural History** contains exhibits of botanic, geological and zoological interest. Of special interest is the extinct Lofoten horse, a giant octopus and a number of whale skeletons.

The **Schøtstuene**, Øvregaten is a collection of old assembly rooms at the western end of Bryggen, which illustrates the social life of the Hanseatic merchants of Bergen. They are still used for celebrations on festive occasions.

The **West Norway Museum of Applied Art and Crafts** exhibits a collection of European arts and crafts, antique Bergen silver and contemporary Norwegian and foreign ceramic, glass, furniture, metalwork. It also contains General JWN Munthe's collection of Chinese art, and works of arts and antiquities from the Norwegian home of Anna and William Singer.

AROUND BERGEN

Places of Interest

Old Bergen, Elesro, Sandviken is home to a park and open-air museum with more than thirty-five wooden houses representing Bergen architecture from the early eighteenth century. The houses have been laid out in streets and the interiors have been faithfully restored to show what town life was like over three centuries ago. There are also period shops and a market place.

Hill Farm Museum, West Norway's Seter Museum recently erected on Fanafjell, to the south of the city, which shows what life was like on remote Norwegian summer farms over the centuries.

Hordamusset, at Stend, south of Bergen is a folkmuseum devoted to agriculture and fishing. There is a section devoted to the history of buildings and many fine tapestries.

Langegaarden-Fjosanger Hovedård, a marvellous manor farm with art gallery and handicraft centre, 10km from the city centre.

Ole Bull's Villa on the island Lysøen is a villa and concert hall. It was designed by the architect von der Lippe and built between 1872 and 1873 by the world famous violin virtuoso and national hero Ole Bull. The villa contains his furniture and possessions at the time of his death in 1880 and the buildings are now protected as a national monument. Ole Bull built a network of paths all over the island and it is a delightful place to spend a few hours.

Damsgård Manor, Laksevåg, about 3km west of Bergen on highway 555 was built around 1770 as Bergen's most splendid home and is now being restored to become a museum. The garden with its fountains and fishponds, has been restored to look as it did 200 years ago, showing the flowers, herbs, shrubs, vegetables and trees of that period.

Alvøen Main Building is a disused paper factory 16km west of Bergen and the former residence of the owners, the Fasmer family. It was opened as a museum in 1983. The building dates from 1797 and contains a collection of old furniture, silver, East Indian porcelain and pictures. There are guided tours on Sundays between 12noon-4pm, May to August ☎ 05 93 18 19/05 32 51 08.

Troldhaugen, Edvard Grieg's home for 22 years was built in 1885 at Hop a few kilometres to the south of the city. It is on a hill overlooking the peaceful Lake Nordås. The composer wrote many of his most famous works here and is buried here with his wife Nina. In the garden with its beautiful flowers and shrubs and twisty paths, there is the hut where he went to compose. A concert hall seating 200 has been built in the grounds and was opened in 1985. The house is now a museum dedicated to his memory.

Fantoft Stave Church (see section on stave churches p44), Paradis was built in the early twelfth century at Fortun in the Sognefjord area and moved to its present site at Fantoft in 1883.

The **Norwegian Arboretum** (open daily admission free), Mildevågen was founded in 1971 and covers 50 hectares (125 acres), part of which is devoted to foreign trees and shrubs. The area has been beautifully landscaped with hilly areas, rocky gorges, a small lake and shoreline several kilometres long. Apart from the trees there are opportunities for walking and swimming.

Fana (off highway 553 south of Bergen is famous for its folk music evenings which are held regularly during the summer months. There is singing, dancing, music and feasting. For more information ☎ 91 52 40. Opportunities for walking and recreation in and around Bergen are countless and there are scores of trails to follow in and around the city. Bergen Tourist Board offer details and guides on these recommended walks. For more information ☎ 91 52 40.

There are many places to bathe in and around Bergen, and plenty of sporting opportunities including angling, bowling, tennis, badminton, squash, bowling, golf, riding, trotting and yachting. The tourist office will also supply details about the many tours available ranging from brief conducted sightseeing trips around the city centre, to ferry journeys through the fjords spanning several days.

Additional Information

Places of Interest in Bergen

Historic Buildings

Cathedral
Open: summer Monday to Friday 11am-2pm.

Håkons Hall
Open: same times as tower, also Thursday 3-6pm.

Korskirken
Open: Tuesday to Friday 10am-12noon or by appointment.

Nykirken
Open: in summer, Monday to Friday 10am-2pm.

Rosenkrantz Tower
Open: mid-May to mid-September daily 10am-4pm. Rest of year Sunday 12noon-3pm. Guided tours every hour.

St John's Church
Open: 1 June to 31 August, Tuesday to Friday 9am-3pm.

St Mary's Church (Mariakirken)
Open: May to end-August, Monday to Friday 11am-4pm, rest of year Tuesday to Friday 12noon-1.30pm.

Museums and Art Galleries

Bergen Fine Arts Museum
5 Rasmus Meyers Allé
☎ (05) 31 14 60
Open: Tuesday to Friday 12noon-4pm, weekends 12noon-3pm.

Bryggens Museum
☎ (05) 31 67 10
Open: May to end August, Monday, Wednesday and Friday 10am-4pm, Tuesday and Thursday 10am-8pm,

weekends 11am-3pm; September to end April, Monday to Friday 11am-3pm, Saturday 12noon-3pm, Sunday 12noon-4pm.

Buekorps Museum
Wall Gate
Opening times available from Bergen Tourist Office.

Fishery Museum
Nordahl Brunsgt
☎ (05) 31 12 49
Open: May to August, Monday to Saturday 1am-3pm, Sunday 12noon-3pm. Rest of year Wednesday and Sunday 12noon-3pm.

Hanseatic Museum
Bryggen
☎ (05) 31 41 89
Open: June to August daily 10am-5pm; May and September daily 11am-2pm; rest of year Sunday, Monday, Wednesday and Friday 11am-2pm.

Leprosy Museum
St George's Hospital
Kong Oscarsgate
Open: mid-May to end August 11am-3pm.

Museum of Cultural History
Sydneshaugen
☎ (05) 21 31 16
Open: daily 11am-2pm except Friday.

Municipal Art Museum
Bergen Billedgalleri
Open: mid-May to mid-September, Monday to Saturday 11am-4pm, Sunday 12noon-3pm; rest of year daily except Monday 12noon-3pm.

Museum of Natural History
Muséplassen
☎ (05) 21 30 50
Open: daily 11am-2pm except Thursday.

Schøtstuene
Øvregaten
Open: June to August daily 10am-4pm;
May and September daily 11am-2pm,
rest of year Sunday, Tuesday, Thursday
and Saturday 11am-2pm.

**West Norway Museum of Applied Art
and Crafts**
Nordahl Brunsgt, ☎ (05) 32 51 08
Consult Bergen Tourist Office for new
opening hours.

Around Bergen

Hill Farm Museum
Open: daily mid-June to mid-August
12noon-6pm.

Hordamuseet
Stend
☎ (05) 91 51 30
Open: Tuesday to Friday and Sundays
12noon-3pm.

Old Bergen
Elsesro
Sandviken
☎ (05) 25 63 07
Open: May to mid-June daily 12noon-
6pm; mid-June to mid-August daily
11am-7pm; mid-August to mid-September 12noon-6pm.

Damsgård Manor
Gardens open: May to September
12noon-6pm.

Troldhaugen
Open: May to September daily 10.30am-
1pm and 1.30-5.30pm. Summer recitals
are here throughout July, usually on
Wednesday and Sunday. Obtain tickets
and information from the entrance.

Useful Information

Consulates
Great Britain
18 Strandgaten
☎ (05) 32 70 11

Emergencies
Police ☎ 002
Fire Brigade ☎ 001
Ambulance ☎ 003
Casualty Station, 30 Lars Hillesgt
☎ (05) 32 11 20

Accidents. Open day and night.
Emergency Dental Care, 30 Lars
Hillesgt ☎ (05) 32 11 20, open: daily 10-
11am and 7-9pm.
Duty Chemist, Apoteket Nordstjernen,
Bus Station ☎ (05) 31 68 84
24 hours service.

Exchange
The tourist office will change money
when the banks are closed but the rates
are poor.

Motorists

Indoor Car Parks
Bygarasjen
Busstation
Parking for 1,500 cars. 5 minute walking
from the city centre. Near bus and train
station. Open: 24 hours.

Citypark
7 Markeveien
Short-time parking.
Open: weekdays 7am-11pm.
Sunday closed.

Parkeringshuset
4 Rosenkrantzgaten
Short-time parking.
Open: 8am-5pm, Thursday til 7pm,
Saturday til 3pm. Sunday closed.

Garages and Service
Mobilstation
1 Lars Hillesgt
☎ (05) 32 45 15
Service station and garage for 60 cars.

Break Down Service
Viking Salvage Corps
3 Edv Griegsvei
☎ (05) 29 22 22

NAF
Torgalmenning
☎ (05) 31 17 90

Motorcycle Hire
Bergen Motorsykkel Salg
30B Fjøsangerveien
☎ (05) 29 78 30

Motoring Clubs
NAF Touring Office
  (Norwegian Automobile Club)
3 Torglam
☎ (05) 31 17 90

Road Service
☎ (05) 29 24 62

Post Office

Opening hours at main post office:
weekdays 8am-5pm, Thursdays 8am-
7pm, Saturdays 9am-1pm.
☎ (05) 54 15 00.

Regional Tourist Boards

Sogn og Fjordane Tourist Board
PO Box 299
N-5801 Sogndal
☎ (056) 72 300

Buskerud Tourist Board
Storgt 4
N-3500 Hønefoss
☎ (067) 23 655

Local Tourist Offices

Bergen Reiselivslag
Postal address only
Slottsgt 1
N-5000 Bergen
Visits: Torvalmenningen
☎ (05) 32 1480
The tourist office is in Torgalmenning.
Pick up the free *Bergen Guide*.

Lærdal og Borgund Reiselivslag
N-5890 Lærdal
☎ (056) 66 509

**Reisetrafikklaget for Valdres
  og Jotunheimen**
Rådhuset, N-2900 Fagernes
☎ (063) 60 400

Voss Reiselivslag
Postboks 57
N-5701 Voss
☎ (05) 51 17 16

Bagn ☎ (063) 46461
(not staffed all year round)
Hønefoss ☎ (067) 23330

Shopping

Opening hours:
Mondays, Tuesday, Wednesdays and
Fridays from 9am-5pm.
Thursdays (some shops also on Fridays)
from 9am-7pm.
Saturdays from 9am-2pm.
The shopping centres 'Galleriet' and

'Bystasjonen' are open Monday to
Friday 9am-8pm, Saturday 9am-4pm.
Some food shops will stay open until
8pm on weekdays and until 6pm on
Saturdays such as the Hye Fosse Super-
market opposite the SAS Royal Hotel.
Some shops carrying typical tourist
articles will keep open longer on days
when cruise ships call at the city. In
these shops you may also buy tax-free
goods.
Ask for the folder 'Shops in Bergen with
special service for tourists'.
Shopping centres outside the city are
open: Monday to Friday 10am-8pm.
Saturday 9am-4pm, some till 6pm.
Bergen has a large variety of exciting
shops.

Banks open: Monday to Friday 8.15am-
3pm, Thursday 8.15am-5pm.

Telephone — Telegrams

For use of telephone boxes a NOK1,
piece is required. Local calls cost NOK2,
for 3 min. Telegrams despatched by
dialling 0138 for ordering trunk calls
abroad, dial 0115. Direct dialing 095
plus country code.
Telegraph Building, Byparken (by the
city park) open: 8am-8pm, Sundays 2-
7pm.

Travel

Airport
Bergen Airport, Flesland
19km south of Bergen. Restaurant.
SAS ☎ (05) 23 60 90. Braathens SAFE
  ☎ (05) 99 82 50
Seaplane Harbour, Sandviken
  ☎ Fonnafly (05) 32 47 85

Airlines
Braathens SAFE
Ticket office: 4 Ole Bulls Plass
☎ (05) 23 23 25
British Airways, 4 Ole Bulls Plass
☎ (05) 23 23 25
Dan-Air Services, 4 Ole Bulls Plass
☎ (05) 23 23 25
KLM Royal Dutch Airlines, 10
Vaagsalmenning ☎ (05) 32 00 90
Lufthansa German Airlines, 9
Torgalmenning (entrance from
Markeveien) ☎ (05) 31 12 30

Scandinavian Airlines — SAS
Ticket Office: 1 Torgalmenning
☎ (05) 23 63 00

Airportbus
Frequent bus service to the airport
leaving from SAS Royal Hotel, via
Braathens SAFE office at Hotel Norge,
and the Bus Station. For departure
times, inquire at the airlines, or at the
Tourist Information Centre.

Bergen-Stavanger-Newcastle Directly
Operator: Norway Line
1 Slottsgaten
5th floor
Box 4098
Dreggen
5023 Bergen.
☎ (05) 32 27 80

Central Bus Station (Bystasjonen)
8 Strømgaten
☎ (05) 32 67 80
Terminal for all buses serving the
environs of Bergen and Hardanger area.
Airport bus, luggage deposits, shops
and restaurant.

City Buses
All buses are marked with destination
and route no. Special tourist tickets for
unlimited travel within 48 hours available on the buses.
One day tickets are available for Bergen
and surroundings.

Ferries
Across the harbour, weekdays 7.15am-
4.15pm. Does not run on Saturdays and
Sundays. From Nøstekaien frequent
ferries to the island Askøy (20 min).

Fjord and Coastal Steamers
Coastal steamers for north Norway
leave daily from Frieleneskaien Dokken
Expresss boats to Stavanger and
Haugesund.
Hardanger Fjord and Sunnhordland.
Express boats leave from
Munkebryggen ☎ (05) 32 65 60
Sognefjord, Nordfjord and Sunnfjord.
Steamers leave from Nykirkekaien.
☎ (05) 32 40 15
Local Steamers serving the islands and
fjords immediately north of Bergen dock
at the inner harbour on the left hand
side of the Fish Market,
Strandkaiterminalen.

International Sea Routes
Ferries for Newcastle, Shetland, Faroe
Islands, Iceland and Denmark dock at
Skoltegrunnskaien.

Railway Station
☎ (05) 31 96 40/(05) 31 93 05. Day and
night trains from Oslo and en route
stations. Luggage deposits. Cafeteria.

Taxi
☎ (05) 99 09 90. To order in advance
☎ (05) 99 13 00

7

THE LAND OF LAKES
AND MOUNTAINS

This route takes you through a microcosm of Norway — the lakes and
mountains it visits are typical of the country as a whole. The route between
Oslo and Bergen through the splendid Hallingdal valley is the busiest and
fastest between the two cities but there is no need to rush. Take the E68 out of
Oslo to Hønefoss and then follow highway 7 through Hallingdal before
turning west through spectacular mountain and lake scenery. Throughout the
route there are detours that can be made and while the 490km journey can be
undertaken comfortably within a day, it is best to spread it over two or three
and enjoy the many sights along the way.

Well over half the journey takes you through the county of Buskerud which
stretches from Oslofjorden in the south-east to almost Sognefjorden in the
north-west, covering an area of 15,000sq km. You travel through Nesbyen,
Norway's warmest town and pass through marvellous winter sports country
both in Hallingdal and the northern fringes of the mountainous
Hardangervidda, while in the summer there is high mountain walking or
windsurfing and canoeing in the many lakes and lower lying rivers.

From Hønefoss take highway 7 and head for the town of **Sokna**. The river
of the same name runs parallel and to the left of the road all the way to the
town. Highway 7 then swings south-west down to Hamremoen overlooking
the long, twisting Lake Krøderen. The lake then runs north underneath
Norefjell, a spectacular mountain area to the west whose highest peak is
Høgevarde (1,460m). It is possible to drive round the other side of the lake by
detouring at Noresund on the toll road which bridges the lake at its narrowest
point. There are then a number of small roads leading over the mountains
across windswept moors to Eggedal. If you really want to explore Norefjell
you can drive from Noresund to Båsheim on highway 287 which runs north
into the mountains. The area with its ski lifts and ski resorts is very popular
in the winter with people from Oslo.

Between Numedal valley to the west (see chapter 8) and Lake Krøderen
there are more than 150 lakes where you can fish, swim, sail and canoe. On the
island of Bjørøya in Lake Krøderen there is Fridheim Villa (grounds open
daily, house times vary) which in the summer stages pageants and exhibitions
built around Norwegian myths and fairy tales. It is one of Norway's most
unusual wooden buildings.

At Krøderen beside the lake, you will find Buskerud's privately operated
steam railway. The 26km long line runs to Vikersund. The engine and car-
riages all date from the turn of the century and the trip is fascinating.

Highway 7 continues along the eastern banks of the lake through Ørgenvika where the Oslo-Bergen railway emerges from the 2.3 km long Haversting Tunnel, as far as Gulsvik which marks the start of the Hallingdal valley.

This heavily wooded area is famous for its brown bears. It is worth a detour by taking the minor road off on the right just beyond the left hand turning for Flå. This road winds up into the wooded hills to Venelisr, close to the Buskerud-Oppland border and an area called Vassfaret, where the bears are most likely to be seen.

Continuing on highway 7 you pass a number of campsites and cabins for rent. There are many bathing areas and places to fish. Boats can be hired. The road, with the river now on your right, runs through Bromma to Nesbyen, the centre for Lower Hallingdal.

Hallingdal is often called the Gateway to the Western Fjords, and is Norway's best developed holiday region with beautiful countryside, extensive transport network and plenty of things to do throughout the year. It is an area of wooded valleys, waterfalls, lakes and scenic views. Activities include mountain hiking, riding, fishing, sailing, windsurfing, canoeing and walking. You can walk almost anywhere in the area on well marked trails or across country. A number of companies operate week-long hiking tours and details can be obtained from the Norwegian Tourist Office. These tours offer an excellent chance to get to know the country in the company of mostly Norwegians who almost all speak English.

If you want to organise your own activities in Hallingdal, Nesbyen makes an excellent base. There are many campsites in and around the town, as well as hotels, youth hostel, cabins and so on.

Nesbyen has the Hallingdal Folk Museum (open daily) which contains many old buildings including the famous medieval Staveloftet. The old houses and farms also contain period household utensils and furniture, tools, weapons and local costumes.

From Nesbyen the Rukkedalen valley runs south-west to Rødberg in Numedal, about 55km away, but this route continues north along highway 7 which climbs to the mountain resort of Gol.

Gol is a popular winter sports area and almost as busy in the summer because the surrounding mountains provide splended walking. The bustling town is also important as a communications centre and is on the Oslo-Bergen railway line, and there is an important link road (highway 49) heading north to Leira in the Valdres. There are a number of side roads off highway 49 which will take you into marvellous mountain country where you can go walking or just enjoy the views. On a clear day there are usually fine views of the snow capped mountains of Jotunheimen to the north. There are a number of small hotels, pensions and campsites along highway 49 as well as a number of mountain huts.

Gol has plenty of accommodation to suit all tastes, including a number of well appointed campsites. There are chair lifts into the surrounding hills and the views from the summit on a clear day are sensational. Gol's old stave church is now the centrepiece of the Oslo Folk Museum at Bygdøy (see section on stave churches p44).

An exciting detour is to take highway 52 from Gol northwards through

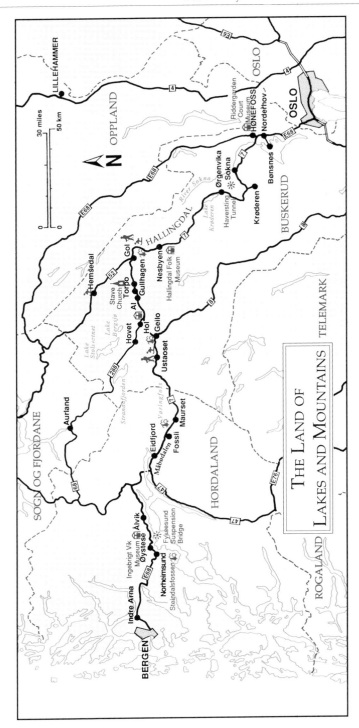

Hemsedal until it meets E68 at Borlaug. Here you can turn left and enjoy the marvellous fjord trip down Aurlandsfjorden and Nærøyfjorden to Gudvangen, before travelling down through Voss to Bergen.

Hemsedal valley is delightful with glorious woodlands, crystal clear streams and waterfalls. Around Hielmen bru there are fine views of Storehorn (1,478m) and Veslehorn (1,300m), the closer of the two mountains. **Hemsedal** itself is a popular ski resort and offers lots of accommodation and a number of chair lifts into the mountains. Beyond Hemsedal the terrain gets even more mountainous and on the right a few kilometres beyond Bjøberg you pass close by Slettind (1,592m), and then Stardalsfjellet (1,589m), on your left, just before you reach Breistølen.

Highway 7 turns west from Gol to **Torpo** which is famous for its stave church (see section on stave churches p47) believed to have been built in the second half of the twelfth century, which makes it the oldest building in Hallingdal. The ceiling paintings date from the thirteenth century and tell the story of St Maragret to whom the church is dedicated. There are elaborately carved portals. The choir was pulled down in the eighteenth century leaving only the 'ship'.

At **Gullhagen**, between Torpo and Ål there are roads leading off on the right into some marvellous areas for skiing in the winter and walking in the summer. The road leads to the tourist resort of Bergsjøstølen at 1,079m beside Lake Bergsjø.

Ål has an interesting church and museum and a number of hotels in and around the town as well as cabins to rent. The church was built to replace the stave church which was destoyed by fire at the end of the last century. The new church, built in traditional style, contains paintings which are copies of those which used to adorn the stave church. The museum is at Leksvoll, just over 1km to the east of the town. The open air museum has a number of very fine old buildings including a complete farmstead, inn, mill and school house.

Highway 7 then runs north of Strandefjorden, a long narrow lake that runs almost as far as **Hol** where there is another open-air folk museum with a number of old buildings, and a photographic museum. There is a thirteenth-century church incorporating parts of an even older stave church, and there are a number of Viking burial mounds in the area. There is also a memorial to the Norwegians from the area, who died fighting in the Napoleonic Wars.

Highway 288 runs north-east from Hol through very spectacular mountain country, through **Hovet** with its richly decorated chapel, past a number of very old but well preserved farms and the rose painting workshop at Myrland. The narrow road then travels along the lovely Lake Strandavatnet with the massive Hallingskarvet range, rising to 1,933m as the backdrop in the west. Sveingardsbotn is almost 1,200m above sea level and then there is a steep climb to the highest point on the road at just over 1,600m. There are a number of power stations close to the road as it winds towards Aurlandsdalen and the ferry station at Aurland near the head of Aurlandsfjorden, a tributary of Sognefjorden. Aurland is busy because of its ferry links and noted for its medieval Vangen church. There is ample accommodation in the area and cabins, boats, bikes and even horses for hire. There is also excellent fishing, bathing and walking.

The road from Hol is very steep in places but the last part of the drive is the most dramatic and scenic, taking you through the Aurland valley which contains some marvellous walks and one of Norway's most famous hiking trails down to Kassbygdi. Østerbø makes a good base if you want to walk in the area.

If you have time another excursion should be to take the train on the Flåm railway. The station is at the head of Aurlandfjorden and you can take the train to Myrdal and back through quite stunning scenery. It is recognised as one of the most famous railway lines in the world and one of the steepest. The line travels through the Flåmsdalen valley for 19km on a gradient of 1:18. For further information contact the Norwegian State Railways (NSB) in Oslo, Box 9115, Vaterland, N-0134 Oslo 1 ☎ (02) 36 80 00.

From Hol highway 7 runs south-west along the top of a steep sided gorge in the Ustedalen valley, which carries the fast flowing Ustelva over a series of rapids and waterfalls, into **Geilo** the main tourist centre in Hallingdal.

The busy town, 800m above sea level, is packed in the winter and is only a little less busy during the summer. Apart from its attractions as a year round outdoor activities centre, Geilo is famous for its production of knives and tools. It is an important communications centre on the Oslo-Bergen railway line, and there is a major junction with highway 8 running up the Numedal valley from Kongsberg. (See chapter 8 to join highway 7). Geilo and the surrounding district has about 35 hotels, pensions, boarding houses, youth hostel and campsites.

There are kilometres of well marked footpaths in Geilo and the surrounding mountains and a very good tourist office which can supply you with details of many recommended walks. There is plenty of good fishing around the town, riding stables, bikes, rowing boats and canoes for hire, as well as swimming, tennis, minigolf and a host of organised trips and outings.

The chairlift operates all year round and in the summer you can take it to the summit of Geilohøgda (1,200m), and then walk back down to the town at your own pace. You do not have to come straight down because once on the top, you usually have a choice of well-marked trails to follow.

Geilo is still primarily a winter resort and it increasingly attracts visitors keen to ski downhill or go cross-country. There are many kilometres of well prepared cross country trails, some of which are floodlit at night. It pays to be fit if you want to go skiing but you do not have to be super fit to do cross country. The great advantage of this activity is that if you do get tired you can always stop and have a rest, something it is a little difficult to do halfway down a crowded piste. A winter sports festival is held in the town every January.

Things to do should include the chair lift ride to the top of Geilohøgda (1,200m) where you can enjoy a drink in the restaurant and enjoy the spectacular views. About 3km west of Geilo near Fekjo there are some Viking burial mounds.

The Geilo Tourist Office suggest walks and supplies maps. All the paths are marked with red painted T's. Geilo, Ustaoset and Haugastøl are all good starting points for hiking trips into the mountains of Hardangervidda. There are numerous walking tours which take a number of days.

The journey from Geilo to the ferry ports of Brimnes or Kinsavik takes you through marvellous rugged mountain scenery. Highway 7 travels through **Ustaoset** at the eastern end of Ustevatn. It is an amazing sprawling village of holiday chalets dotted around the hills. To the south is Ustetind (1,376m), while to the north is Prestholt (1,857m), with Hallingskarvet (1,933m) towering behind it. The Oslo-Bergen line runs between the road and Lake Ustevatnet as far as Haugastøl and it is on this stretch that it reaches its highest point, more than 990m above sea level.

Haugastøl marks the start of the climb up on to the northern rim of the

Inhospitable terrain near Geilo

The chairlift from Geilo

Vøringfossen's cascading water drops almost 200m

Hardangervidda mountain plateau and there are a number of places worth stopping for. There is a windswept Lapp trading post with the usual display of reindeer antlers outside near Fagerheim. At Krækkjavatn you can get wonderful views of the Hardangerjøkulen glacier with its peaks rising to 1,862m. At Halne you cross the county border from Buskerud into Hordaland and Tråastølen marks the roads highest point at 1,250m. A short distance further on is Dyranut which is famous for its trout fishing.

There is also good trout fishing at **Maurset**, the highest farm in the Bjoreidalen valley. Although the weather in this area can be very inhospitable during the winter it is still popular with the hardy Norwegians and there are a number of mountain huts and cabins which make good bases for summer walks and exploration.

At Isdøla there is a small road north to Vøringfossen. There are incredible views from the **Fossli** tourist centre and restaurant, which is on the edge of the cliffs overlooking the falls which plummet almost 200m.

The road down through the Måbødalen valley was literally dynamited from the hillside. It is a series of breathstopping hairpin bends which cling to the mountain side. There are five hairpin bends and a series of tunnels as the road drops rapidly to the valley floor at Sæbø only 15m above sea level. The view from the top before you start your descent is fantastic. Low gear driving is essential.

If the descent did not worry you at all, it is worth making a detour along the side road from Sæbø to Hjølmo. The road is very narrow and steep but the scenery is spectacular with steep sided mountains and plunging waterfalls.

Highway 7 continues west to **Eidfjord** at the head of Eidfjord. It is famous for its salmon fishing, medieval stone church and the nearby Sima power station, for many years the largest in Norway. The road to the power station runs north-east out of Eidfjorden through the valley of Simadalen. The road contains one of the few s-shaped tunnels as it wiggles through the mountain. The road finally runs out but there are paths to two lovely waterfalls Rembesdalfossen and Skykkjedalsfossen which is to the south.

From Eidfjord the road follows the fjord to Brimnes where there is a 10 minute ferry crossing to Bruravik. This is the fastest route via the E68 connection at Granvin if you want to get to Bergen. Just outside Brimnes at **Bu** there is an open air folk museum.

If you have more time you can continue down to the ferry terminal at Kinsarvik which in the height of the season carries thousands of cars a day. The crossing to Kvanndal takes about 35 minutes and you then follow E68 west along the shores of Hardangerfjorden for Bergen (head west for Voss).

The drive takes you through Ålvik with its spreading industrial development, past the hydro-electric power station at **Bjølve** (with its 800m long vertical water pipes, the longest in Norway), and then across the wonderful Fykesund suspension bridge which spans an inlet of the fjord. The bridge is almost 350m long and the main span extends 232m.

A few kilometres beyond the bridge is the delightful resort town of **Øystese**. The Ingebrigt Vik Museum contains about 150 works by the Norwegian sculptor. There is ample accommodation, a youth hostel, campsites and cabins to rent.

A short distance on again is **Norheimsund**, famous for the Steindalsfossen a few kilometres to the west of the town, which you can walk under. Again there is plenty of accommodation and you can take a number of boat trips to explore Hardangerfjorden from the busy harbour.

E68 continues through the Steinsdalen valley to Tokagjelet, a canyon which you negotiate through a series of tunnels, and this takes you to a mountainous area called Kvamskogen which separates Samnangerfjorden and Hardangerfjorden. It is very popular with the people of Bergen as a skiing centre in the winter and as a walking and outdoors activities area in the summer and there are hundreds of chalets dotted among the hills. There is a youth hostel and a number of cabins to rent if you want to spend some time walking in the area.

The road drops down to Samnangerfjord at Tysse where it meets highway 13 coming up from Stavanger, and then heads north over Gullbotn, the summit of the pass which separates Samnangerfjord and Sørfjord, before descending through a number of tunnels into Indre Arna. The road then runs south through Nesttun, where there is a turn off for Edward Grieg's home at Trollhaugen, before swinging north into Bergen.

Additional Information

Useful Addresses

Regional Tourist Boards

Buskerud Tourist Board
Storgt 4
N-3500 Hønefoss
☎ (067) 23 655

Hordaland and Bergen Tourist Board
Slottsgt 1
N-5003 Bergen
☎ (05) 31 66 00

Local Tourist Offices

Aurland Reiselivslag
N-5745 Aurland
☎ (056) 33 313

Eidfjord Reiselivslag
Postboks 132
N-5783 Eidfjord
☎ (054) 65 177

Geilo Turistservice A/L
N-3580 Geilo
☎ (067) 86 300

Gol Turistkontor
N-3550 Gol
☎ (067) 74 840

Hemsedal Turistkontor
N-3560 Hemsedal
☎ (067) 78 156

Krødsherad, Modum og Sigdal Turistkontor
N-3515 Krøderen
☎ (067) 47 960

Nesbyen Turistkontor
Postboks 29
N-3541 Nesbyen
☎ (067) 71 249

Norheimsund Turistinformasjon
N-5600 Norheimsund
☎ (05) 55 17 67

Ål Turistkontor
N-3570 Ål
☎ (067) 81 060

Aurland ☎ (056) 33313
(Staffed all year round)

Øystese ☎ (05) 551767

8

THE SILVER TRAIL

This route from Oslo to Bergen is 480km long. Follow E18 out of Oslo for Drammen (described in chapter 4) and then the E76 for Kongsberg which takes you through Hokksund. Just to the south of Hokksund there is a lovely church at **Haug**. Although it was built in the 1850s the tower dates back to medieval times. The crossed keys over the door indicate it was dedicated to St Peter while Catholicism was being practised.

The road then swings south-west passing the head of Eikeren, the lake which runs down to Eidfoss. To the north you can spot Svartskur 407m, and on clear days Myrhogget, 705m in the distance behind it.

You then arrive at the thriving town of **Kongsberg**. It used to be Norway's second largest town because of the rich silver mines. The mines were discovered in 1623 and officially opened by Christian IV on 2 May1624. The silver was the source of the town's wealth for more than 300 years. Although the mine was closed commercially in 1957 it still attracts tourists in their thousands and a visit into the mines is well worthwhile (open mid-May to August daily 10am-4pm). Metal working which developed alongside the mine, is still one of the town's main industries.

The mines are about 6km out of town at **Saggrenda** and during the summer there is a small gauge railway which runs deep into the mines several times a day. The mine workings have been well restored.

The mine is signposted off the E76 by 'Solgruvene'. The road twists uphill to a dusty car park below the railway line which leads into Kongens Grube the most famous of all the mines in the area. The little train will take you approximately $2^1/_2$km deep into the mountain side where you can then join a conducted tour of the mine more than 342m under ground. Tourists are only allowed to descend to a third of the mine's true depth. The train journey into the mine is well worthwhile if you have time, but do wear warm clothing. The trip lasts almost $1^1/_2$ hours and it can get rather chilly.

Kongsberg has grown up on both sides of the River Numedalslågen which falls in a series of waterfalls through the town, and there are a number of delightful river walks. You can also enjoy a drink in the old Christian IV pub. Kongsberg church dates from 1761 and is one of the finest examples of Baroque architecture in Norway. The large size of the building is an indication of how wealthy Kongsberg was. The church is open mid-May to August, Monday to Friday 10am-4pm, Saturday 10am-1pm. Sunday open after service to 1pm, rest of year Tuesday to Friday 10am-12noon. There is also a fine mining museum on the banks of the River Lågen, which now incorporates a skiing museum and the Royal Norwegian's Mint collection. Outside the museum there is a working water mill. There is an open-air folk museum with many fine old buildings at Lågdalsmuseet on the eastern bank of the Lågen. The town has plenty of accommodation from good hotels and boarding houses to campsites and a youth hostel (☎ 03 73 20 24) which is open all year.

The route now swings north out of Kongsberg on highway 8 for the Numedal valley with Geilo as the destination. The valley runs along the eastern fringes of Hardangervidda with fantastic mountain views to the west in fine weather.

The valley is steeped in history and culture. There are stave churches at Nore, Uvdal and Rollag and the wonderful old buildings at Bygdetun which make up the Dåset Estate. The fast-flowing waters from the mountains have been tapped underground in the impressive subterranean power stations at Uvdal and Nore.

The whole valley is a golden opportunity to get out and exercise. There is plenty of scope for walking, fishing, canoeing, cycling and riding. One of the most popular centres is around the alpine farm at Langedrag where they not only keep fjord horses, goats and rabbits, but wolves as well. They are also famous for their cheeses. The valley is heavily wooded and the road follows the River Lågen closely although they are constantly switching sides.

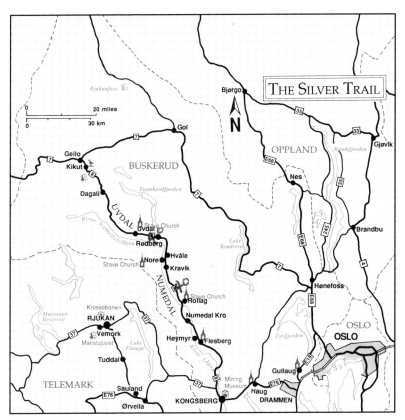

Highway 37 branches off to the left just beyond Skavanger and gives you the chance, if you have time, to take in a mini-tour of north Telemark. You can take highway 37 past Lake Follsjå and then north along the banks of Lake Tinnsjø before swinging west across the head of the lake for **Rjukan**. This small town, apart from having some of Europe's largest hydro electric power stations, also contains the Krossobanen, the first cable car built in Scandinavia. It takes you from the town to Gvepseborg, 950m above sea level. The views from the top are incredible, especially south towards Gausta (1,883m). Rjukan has a little museum (open daily) with a number of medieval exhibits, and there are cabins to be let in the grounds. There is also plenty of other accommodation available in the area which is popular both in winter and summer.

Just south outside the town is **Vemork** where there was a plant during World War II producing heavy water. A small band of Norwegian commandos blew the plant up in 1943 putting it out of commission for several vital months. The town was badly damaged the same year when it was attacked by wave after wave of giant USA bombers, the Flying Fortresses. A new power station has been built into the mountain.

The road here then runs by the Maristujuvet gorge famous for its 115m high Rjukanfossen. Because the river has been dammed for a reservoir to feed the power station, water only flows over the falls after very heavy rain.

You can follow highway 37 south past Møsvantet, one of Europe's largest reservoirs, back to Åmot on the E76, or you return to Rjukan and then take the mountain road through Tuddal along Tuddalsdalen to Sauland on the E76 where you turn left for a short way until you pick up highway 361 at Ørvella. This will take you back to Ormemyr on highway 37 and back on to highway 8 to continue your route north to Geilo.

There are many small roads running off to the left into Blefjell which is a marvellous walking area. A number of these are toll roads where you leave the money in an honesty box. It is an area of woods, lakes and hills rising steadily up to Bletopen (1,341m) in the west. The other major peaks are Bolkesjøfjell (910m) and Åklinut (1,246m).

At Grettefoss bru the road crosses to the right bank of the river and then enters **Svene** where there is a church dating back to the Middle Ages although it was substantially rebuilt about 200 years ago.

The next port of call is **Flesberg** famous for its stave church built at the end of the twelfth century. Although the church was extensively altered in the eighteenth century when it was rebuilt in cruciform style, the nave from the original columnar church remained. The church is noted for its very elaborately carved portals (see section on stave churches p44).

From Flesberg you can make short trips into the hills, either by driving north-east to Lyngdal, or south through **Hoymyr** into the lake country. This area is popular for winter sports, but the water and trails make an excellent summer recreation area as well.

Continuing north it is worth turning off the main road at Numedal kro to skirt round the eastern shores of the lake using the old road which goes to **Rollag** stave church (see section on stave churches p47). You can also take the turning at Stærnes. Although the church was not mentioned in local records until 1425 it is almost certainly very much older. It was rebuilt on the same site in 1697 and is now a strange combination of a number of ecclesiastical styles.

The altar-piece particularly has been constructed of figures from a number of periods. The pulpit is Rococo and many of the other decorations are from the Renaissance. This whole area is steeped in history and there are many lovely old farmsteads and store barns to be enjoyed. If you continue on the old road it swings round to rejoin highway 8 near Mogen where there are a number of campsites and cabins to let.

Highway 8 then runs to the east of the river into **Kravik** where there is the Kravikgårdene farm. It contains two of the oldest occupied medieval houses in the country and is now a national monument.

A few kilometres north is Hvåle at the foot of Norefjorden. It is worth taking the road across the old bridge to **Nore** where there is a twelfth-century stave church. It is a single nave church although it was extended later in the Middle Ages and substantially altered in the seventeenth century. It is noted for its painted decorations which date from the sixteenth and seventeenth centuries (see section on stave churches p44).

The next stretch of road is a delight to drive in the summer because the river has broadened out into a lake and there are lush water meadows full of wildflowers. Many of the farms are centuries old and there are lots of old store barns with grass roofs adorned with flowers. Some of the oldest buildings are found around Sevle where there is a very well preserved storehouse.

Just beyond Skjønne the road starts to turn towards Rødberg. Just before the town to the south you pass Nore 1, one of the country's largest power stations, while to the right there is a turn off which goes north to Tunnhovdfjorden, a massive reservoir. You can drive almost to the summit of Sveinsnuten which gives marvellous views over the whole area.

Rødberg has a number of small industries. Accommodation is available but if you want to overnight, it is better to drive on to **Uvdal** in the heart of the valley of the same name. It is a charming spot with a wonderful stave church looking out from the hillside. It is another church built in the mid-thirteenth century but rebuilt in 1720 when the fashion was to convert all churches into cruciform style. It too has wonderfully carved portals (see section on stave churches p44).

The area is ideal for a summer holiday with excellent walking, bathing, fishing and boating. There is ample accommodation including a summer youth hostel, campsites and cabins to hire. There are also a number of roads up into the mountains where you can find accommodation in delightful pensions.

Highway 8 climbs deeper into the Uvdal valley pointing straight at Hardangervidda in the west. It starts to swing north again around Bjørkeflåta and reaches its highest point at Vasstulan which is 1,100m above sea level.

It descends to **Dagali** where there is a turning off to the right to the Dagali museum (open daily) which houses a collection of buildings from the eighteenth and nineteenth century. There is a chair lift here and the region is ideal walking countryside.

The road starts to climb again to Fetjan (1,063m) and then descends through Skurdalen. It passes beside Skurdalsvatnet where there is a small chapel on the shore. There are also campsites and cabins and boats to let.

The final stretch of road climbs again to **Kikut** (1,010m) where there are marvellous views back over Hardangervidda, and then drops in a series of hairpin bends into Geilo. From here you can turn left on highway 7 for Bergen (chapter 7), or right to take you back to Oslo.

Additional Information

Local Tourist Offices

Kongsberg og Numedal
Turistkontor
Schwabes gt 1
N-3600 Kongsberg
☎ (03) 73 15 26

Rjukan og Tinn Reiselivslag
N-3660 Rjukan
☎ (036) 91 290

Regional Tourist Board

Telemark Tourist Board
PO Box 743 — Hjellen
N-3701 Skien
☎ (03) 52 92 05

Relaxing in the winter sunshine at Rjukan

9

THE GOLDEN ROUTE

The journey north from Bergen to Kristiansund (650km) has been known for centuries as 'the golden route' — not because of any precious metals but the sheer magnificence of the scenery encountered.

This is the Norwegian fjords at their best; dramatic, beautiful and varied. There are towering mountains, waterfalls, glaciers and above all, the magnificent deep blue fjords. This route takes longer than driving deeper inland and crossing the mountains because it uses a number of ferries but it is these fjord trips which make the route really memorable. In the summer the ferries can be crowded but the boats run so frequently that if you cannot get on one, you are almost certain to get the next, and you can enjoy the scenery while you wait. The highlight of the trip is the journey through Geirangerfjord, considered by many to be Norway's most beautiful fjord.

Drive south out of **Bergen** to pick up E68 and then head for Indre Arna. The road passes through a number of tunnels but in between there are wonderful views back across the fjords. About 13km beyond Indre Arna, take highway 13 which branches off the E68 and heads north for Dale. The road hugs the side of Veafjorden through Vaksdal and then starts to climb as it swings inland to Dale. The railway line that has run parallel with the road for much of the way until now swings north following the valley of the River Vosso into Voss while the road runs through Bergsdalen into Voss.

The road is narrow and twisty in places but there are passing places suitably positioned along the way. Bergsdalen is an impressive valley, especially after heavy rain when hundreds of new waterfalls seem to be spawned. The road hugs the mountainside and there are often steep drops down to the valley floor where the river crashes its way down to the coast.

Continue on the E68 as far as Vinje where you have a choice of routes. You can turn right on the E68 for Gudvangen and the ferry across to Revsnes and Kaupanger or you can turn left on highway 13 and head for Vik and Vangsnes where you catch the ferry across to Balestrand.

The E68 crosses a lake filled plateau as it climbs up to Stalheim which marks the highest point on the road. It is worth the small detour off to the left to see Sivlefossen which lies in the shadow of Jordalsnuten just to the east. From the top of the pass the road snakes its way down through the Nærøydalen to Gudvangen.

If you take the ferry across to Kaupanger, you will have to take highway 5 through Sogndal, Hermansverk and Leikanger to Hella where you catch the ferry across to Balestrand to rejoin the route north.

Kaupanger has the largest stave church in Sognefjorden. Built at the beginning of the thirteenth century it was altered in the seventeenth and nineteenth centuries before being fully restored in 1965 (see section on stave churches p46). **Sogndal** is a charming little town and the tourist centre for the region. It has many old houses and an interesting old parish church and folk museum out of town on the Kaupanger road.

A detour from Sogndal along highway 55 into Jostedalen is well worthwhile. The road goes close to the lovely resort of Hafslo. On the opposite shores of Lusterfjorden stands **Urnes** stave church, the oldest in Norway. It was built at the beginning of the twelfth century and what is believed to have been the site of an even older church. The carvings are still very well preserved (see section on stave churches p47). In the summer you can catch the ferry across from Solvorn.

Just before Gaupne the road forks and you should take highway 604 into Jostedalen, a wild and beautiful mountain valley with rushing rivers and cascading waterfalls. The Jostedalsbreen glacier is the largest in Europe, covers an area of more than 1,000sq km and in the north towers to 2,083m at Lodalskåpa. The ice in places is more than 600m thick. It is always present on your left and you can drive as far as Høgebru on good roads and then as far as Nigardsbreen on an unmetalled surface, which is quite manageable in the summer. There is a car park and you can walk round the lake or take a boat to the glacier's edge. Strong boots with good gripping soles are essential. It is possible to walk underneath the ice in places but great care must be taken at all times as blocks of ice might suddenly break off. The ice is moving and huge columns can crash down, and ice bridges can give way, especially in hot weather. There are organised walks across the glacier in the summer and it is inadvisable to attempt these without a guide. If you are sensible the dangers can be kept to a minimum and you will have an unforgettable experience on the ice. Allow a full day for the round trip into Jostedalen.

Having returned to Sogndal you drive west along highway 5 to **Nornes**, the scene of one of the greatest battles in Norwegian history when the two warlords Sverre and Magnus fought it out in 1184. You then pass **Fatlaviken**, which for years had the world's longest power cable span, stretching more than 5km across Sognefjorden, before arriving at **Hermansverk**, the centre for the area's flourishing orchards. At **Leikanger** there is a medieval church and just to the west one of Norway's largest Viking memorial, or runic stones, known as Baldershage. The road then continues to Hella and the ferries for Balestrand.

If you drive north from Vinje you drive through Myrkdalen. The road is very twisty and steep in places and climbs up to 986m just beyond Holaseter. From the top of the pass there are wonderful views north over Sognefjorden. The road falls steeply down to Vik passing Fossefjell and waterfalls at Målsetvatn. At **Hopperstad**, just before Vik, there is a twelfth-century stave church which was rebuilt just before the end of the last century. It has an unusual altar canopy with carvings of heads and decorations (see section on stave churches p46).

Vik (sometimes referred to as Viksøyra) is on Sognefjorden and the home of an aluminium works. There are lots of campsites, cabins and rooms to let in the area. The road then follows the fjord north 11km to **Vangsnes** and the ferry terminal. The saga hero Fridtjof the Bold was believed to have lived in Vangsnes, and in 1913 a giant statue was erected here on the orders of the German Emperor Wilhelm II.

There is plenty of accommodation in the area if you want to explore, including campsites, cabins to let and a summer youth hostel. But if you want to press on make for the ferry terminal where there are numerous sailings throughout the day. The crossing takes about 20 minutes to Balestrand, but you can also cross to Hella (about 15 minutes) if you want to visit Sogndal and explore the Jostedalen.

Hella to Lom

This is rather more than a side tour but if you like mountains you will love this trip. Follow highway 5 east along the shores of Sognefjorden to Sogndalsfjörä and then take highway 55 into the mountains. It is a wild and rugged road that climbs steadily although you are always aware of the massive peaks around you. The road follows Lusterfjorden with the magnificent Urnes stave church and then Feigumfossen on the opposite shores. **Feigumfoss** is another of Norway's most famous landmarks. The falls have a vertical drop of 218m making it one of the highest in Scandinavia. The road starts to climb inland. On your left you have Breheimen with Josterdalsbreen behind and ahead of you and to the right is Jotunheimen.

The road climbs steeply in a series of hairpin bends through **Dale** with its medieval Gothic church and fourteenth-century frescoes, and carries on climbing until the pass at **Sognefjell** which is 1,430m above sea level. It is the country's highest road pass and closed from October to June. Even in the summer, snow can lie thick on either side of the road which is narrow and often only wide enough for a single vehicle although there are plenty of passing points.

Near Sognfjell is the **Jotunheimen National Park** (details of maps and trails available from the local tourist office). The road then starts to descend past a number of mountain huts with trails leading from them and past Galdhøpiggen at 2,469m (Norway's second highest mountain). **Lom's** richly decorated stave church was built in the mid-twelfth century and extensively altered in the seventeenth century. However many of its original features remain including the marvellous carved dragon's head and the row of crosses carved on the roof ridge over the central aisle, the only example in Norway (see section on stave churches p46). Also of interest is the Lombygdemuseum, open daily. Legend has it that St Olav stayed here in the eleventh century. There is also a fantastic three storey high store barn. Lom is on highway 15 and you can either turn left and head for Geiranger taking the toll road over Dalsnibba (1,476m) with its spectacular views over the fjord, to rejoin the route, or turn right for Otta on E6 for Oslo or Trondheim.

The short ferry ride across Sognefjord takes you to **Balestrand**, a long established tourist resort which used to be very popular with the English gentry at the turn of the century. It is still a delightful area because of its wonderful scenery and pure, fresh air. It makes a good base for touring the area either by car, bus, train, boat or foot. There are a number of excursions to Nærøyfjorden,

Gudvangen, Mount Gaularfjell and the Jostedal glacier. You can take a ride on the Flåm railway or rent a bicycle or boat. It is a marvellous area for walking, bathing and water sports. Balestrand has a wide choice of hotels, pensions, youth hostels, campsites and cabins for rent.

The Fjærlandsfjorden used to provide the main route north until 1986 when a tunnel underneath the Jostedal glacier linked the village of Fjærland, at the head of the fjord, with Skei in Jølster.

From Mundal it is possible to visit the Bøya and Supphell glaciers, two offshoots from Jostedalsbreen. Guided walks on the glacier start from Flatbreen. The area has a very interesting flora and birdlife, and there is marvellous lake fishing.

Take highway 5 around Esefjorden where there is a wonderful little camp-site at Ese. At **Dragsvik**, where there are ferry links with Hella, Balestrand and Vangsnes, the road turns north along the western banks of Vellefjorden. Just beyond Ulvestad you pass Harevollnipa (1,406m) on your right, then Valneskredet (1,403m) on the left. The road climbs steeply and then swings west into the twisting Bårddalen valley which runs through Gaularfjell rising to 748m, before running down into **Eldalsosen**, a famous fishing village which nestles between Viksdalsvatnet and Lauvavatn.

Kaupanger's stave church has been well cared for over the centuries

Blue ice cavern in the glacier at Nigardsbreen

A little further north, the road passes Vallestadfossen (130m) and then follows the west bank of the lake to Flåten where it turns to the left along the northern bank of Holsavatnet into Moskog. Highway 5 continues west through **Førde**, an administrative and industrial centre with regular air connections to Bergen and coastal towns further north, to the coast at Florø, but you need to turn right on to highway 14 for Skei and Byrkjelo.

The road follows the northern bank of Jølstravatnet past a number of lakeside campsites, such as Vassenden, Jølstraholmen, Jølstratunet and Haugen, and the eighteenth-century church at **Ålhus** where Norwegian painter Nikolai Astrup is buried. He was born in Jølstratunet where there is a museum dedicated to him. Continue to **Skei** which is now a popular summer resort. From Skei you can drive under the glacier back down to Fjærland and Balestrand. This is magnificent countryside with towering mountains and deep lakes. To the east, Bjørga, (1,554m) towers into the sky, to the south is Trolleboleggja (1,487m), and Grovebreen (1,516m), and to the north Skjorta (1,473m).

Highway 14 then enters Våtedalen, a steep sided valley that runs north past Eggenipa on your right to Byrkjelo, the centre of the region, a popular tourist resort and famous for its cheeses. It is at the heart of a very popular winter sports area and there are chair lifts up into the mountains which take you to some marvellous high level walking country. There is ample accommodation with guesthouses, campsites, cabins to rent and a summer youth hostel.

You have a choice of routes from Byrkjelo. You can take highway 14 which will bring you to the coast at Anda. Just before Sandane it is worth making the short detour to Eidsfoss besides which is Europe's highest salmon ladder. **Sandane** is a pretty little village and home of the Nordfjord Folk Museum (open throughout the summer, check times with the local tourist office). The road then follows the banks of Gloppenfjorden, past the medieval Vereide church to Anda for the short ferry crossing to Lote where you drive through the 3km tunnel to **Nordfjordeid** with its charming old houses nestling by the water's edge. Highway 14 then runs north to **Volda**, a rural centre with a fine church and the Aarflot Museum (open daily, but check times with the local tourist office), and then on to **Ørsta** at the head of one of Norway's finest salmon rivers. The Aasen Museum depicts the life of poet Ivar Aasen. From Ørsta you follow the coast north to Festøy where you can ferry across Storfjorden to Solevågen, and then either turn left for Ålesund, or right for Åndalsnes where you can rejoin route 9. It is an incredibly beautiful route through magnificient scenery, but if you are pressed for time, take the alternative route at Byrkjelo, following highway 60 to **Utvik**.

The road twists its way over Fillefjell and then into Utvikfjell before its descent through pine trees to Utvik. The road then follows the shores of Innvikfjorden north until it comes to **Innvik**, famous for its 1880s church and much earlier pulpit. There are many campsites in the area and cabins and boats to hire.

At **Olden**, one of many popular holiday villages on the fjord and has a fine old church, built around 1745 and there are many campsites in the area. There are a number of boat trips offered here to allow you to explore the fjords. It is worth detouring south along the mountain road to **Briksdal** about 20km away where there is a campsite and accommodation. The campsite is not far from the Briksdalsbreen, one of the many glacial arms jutting out from Jostedalsbreen.

Loen is a similar tourist village with plenty of accommodation. The hotels features folk dancing several nights a week during the summer. There is a small road south from the village leading to the Kjenndalsbreen about 15km away.

At **Stryn** on the northern shores of the fjord there is the Walhalla Inn, once the home of a merchant, and a wide range of accommodation. You also have a number of choices of how to continue. You can head east on highway 15 for Grotli, Bismo, Lom and Otta on the E6. You can take highway 15 west to Nordfjordeid and the coast as above, or you can veer north on highway 14 at Hjelle and head for Volda and Festøy for the ferry to get you to Ålesund or Åndalsnes. Alternatively, you can stay with the route, turn right on to highway 60 at Kjøs and head for Hornindal.

About 18km of the road beyond Blekesvingen was carved out of the mountain side and there are sheer drops to the fjord below and some splendid views. After turning north at Kjøs the road skirts the western edge of **Hornindalsvatnet** — the largest lake in fjord country. It is also said to be the deepest in Europe at 605m and the clearest in Scandinavia. At the top north-east corner of the lake is **Hornindal**, home of the Anders Svor Museum (check opening times locally) with more than 400 works by the sculptor.

Kjellstadli used to be old posting station and at 422m is the highest point on the road which then runs down into Tryggestad. Highway 655 runs north-west through Norangsdalen, an incredibly wild and beautiful valley. The sides of the valley are so steep in places that they often fall in. Through the valley and at the head of Norangsfjorden lies Øye, which is famous as a rock climbing centre. You can ferry from Leknes across Hjørundfjorden to Sæbø and then continue along highway 655 to Ørsta and Festøy as above.

From Tryggestad, route 9 continues to Hellesylt, past Hellesyltfossen where the water crashes down into the fjord to the ferry and the journey of a lifetime.

Hellesylt has plenty of accommodation including campsites and a summer youth hostel (☎ 071 65 128) and you could if you wish drive north on highway 60 through the long tunnels blasted in the mountains to Stranda to catch the ferry across to Gravaneset for the run in to Åndalsnes. This route offers fantastic views over Geirangerfjorden and Sunnylvsfjorden, but you would be missing out on one of the highlights of a trip to Norway if you did not actually take the ferry to Geiranger. The fact that most Norwegians also pick Geirangerfjorden as one of their country's greatest treasures helps illustrate how beautiful it can be.

The ferry leaves Hellesylt at the head of Sunnylvsfjorden and then swings round the point into **Geirangerfjorden** with its massive sheer cliffs and even more imposing mountains beyond. It is the melting snow from the mountains that feeds the fjord's famous waterfalls. The fjord bends first to the left with some of the most spectacular cliffs on your left. Waterfalls crash down hundreds of metres into the fjord. The first major one is Brudesløret (Bride's Veil), on the left just before you start to swing around the bend. On the opposite bank is Friaren (Suitor), and then as the fjord starts to twist to the right you pass the magnificent De Syv Søstre (Seven Sisters). This group of waterfalls is in your left and after heavy rainfall can grow in size, so do not be confused if you count more than seven.

The sides of the fjord are much steeper on the right hand side and the cliffs here rise up to Prekestolen. The ferry then rounds the cliffs and you can see

The beautiful Sognefjorden is served by both pleasure ships and ferries

Quiet moorings at Utvik on the Innvikfjorden

(Opposite) The Briksdal glacier: a finger of ice stretching down the mountainside

Geiranger nestling at the head of the fjord under a backdrop of massive snow capped mountains.

There are a number of abandoned farms along the fjord such as Skageflå and Knivsflå beside the Syv Søstre. Some of them seem precariously perched on the mountain sides and agile footwork would have been needed to reach them when they were occupied. Because the water is so deep and the cliffs so perpendicular, the fjord is a great favourite with cruise ships and many have painted their names just above the waterline on the cliffs.

Geiranger is a bustling community. There are four hotels, a motel, cabins for hire and a number of campsites. It has a lot to offer with boat trips, fishing, swimming and walking. There are many marked trails and details can be obtained from the tourist office in the village.

Geiranger makes a good touring base. You can drive up to Mount Dalsnibba (1,495m) by taking highway 58 south to Djupvass Lodge and then taking the scenic Nibbe toll road with its many hairpin bends for a further 5km. The views from the top are fantastic.

If you go a little further south you come to Lake Djupvatn which is the highest point on the road, around 1,038m. There is usually ice in the lake well into summer. A summer skiing competition is held at Djupvasshytta each June.

Highway 58 north out of the village takes the visitor along Ørneveien, the Eagle's Road. Stop at **Ørnesvingen** (the Eagle's View) for the magnificent panorama over the fjord including the Syv Søstre and Prekestolen.

The road then drops down to Eidsdal on the shores of Norddalsfjorden where the ferry sails for Linge. It is worth spending a little time in Valldal, a charming fjord village. Legend has it that the zig zag markings on the mountain side were caused when King Olav cast a serpent against the cliff after landing in 1028.

The village makes another good base for exploring because there is lots to see and do in the area with good fishing, boating, swimming and walking. There are a number of campsites, cabins to let and a summer youth hostel.

From Valldal take highway 63, also known as the Troll's Road, through this very popular summer walking area. There are many campsites and cabins along the way, with towering mountains on both sides of the road. The Gudbrandsjuvet gorge is worth exploring.

The road climbs up to Trollstigheimen, almost 900m above sea level and then it drops steeply down through Isterdalen in a series of hairpin bends to Åndalsnes. At the top of the pass it is possible to ski in the summer, and on the way down you should stop to see the 200m Stigfossen. The mountains here have names to suit their grandeur. At the top of the pass there is Bispen (Bishop), and on the way down is Kongen (King) and Dronninga (Queen).

Åndalsnes is an attractive tourist centre which also has some light industry. It is famous for furniture manufacturing. The area has long been popular with the English and many of the large farms in the district used to be rented by the English gentry for salmon fishing parties. Many of the buildings in the town were destroyed when it was heavily bombed in 1940 after British troops landed. The town is at the mouth of the River Rauma and is the terminus for the Rauma railway line. A trip through the beautiful Vengedalen valley is worthwhile if you have time.

Another tour if you have time is to drive along the southern shores of Romsdalsfjorden to Vestnes on the E69 and then to follow it south-west through Sjøholt and Spjelkavik to the charming fishing town of Ålesund with its town museum and the nearby Sunnmøre open-air museum. The round trip is about 220km and it makes a fascinating day out from Åndalsnes, and you can return along Norddalfjorden through Stordal and Valldal if you want a different route.

From Åndalsnes drive through the series of tunnels leading to Innfjorden, and then along the coast through Måndalen, at the mouth of the Måna river, famous for its salmon, to Vågstranda, famous for its oyster beds. This whole stretch of coastline is very popular and there is plenty of accommodation.

Tresfjord, at the head of the lovely Tresfjorden, has a richly decorated church and a folk museum (Tresfjordbygdemuseum, open throughout summer, but check times locally) with a number of old buildings with period tools and household articles.

The E69 then swings over Skorgedalen, popular as both a winter and summer sports area. There are lots of lakes and some wonderful walking around **Ørskogfjellet** where there is a good campsite, and lots of accommodation.

The road then drops down to Sjøholt on Storfjorden, past Snaufjellet on your left. It is then a lovely drive besides lakes and the fjord, through Spjelkavik into Ålesund. **Borgund**, on the outskirts of the town, used to be the original medieval trading centre and excavations have unearthed remains from Viking settlements which can be seen in the Sunnmøre Museum. The museum has about forty old buildings and a section devoted to fishing, the industry responsible for the livelihoods of both Borgund and Ålesund.

Ålesund is the industrial and commercial capital of the Møre og Romsdale district. Its coat of arms combines a trawler, freight ship under sail and three fish depicting the community's long involvement with and reliance on the sea. The town has Norway's largest fishing harbour, and one of the largest export harbours in the world for *klippfish*, split and dried cod.

Although only granted municipal status in 1848, Stone Age settlements have been discovered in the caves at Skonghelleren on the island of Valderøy, and the twelfth-century marble Giske chapel is one of the earliest traces of the spread of Christianity in Norway.

Things to see here include Aksla, a mountain which stands in the centre of the town. If you climb the 418 steps which start in the municipal park to the top there are splendid views in all directions. There is a restaurant and terrace at the top where you can enjoy the scenery.

Spend some time exploring the Art Nouveau quarter, Ålesund aquarium, Ålesund museum with photographs and prints from the old town before the fire. The museum also contains a model of the Brudeegget, the world's first prototype of today's covered lifeboat. It sailed from Ålesund to Boston in 1904.

Ålesund church was built in Norman style in 1909 and has marvellous frescoes by Enevold Thomt, as well as beautiful stained glass windows, a gift from Emperor William II. There is a statue of the Viking chief Gangerolv in the town park. It was a gift from the people of Rouen in France because the chief, whose name in French was Rollo founded the Duchy of Normandy in AD911. The medieval museum is built on the site of a group of twelfth-century open-

Reflections in the fjord at Stryn

(opposite) The tranquil beauty of Lake Lovatnet near Loen

A balconied, wooden house in Stryn

hearth rooms and the exhibits give a fascinating insight into the lives of people in the Middle Ages. The town hosts a music festival every summer.

Tours in the area include a visit to the island of **Giske**, linked to the mainland by one of the longest submarine tunnels in the world. The tunnel system extends more than 7km and links the many small islands that now make up the town. Giske is famous for its twelfth-century marble chapel, the only one in Norway, and burial mounds. Fugleøya (Runde bird rock) is internationally renowned and there are many other good bird-watching spots along Hjørundfjord. Return to Åndalsnes either by the same route or through Stordal, with its 200 year old 'rose' church, and Valldal on the south coast.

From Åndalsnes the route goes around Isfjorden to Torvik where it divides. There is a small road which continues along the shore to **Klungnes** where there is a memorial to a landing by a Scottish force in 1612.

Highway 58 heads north along the eastern shores of Rødvenfjorden to **Åfarnes**, where there is a ferry across to Sølsnes and the road to Molde. Continue along the southern shores of Langfjorden through Holm to Vistdal where the road cuts inland between the mountains to Eresfjord and Hauste. From Eresfjord you can catch a ferry down Eikedalsfjorden to Eikesdal at its head and visit the beautiful Mardalsfossen.

Back in Eresfjord follow highway 660 up the eastern shores of Eresfjorden through Boggestranda and Nesset to the lovely old village of **Eidsvåg**. Turn right on to highway 62 which runs north-east to hit Tingvollfjorden at Eidsøra. You have to follow the road south round the head of the fjord at **Sunndalsøra** where you pick up highway 16 for the last leg of the journey into Kristiansund.

Sunndalsøra is an industrial town with an aluminium works and a large power station at Aura. You can take highway 16 east through the lovely Sunndalen to Oppdal where you connect with the E6, the main Oslo-Trondheim road. It is a marvellous base for exploring and there is great walking in Litledalen which runs south from the village. It is famous for the Kalken, a towering rock wall more than 1,600m high. There is good walking and climbing in Øksendalen to the west. In fact, the whole area is a walker's paradise and the whole region to the south of Sunndalsøra is worth hiking. It is an area of countless lakes, rivers and mountains and hundreds of square kilometres to roam over.

About 6km to the east of Sunndalsøra on highway 16 is the Leikvin folk museum (open daily throughout the summer but check times locally). It is actually at Elverhøy bru in a manor owned in the mid-nineteenth century by the Scottish Lady Barbara Arbuthnott. She was known locally as the 'Queen of Sunndal' and she was famous for her fishing house parties. Part of the museum is now devoted to a history of salmon fishing in the area. The nearby Elverhøy built in 1870 is still used by British fishermen.

The road north from Sunndalsøra goes through a number of tunnels carved out of the mountain side as it plunges into the fjord, and then cuts inland at Opdøl. At **Ålvundeid** there is a small road off to the right which leads into Innerdalen, another tucked away mountain valley surrounded by flattened peaks which the locals call sugar lump mountains. You can travel up the rough but manageable road as far as Nerdal where there is accommodation in the shadow of Snøfjell to the north. This is a very popular summer mountain climbing and walking area and there are many well marked trails to follow.

The road crosses the peninsula to Ålvundfjorden and then sweeps round past Hanemsvatnet and several other smaller lakes to **Tingvoll** where there is a small museum and a very unusual church built around 1120. It has a series of passages in its walls which could have been for defensive purposes. There are several Viking burial mounds in the area and 4,000 year old rock paintings at Hindhammer. You can also catch the ferry here for Angvik if you want to take this route to get to Molde.

The route from Tingvoll to Molde takes you across Tingvollfjorden and then along highway 665 which runs down to the southern shores of Fannefjorden through Lønset to Molde. There is a ferry link between Lønset and Grønnes which is the fastest route back to Åndalsnes. The drive into Molde takes you along Fannestranda with its wonderful old houses which used to be owned by rich merchants and nobles. One of these houses is Moldegård, which inspired Ibsen to write *Rosmersholm*.

Molde is a delightful town nestling sheltered beneath the hills and full of trees and greenery. The residents take advantage of the mild weather to produce glorious displays of colour in their gardens, and Molde has been called 'The City of Roses'.

Visit the observation point on Varden for the panoramic views. It is said there are more than eighty snow capped peaks to be spotted. The Romsdal museum (open daily, check times at the local tourist office) has a collection of fine old houses and in the summer is the venue for folk dancing and singing. It also contains a fisheries museum built to resemble a small fishing community. You can retrace your steps to Tingvoll or take highway 67 north to Ørjavik for the short ferry crossing to Tøvik and the road into Kristiansund. There is an airport.

From Tingvoll drive along the shores of Tingvollfjorden to Sandvika where an avenue of larch trees was planted from seedlings brought by the scots at the beginning of the nineteenth century. The trees have now colonised much of the Tingvoll peninsula. The road then continues to Kvisvik where the ferry sails across to Kvalvåg on the island of Frei from where it is about 15km to the bridge which leads into Kristiansund.

Kristiansund is traditionally a fishing port although it did get caught up in the North Sea oil boom, becoming a major supply centre. The capital of Nordmøre, the town has spread over three islands — Nordlandet, Innelandet and Kirkelandet. Kristiansund suffered heavily from German bombing during World War II. Lossiusgården, built in the late eighteenth century, was the only old house to survive the bombardment. The town is still delightful, however, whether you are visiting by car or from the island hopping ferry. There is a small airport.

There have been settlements in the area since the last Ice Age and evidence that its harbour was in use 8,000 years ago. It achieved municipal status in 1742 when it was named after King Christian IV, king of Denmark and Norway. In the centre of the town is the Varden Tower, from the top of which you can see far out to sea.

The Nordmøre museum (check the opening times with the local tourist office) has a section devoted to the history of fishing as well as old buildings in the open-air section. Visit the cooper's workshop and shipping wharf, reconstructed as part of the museum. The modern church was built in 1964.

A view from the medieval museum in Ålesund

A ferry trip on Geirangerfjorden should not be missed

There are many boat excursions on offer but a fascinating one is the trip north to the tiny island of **Grip**. For centuries the island was the home of fishermen and their families — Norway's smallest independent community. The cottages still remain as does a wonderful stave church (see section on stave churches p44), but the families have moved out and the buildings are really only occupied in the summer.

A panorama of Ålesund from Mount Aksla

A quiet café in Kristiansund

About 16km south of Kristiansund is **Kvernes**, on the south-east tip of Averøya where there is a medieval stave church (see section on stave churches p46) with very ornate interior, and an open-air museum with a fine collection of old buildings.

The shortest route between Kristiansund and Trondheim is along highway 65 and then highway 71 which hugs the coastline through Orkanger to Trondheim. An alternative route is to stick with highway 65 which swings inland to skirt the mountains of Trollheimen, before heading back to the coast at Orkanger.

Additional Information

Places of Interest

Ålesund

Aquarium
Open: Monday to Friday 10am-6pm, Saturday 10am-3pm and Sunday 12noon-4pm.
☎ (071) 24 123

Museum
Open: Monday to Saturday 11am-3pm, Sunday 12noon-3pm.
☎ (071) 23 170

Medieval Museum
Open: daily 25 May to 31 August, Wednesday 5-7pm, Saturday and Sunday 12noon-3pm.
☎ (071) 32 137

Useful Information

Bicycle Hire
Ålesund Tourist Office
Rådhuset, 6025 Ålesund, ☎ (071) 21 202

Car Parks
St Olav's plass 8am-6pm, Saturday 8am-5pm.
Ålesund Town Hall 8am-6pm, Saturday 8am-3pm.
Rica Parken Hotel, Storgt 16. Open day and night.

Post Office
Ålesund Main Post Office, Korsegt 4 ☎ (071) 25 680, Exchange and cashes travellers' cheques.
Open: 8am-4pm, Saturdays 9am-1pm.

Service Boats
M/Y *Charming Ruth*: 3 hour fjord and fishing trip from Ålesund. Summer departures: Monday and Thursday 3pm from Skansegata.

M/B *Trio*: Serves the Ellingsøyfjord, setting out from the Catholic church at Norvasund. Departs weekdays at 8.30am, 2.30pm and 4.10pm. Saturdays 9.30am and 2pm. Sundays 10am and 6pm.

M/S *Sulafjell*: A passenger ferry crossing the Borgundfjord from Røysekaia (Blixvalen) to Langevåg. Departs at 8.05, 9 and 10am, 2.50, 3.30 and 4.10pm.

M/S *Fjørtoft*: An express catamaran between Ålesund and Nordøyane. Departs at 8.40am, 2.35pm and 4.10pm on weekdays, on Saturdays at 9.30am, 12.30pm and 3.20pm, and on Sundays at 10am and 5pm.

Useful Addresses

Regional Tourist Boards

Møre og Romsdal Tourist Board
PO Box 467
N-6501 Kristiansund N
☎ (073) 73 977

Local Tourist Offices

Balestrand og Fjærdal Reiselivslag
Postboks 57
N-5850 Balestrand
☎ (056) 91 255

Hellesylt Turistinformasjon
N-6218 Hellesylt
☎ (071) 65 052

Kristiansund Reiselivslag
Postboks 401
N-6501 Kristianund N
☎ (073) 77 211

Leikanger Reiselivslag
N-5842 Leikanger
☎ (056) 54 055

Lom — Jotunheimen Reiselivslag
N-2686 Lom
☎ (062) 11 286

Lærdal og Borgund Reiselivslag
N-5890 Lærdal
☎ (056) 66 509

Ålesund Reiselivslag
Rådhuset
N-6025 Ålesund
☎ (071) 21 202
Pick up the free *Ålesund Guide* and *On foot in Ålesund* from the tourist office.

Tourist offices shown in bold type in the list below are staffed the year round.

Geiranger ☎ (071) 63099

Loen ☎ (057) 77677

Olden ☎ (057) 73126

Valldal ☎ (071) 57767

Ørsta ☎ (070) 66477

Molde
Reiselivsforeningen i Molde
Postboks 484
N-6401 Molde
☎ (072) 57 133

Sogndal Reiselivslag
Postboks 222
N-5801 Sogndal
☎ (056) 71 161

Sunndal Reiselivslag
Postboks 62
N-6601 Sunndalsøra
☎ (073) 92 552

Vik og Vangsnes Reiselivslag
Postboks 148
N-5860 Vik i Sogn
☎ (056) 95 686

Volda Reiselivslag
v/Volda Turisthotell
N-6100 Volda
☎ (070) 77 050

Ørsta Reiselivslag
Holmegt 3
N-6150 Ørsta
☎ (070) 66 598
Staffed during the summer only.

Åndalsnes og Romsdal
Reiselivslag
Boks 133
N-6301 Åndalsnes
☎ (072) 21 622

10

THE GATEWAY TO THE NORTH

This is the quickest route between Oslo and Trondheim, the 'gateway to the north', although it is no short drive. It is about 550km between Oslo and Trondheim but there are a number of interesting side tours of the E6.

The E6 runs all the way from Norway's southern border with Sweden deep into the Arctic Circle. It is a very popular route and in the summer carries a lot of traffic but there is no need to rush along because there are a number of places worth visiting, such as historic Eidsvoll, Lillehammer, Ringebu, Vinstra, Dombås and Dovrefell. There are detours off along Espedalen and the Peer Gynt Trail, or you can take a lake cruise on Mjøsa aboard *Skibladner*, the world's oldest paddle steamer, or visit the wonderfully preserved mining town of Røros.

The E6 also follows a very ancient route and was the path taken by the Germanic tribes as they moved north to cllonise the land as the ice receded. The route heads north-east out of Oslo through the suburbs of Skedsmo and Frogner to Kløfta where highway 2 turns off to the right for Kongsvinger with its fortress and museum. Here it turns north as highway 3 and runs roughly parallel with the E6 as far as Røros (this route is covered in the following section).

An interesting detour is to take highway 4 our of Oslo through Brandbu and then to take highway 180 at Lygna to rejoin the E6 at Minnesund. This route takes in Hakadal, site of Norway's oldest iron works founded in the mid-sixteenth century. There are a number of sidetours available on this route. At Gran you can turn off to visit Granvollen and the Nikolai and Maria churches. The churches were built by two sisters who could not stand each other so they each had their own in which to worship. At Volla there is a turn off for the medieval church at Lunner, and at Brandbu there is a small road leading to the Hadeland open-air folk museum containing the twelfth century Tingelstad Church.

If you follow E6 through Kløfta you come to the market town of Jessheim and then through Dal to **Eidsvoll verk**, which is an almost obligatory stop. It was here in the office of the ironworks, that the Norwegian Constitution was proclaimed on 17 May 1814. The building is now a museum and the site is a national monument. There is also the charming Eidsvoll open air museum beside the highway with its collection of old buildings.

A few kilometres beyond Eidsvoll the road passes to the east of Mistberget and then crosses over the River Vorma at the foot of Lake Mjøsa into **Minnesund**. The 200m long bridge gives you splendid views of Norway's

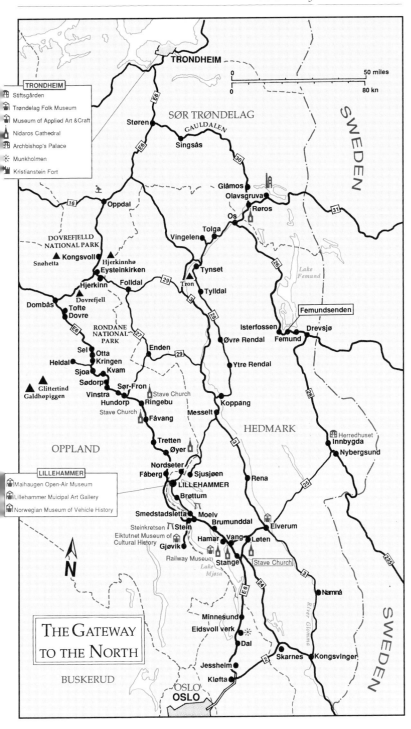

TRONDHEIM

- Stiftsgården
- Trøndelag Folk Museum
- Museum of Applied Art &Craft
- Nidaros Cathedral
- Archbishop's Palace
- Munkholmen
- Kristianstein Fort

TRONDHEIM

SØR TRØNDELAG

SWEDEN

Støren

GAULDALEN

Singsås

50 miles
80 km

Glåmos
Olavsgruva
Røros
Os

Oppdal

DOVREFJELLD
NATIONAL PARK

Tolga

Snøhetta   Kongsvoll   Hjerkinnhø
Eysteinkirken

Vingelen

Lake
Femund

Hjerkinn   Folldal   Tynset
                    Tron
Dombås   Tylldal
        Dovrefjell
        Tofte
        Dovre

Femundsenden

RONDANE
NATIONAL
PARK

Sel   Enden
Heldal   Otta
        Kringen
        Kvam
Sjoa

Isterfossen
Øvre Rendal   Drevsjø
                Femund

Ytre Rendal

Glittertind Sødorp
Galdhøpiggen Vinstra   Sør-Fron
        Hundorp   Ringebu   Stave Church
        Stave Church   Messelt   Koppang
                Fåvang

HEDMARK

OPPLAND   Tretten
        Øyer

Herredhuset
Innbygda
Nybergsund

Nordseter
Fåberg   Sjusjøen
                LILLEHAMMER   Rena
        Brøttum

LILLEHAMMER

- Maihaugen Open-Air Museum
- Lillehammer Muicipal Art Gallery
- Norwegian Museum of Vehicle History

Smedstadsletta   Moelv
        Brumunddal
Steinkretsen   Stein
Eiktutnet Museum of   Hamar   Vang   Elverum
Cultural History   Gjøvik   Løten
        Railway Museum   Stange
Lake   Stave Church
Mjøsa

Namnå

N

SWEDEN

Minnesund
Eidsvoll verk
        Dal

River Glomma

Jessheim
        Skarnes   Kongsvinger
Kløfta

**THE GATEWAY
TO THE NORTH**

OSLO
OSLO

BUSKERUD

largest lake which disappears into the distance in the north. The lake covers 366sq km and in places is 400m deep. This is a popular tourist area and there is a good campsite here if you want to explore the area further.

The route mostly follows the eastern shore of the lake through Morskogen where it heads north past the village of **Stange** with its beautiful medieval church dated around 1250.

The road then swings back towards the lake and Hamar, which lies at the mouth of Furnesfjorden, an arm of Mjøsa. There are many large farmhouses in the area, several of them centuries old and protected as national monuments. The area is rich in bird life and the Akersvika Reserve is internationally famous.

Hamar is a farming, industrial and commercial town at the centre of a rich agricultural region. It owes its original prosperity to the medieval cathedral and the ecclesiastical estates which surrounded it. It became an episcopal see in 1152. Little remains of the twelfth-century cathedral with its Gothic additions, except a section of magnificent arched wall, now a feature in the grounds of the Hedmark museum at Domkirkeodden (open May to September). The museum houses a number of interesting old buildings and you can walk down to the lakeside where there are a number of bathing beaches.

Also of interest is the town's famous Railway Museum. There are a number of old steam trains on lengths of track of different gauges, and many railway buildings that have been brought in from other parts of the country to help tell the story of the history of railway in Norway. You can also enjoy a spin on the shortest railway line in Norway. The local tourist office will give opening times for the museums.

The new cathedral was consecrated in 1866 and the spire is almost 50m high and Vang stave church, formerly a village but now absorbed in the town, dates from 1810. See section on stave churches p47.

Hamar is a very popular tourist centre because of its beaches in the summer and the nearby skiing in the winter. There are several hotels and boarding houses, the youth hostel is open all year round (Finstadsgate 11, ☎ 065 23 641), and there is a good campsite. Boats and cabins can be rented close to the beaches.

The E6 has now been rerouted away from the eastern shores of Furnesfjorden and swings inland to **Brumunddal**, a small industrial town, and then across the peninsula to the shore of Mjøsa again and the community of Ringsaker. There is a very good campsite at **Soug** on the old E6 route. It is worth visiting the twelfth-century church with its 70m high tower. The church, considered the most beautiful in Hedmark, is noted for its magnificent sixteenth-century carved altar which contains frescoes depicting the life of St Olav.

At **Stein** there are the remains of Håkonsson's fortress, and Steinkretsen, a group of twelve bronze age stones which, it is thought, used to be used as a place of pagan worship. On the outskirts of Moelv there is a campsite at Steinvik where there are also boats and cabins for hire, and good bathing.

From Moelv there is a toll bridge, Mjøsbrua, which takes you over the lake so that you approach Lillehammer along the western banks of Mjøsa.

Once on the western bank you can detour down to **Gjøvik**, known as the 'White Town of Mjøsa'. It is the natural capital of west Oppland and noted for its glass. The first small glass studios opened in the nineteenth century and led to the Gjøvik Glass Works which was one of the leading glass factories in Scandinavia. Apart from the glass works, you can visit the Eiktutnet Museum of Cultural History, the Gjøvik Mansion, the design centre at Brenneriet and Toten Museum. Take highway 4 from Gjøvik to Lillehammer through **Biri**, famous for its straw tapestry and richly decorated church built in 1777. There are many campsites and cabins and boats for hire along the lakeside.

If you stay on the eastern bank just to the north of Moelv is **Smestadsletta**, another ring of prehistoric sites marking a burial site. The road then follows the eastern shores of the lake to Brøttum, which has a church built in 1790. You then cross over the county boundary between Hedmark and Oppland for the 13km drive into Lillehammer.

Oppland is famous for many things. It is the home of *Peer Gynt*, the wonderful scenery of the Gudbrandsdalen, the high mountains of Dovrefjell, Rondane and Jotunheimen and splendid valleys, lakes and beaches. Oppland contains the country's two highest mountains, Galdhøpiggen (2,469m) and Glittertind (2,465m).

The county is one of the most healthy in Norway with lots of sunshine and it is a strange experience to bask in brilliant warm sunshine among the snow near the summit of one of the peaks. Oppland boasts four national parks and a nature reserve where you can get to know the area on foot. There is a network of cabins for overnight stops so you can spend days exploring off the beaten track and hundreds of kilometres of marked trails. There is glacier walking, summer skiing, water sports, riding, boating, cycling, fishing and a host of other things to do and enjoy. Lillehammer is the gateway to Gudbrandsdalen. It is one of Norway's most popular tourist centres and has a great deal to offer.

Lillehammer is a charming little town with many fine old wooden houses that cling to the hillsides in attractive gardens overlooking the lake. The River Mesna bubbles its way down through the houses to the lake in a series of rapids and falls. For decades it has been popular with artists because of the special light, and even before the turn of the century it was known as the 'Athens of Norway'.

There is a wealth of accommodation which will be put to good use in 1994 when Lillehammer hosts the Winter Olympics. Lillehammer is the only town in the world to have a skier in its coat of arms. It depicts a Birkebeiner, the mountain men who in 1206 escorted the young Prince Haakon Håkanson over the mountains to safety. Haakon grew up to become one of Norway's most famous kings. That famous exploit is still remembered every year by the incredible tough Birkebeiner Race.

The town did not get municipal status until 1827 although it was still one of the main inland towns together with Hamar and the mining towns of Røros and Kongsberg. It is proud of its heritage and the main street Storgaten has won a national architectural award. Things to see are the art gallery and transport museum at the Mesna Centre, and the marvellous open-air museum, Maihaugen.

Local dentist Anders Sandvig moved to the town in 1885 and was so concerned that the heritage of the district was being lost because of the mass emigration, that he started to 'collect' old buildings. The result is a vast collection of more than 30,000 objects and 120 historic buildings from the

Middle Ages to the last century. Many of the farms are complete with out-buildings with original furniture and tools. There is the medieval stave church from Garmo (see section on stave churches p44), an old parsonage and a number of workshops. The fisherman's chapel, blessed in 1459 was the first log church to be built in Norway after the Black Death. In the summer traditional crafts, skills and customs are practised in the old buildings.

You can also visit Bjerkebæck in Nordseterveien, the home of Nobel Prize winning author Sigrid Undset who came to live in the town in 1921. There are a number of monuments in the town. People commemorated include Anders Sandvig, Sigrid Undset, Ludwid Wiese 'The Father of Lillehammer', the missionary Lars Olsen Skrefsrud, and explorer Carl Sofus Lumholtz. Hunderfossen family park at Fåberg is the area's most popular attraction.

There are many pleasant walks along signposted trails in and around the town and details are available from the tourist office which is located near the railway station in Jernbanetorget. There is good bathing and fishing in the area, riding, boating, and several good campsites.

The *Skibladner* was launched in 1856 and is the oldest paddle steamer in the world still operating a regular service. In fact, the steamer has even sunk but was refloated and recommissioned. There used to be many steamers plying the lake but the *Skibladner* is the only one still working. Little has changed in the last 140 years or so. In 1856 when she was launched, she steamed along at 11.5 knots, today she manages a sedate 14 knots. The round trip from Eidsvoll via Lillehammer takes about 12 hours and the *Skibladner* is allowed to carry 230 passengers. The *Skibladner* normally sails into Lillehammer at an incredible angle in the water because every passenger is packed on the starboard side looking out at the town.

About 14km east of the town is **Nordseter**, the gateway to the mountains. Once a cluster of mountain farms it is now a year round tourist centre and an ideal starting place for winter or summer trips into the mountains. A couple of kilometres to the south-east is **Sjusjøen**, a collection of traditional mountain farms which has been developed into a modern tourist centre and is popular all year round. It also has a water sports centre.

The E6 heads north out of Lillehammer into **Gudbrandsdalen**, for centuries the main inland route north, especially when Trondheim was the country's political and spiritual centre. Gudbrandsdalen is mentioned often in the sagas. You can still follow the routes of the pilgrims. This is a wonderful broad, fertile valley — one of the longest in Norway — surrounded by spectacular snow-capped mountains offering enormous opportunities for walking and watching wildlife. The road follows the eastern bank of the River Lågen to Fåberg where you can turn off to the left to follow the Peer Gynt Trail.

The Peer Gynt Trail — Fåberg to Vinstra (85km)

As soon as you enter this area you can understand where the inspiration came from for *Peer Gynt*. The 'Realm of Peer Gynt' lies in the mountains to the west of Gudbransdalen between Skei and Espedalen. This was the area travelled by the eighteenth-century farmer, hunter and dreamer Per På Hågå. He was the eccentric inspiration for Henrik Ibsen's world famous classic.

The area now plays hosts to tourists every year. The three resorts Skei, Golå-

Fefor and Espedalen are surrounded by mountains and between them weaves the Peer Gynt Vei (road) and Peer Gynt Sti (path). The path extends for 60km and is a marvellous opportunity to get out and roam the area in the footsteps of Per på Hågå. Apart from the Per Gynt Sti there is a well developed network of marked trails and mountain cabins and hostels. You can even arrange to have your luggage taken on ahead of you so that you can walk unencumbered to your next overnight stop.

From **Fåberg**, with its 1720s church, take highway 255 as far as Segalstad bru and then turn right on to the Peer Gynt Vei. If you stay on highway 255 you travel through Espedalen, another picturesque valley, and then swing round

Hamar: exhibits from the railway and open-air museums

to connect with the Peer Gynt Vei just before it rejoins the E6 at Vinstra. Just before Vassenden there is a series of craters beside the road known as Helvete (Hell). The section between Skåbu and Vinstra is particularly rugged and spectacular.

If you decide to stay on the E6, the next stop should be at **Hunderfossen** where there are guided tours around the power station and the 280m long Hunder Dam. There used to be a mighty waterfall until it was harnessed by the power station. There is also the Hunderfossen amusement park and an excellent campsite at Hunderdammen where there are also cabins and boats for hire and good swimming.

Øyer is famous for its church built around 1725, and the nearby miniature town of Lilleputthammer. There is another left turning at **Tretten** which takes you on to the Peer Gynt Trail. Tretten was the scene of bloody fighting between an Anglo-Norwegian force and a much greater number of Germans in April 1940.

At **Fåvang** there is a stave church which dates from the thirteenth century. It was rebuilt in cruciform style in the eighteenth century and restored in 1951. It has a pulpit and altar piece in Renaissance style. See the section on stave churches p44.

Just before you reach **Ringebu** drive down to its columnar stave church built at the end of the thirteenth century. It was expanded and rebuilt in 1630 with a steeple and two pulpits. It has a twelfth-century baptismal font, a statue of Laurentius, a deacon of Rome in AD258, several ancient crucifixes and runic inscriptions. The wooden bell tower dates from the seventeenth century and the church was restored in 1921. See the section on stave churches p46.

There is a very scenic alternative route from Ringebu to Dombås where you can rejoin the E6 for Trondheim. This route which starts out as highway 220 is known as the Rondane Road and includes spectacular mountain scenery. It travels past Flakksjøen and Mount Bølhøgda to **Enden** where it connects with highway 27. Turn left and follow this road north through the **Rondane National Park** and high mountain country to Folldal before you turn left on to highway 29 for **Hjerkinn**, where you turn right on to the E6 through Dovrefjell for Trondheim. Turn left for Dombås.

The E6 from Ringebu follows the river to **Hundorp** which is connected with the chieftan Dalegudbrand. **Sør-Fron** octangonal church, built in 1787, is known locally as Gudbrandsdalen's Cathedral.

The road then runs into **Vinstra**, the village of Peer Gynt and famous for its cheeses. **Sødorp Church** on the other side of the river was built in 1752 and has a beautifully carved pulpit and altarpiece. Peer Gynt is buried in the graveyard. This whole area is packed with places to stay, campsites and cabins to rent. The Peer Gynt Trail ends here.

The road continues to follow alongside the river to **Kvam**, where the British and Germans fought for control of Gudbrandsdalen in 1940. The church was destroyed during the battle and a new church was built here in 1952 with a memorial to commemorate the British soldiers who died in the action. At Sjoa there is a turning off to the left. The road follows the River Sjoa to Heidal, Randsverk and Jotenheimen.

The church at **Heidal** was built in 1938 as a replica of a much older one which was burnt down after being struck by lightning. Wood carvings from the old church were considered the finest in Norway. There is a second older church which for many years was used as a barn but it has not been reconstructed as a chapel. It has the oldest carved stave church portal in the country which dates from the eleventh century, and may have come from an even older pagan church.

Back on the E6, follow the road to **Kringen** which was the scene of an unusual battle on 26 August 1612 when the locals routed a band of marauding Scottish mercenaries. There is a monument beside the road commemorating the battle and a much larger one on the path above which looks out over the battleground. At **Otta** there is a turning off for Lom and Lustrærfjorden or Nordfjord. You can drive almost to the top of Pillargurikampen, from where there are marvellous views.

The river keeps widening out into lakes and there are many places along the way to stop and bathe although take care because the water is cold. There are also many campsites and huts to rent. Otta is an excellent base for exploring the Rondane National Park. It was established in 1962 and is Norway's oldest national park, covering an area of 570sq km.

The E6 continues to the old village of Sel, made famous by Sigrid Undset as the setting for *Kristin Lavrandsdatter*, and the Ulfossen, and then reaches Dovre, a popular mountain resort. Just to the north is **Tofte**, a former Royal farm. It is one of the oldest and largest estates in the region and now a national monument.

Dombås is the ideal base if you want to explore the beautiful Dovrefjell. It is also an important traffic centre with the E69 branching off the E6 for Åndalsnes and Ålesund. This is a wonderful mountain area with many peaks over 2,000m. You can explore the Dovrefjell National Park which is dominated by Mount Snøhetta. Just north of the town you should visit Utsikten, which gives wonderful views up the Dovre valley.

From Dombås the road starts to climb into the mountains, following the old pilgrim path to Trondheim. The area of peat bog to the left of the road is known as **Fokstumyrene**. It was Norway's first national park, founded in 1923 and is noted for its rich bird and plant life. There are roadside information boards giving details of the rare flora and fauna that can be seen.

The road now crosses the mountainous Dovrefjell National Park. The railway runs just to the west of the road and just beyond Vålåsjø station, stop at **Dovregubbens Hall**. It is now a very popular tourist spot on the way to Trondheim and the restaurant attracts coachloads of visitors. Nearby is Anfin's Bridge, built by a convict single handed in 1826 to earn his freedom. In the summer you might be lucky and spot herds of reindeer which graze in the area.

Hjerkinnhø overlooks the driest area in Norway where the average rainfall is only about 220mm a year. In **Hjerkinn** visit Eysteinkirken. The church was built in memory of King Eystein who built a chain of mountain huts through the high mountain passes in the twelfth century. The road followed by successions of monarchs on their way north to Trondheim is known as the Kongeveien (Royal Road), follows almost the same path as the E6 and is marked by cairns along the way. Just outside the village the road reaches its highest point in Dovrefjell at 1,026m. Stop at **Kongsvoll** where the inn has hardly changed for hundreds of years. Nearby is Kongsvoll station which is famous for its gardens which grow many of the mountain flowers of the high tundra. From here it is possible to drive to the foot of Snøhetta, which at 2,286m is the country's highest peak outside the Jotunheimen range. As the road crosses an artillery firing range use the phone to get permission to cross. The telephone connects you with someone who will give information on safety.

Boats lining the jetty at Lillehammer

Silver birches provide an attractive backdrop for the buildings in the Lillehammer folk museum

The road enters the narrow Drivdal valley. The valley sides are often very steep with a sheer drop down to the fast flowing river below. **Oppdal** is another popular year round resort. It is very busy in the winter because of its many fine ski slopes. On the outskirts of the town is the open-air museum with a score or so of old buildings. The town church dates from about 1650 and to the north of the town there are a number of Viking burial mounds. Oppdal has plenty of accommodation with a number of hotels and guesthouses, summer youth hostel, campsites and cabins.

The route continues north following the River Byna to Ulsberg and Berkåk, where highway 700 turns off left for Lokken Verk and Orkranger. The E6 continues to **Støren** which is noted for its massive granite quarries. You can turn right here on highway 30 if you want to visit Røros. The road then follows the eastern bank of the River Gaula through Trøndelag country to Høvin, scene of a massive landslide in 1345 which killed almost 250 people, and then through Melhus to Trondheim.

Trondheim

Trondheim is Norway's third largest city. A Viking settlement existed at the mouth of the River Nid in the early tenth century and Olav Tryggvasson, who built a Royal manor and church in AD997, is regarded as the founder of Trondheim. His statue now stands on top of a column in the market place in

Ringebu's thirteenth-century stave church

the city centre. In 1030 King Olav Haraldson was killed at the battle of Stiklestad and was buried in Trondheim. He became known as Olav, the Holy King, and for centuries his tomb attracted pilgrims from all over Europe.

Trondheim became the seat of the monarchy in the twelfth century and therefore the country's first capital. It became the see of the archbishopric and in 1152 work on the magnificent Nidaros Cathedral started in 1170. All kings of Norway are crowned in Nidaros Cathedral and the crown jewels are displayed in the North Chapel. The city has been known as Trondheim since the sixteenth century — before that it was called *Nidaros*. Over the centuries it has been ravaged by many devastating fires. The present city centre was built by General Caspar de Cicignon, after a massive fire in 1681. At the beginning of the last century Trondheim was larger than Oslo. Cicignon also built Kristiansten Fort in the hills to the east of the city. Today it is a modern, expanding university city and major port because of its large sheltered harbour, kept ice-free during the winter because of the Gulf Stream. All that remains of the medieval city of densely packed wooden buildings and narrow alleys, is the cathedral and some of the old wharves along the banks of the River Nid.

Trondheim has always been a seat of learning. Norway's first Institute of Technology was built here in 1910 and the city is regarded as the technology capital of the country. The university is the second largest in Norway, and the home of the Royal Norwegian Society for Science and Humanities, founded in 1760 and Norway's oldest scientific institution. The new cultural centre, Olavshallen, was opened in 1989.

The city has plenty of accommodation and a number of good campsites at Flak (near the ferry terminal), Sandmoen, Storsand Gård, Vikhammer Gård and Øysand. There are many good restaurants and cafés, a very good shopping centre and some wonderful open-air markets. You should visit the fish market at the lower end of Munkegata where there is also the old Ravnkloa clock. The city centre is very compact and you can easily take in all the sights on foot. There are many organised tours of the city and the surrounding fjords and countryside, or you can enjoy a conducted tour of the city centre aboard a vintage tram. The tourist office provides the free *Trondheim Guide*. This is also available at the station information office and youth hostels. The tourist office will also change money outside banking hours.

Nidaros Cathedral is one of the largest Gothic buildings in Scandinavia. Although it has been destroyed by fires on a number of occasions, it was quickly rebuilt each time. The Archbishop's Palace next door is Scandinavia's oldest secular building. The cathedral was originally built over the grave of St Olav. Work started in 1170 but the oldest parts still standing are from the twelfth century. The oldest parts around the transept are in Roman style while the rest of the cathedral is Gothic. The cathedral is noted for its marvellous stained glass windows and the statues on the west wall. You can climb the tower for a splendid view over Trondheim. The best time to see the cathedral is in the afternoon when there are few tour groups.

The **Archbishop's Palace** also dates from the twelfth century and was the archbishop's residence until the Reformation. For about 100 years from 1556 it was the official residence of the Danish Governors and then it was taken over by the military. **Vår Frue Kirke** (The Church of Our Lady), dates from the

thirteenth century but was restored and extended in 1739. The very thick walls
remain from the oldest part of the church.

The **Hospital Church** was built in 1705 and was the first octagonal church
to be built in either Norway or Sweden. It was built in the grounds of
Trondheim Hospital which was founded in 1277 and is Scandinavia's oldest
social institution. It is now a home for the elderly. The area around the hospital
is known as Hospitalsløkka and consists of a number of old buildings that
have been beautifully restored and are now occupied as family homes.

Bakklandet, on the east side of the River Nid, is another area of faithfully
restored old timber houses. Waisenhuset is a lovely, large timber building
built in 1722 to the west of the cathedral.

Gamle Bybro is the old town bridge. The first bridge was built on this site
in 1681 while Kristiansten Fort was under construction. A sentry and excise
house stood at either end of the bridge. The excise house on the west side is still
standing. The present bridge and gates were built in 1861.

Stiftsgården is Scandinavia's largest timber mansion. Built as a private
home between 1774-8, it is now the king's official residence in Trondheim. It
is open to the public and there are guided tours. There are many fine buildings
in this area including Svaneapoteket (the Swan Apothecary). Skansen, the
remains of Trondheim's old defences and the site of the city gate is now a park
with good views of the fjord.

Munkholmen (Monk's Island) used to be Trondheim's execution ground
in ancient times. A monastery was built by Benedictine monks early in the
eleventh century, one of the first two monasteries in Scandinavia. In 1658 it
was converted into a prison fort and later a customs home. Parts of the
seventeenth century fortifications remain. There is a display of local
handicrafts in the caretaker's house, and the island is now a popular resort
with good swimming. **Kristiansten Fort** was built between 1676 and 1682. It
offers impressive views over the city and surrounding countryside while the
Tyholt Tower is a 120m tall telecommunications tower. There are spectacular
views from the observation platform, and a revolving restaurant.

Olavskirken are the excavated ruins of what is believed to be the church
built to commemorate St Olav in the twelfth century. The ruins and some of
the finds, including a group of skeletons, are now on display between the old
and new library buildings. The ruins of another medieval church can be
viewed in the basement of the Sparebanken Midt-Norge. The find was made
while the foundations for the bank were being dug, and have been incorporated into the building. The ruins can be seen during bank opening hours.

Sukkerhuset, the sugar factory, was built as a refinery in 1752. Between 1856
and 1984 it was a brewery and is the oldest remaining factory in Norway.

Museums to visit include the **Trøndelag Folk Museum** at Sverresborg,
which depicts rural and coastal life over the centuries. The museum with
many old buildings, includes the remains of Sion, King Sverre's palace, built
about 1180. The Tavern, an inn built in 1739, is now a good restaurant. The
Museum of Applied Art and Craft, ancient and modern, and includes Norway's largest collection of tapestries woven by Hannah Ryggen.

Trondheim's Sjøfarts, the maritime museum, is housed in the Slaveriet
(Slavery) built in 1725. It was used as a prison until 1835. Exhibits include
articles recovered from the wreck of the *Perlen*, a frigate which sank in 1781.

The **University of Trondheim Museum** contains exhibits of cultural and natural history, and an archaeological exhibition displays the history of Trøndelag up to the Middle Ages. There is also an exhibit of church history. Close by is the university library with a large and valuable collection of rare prints.

Ringve Museum in Lade Allé 60 is the only museum in Norway that specialises in musical instruments from all over the world. The museum, housed in an eighteenth-century mansion, also contains a concert hall and banqueting hall. Ringve Botanical Gardens is the most northerly botanical gardens in the world.

The Art Gallery in Bispegt, has a large collection of Norwegian art from around 1800 to modern times. Many well known foreign artists are also represented. The **Army Museum** in the Archbishop's Palace exhibits uniforms and weapons used by Norwegian soldiers since the army was formed in 1620.

The **Civil Defence Museum** in Tempeveien 37, was opened in 1983 and is

Skiing in the Rondane National Park

the only one of its kind in Norway. The museum is divided in two, one section devoted to the attack on Trondheim in 1940, while the other concentrates on how the Norwegian Civil Defence operated during World War II and the equipment at its disposal.

Sporting facilities available in and around the city include tennis, golf, riding, fishing, walking, skiing and skating, and swimming.

Oslo to Trondheim via Elverum and Røros

This is not the most popular route (580km) to Trondheim but it does take in the magnificent Røros, one of the best preserved mining towns in the world, and some spectacular walking country along the way.

From Oslo the route heads north-east to **Kløfta**, with its state prison behind 7m high walls. Turn right on to highway 2 for Skarnes and Kongsvinger. Just past Nes the road runs beside the wide River Glomma. This is an area of dense

Lunchbreak in the snow at Golå

forest and at Skarnes you can turn off on highway 24 to explore Lake Storsjøen. This detour takes you to Nord-Odal where you turn right on to highway 209 which brings you back round the lake to rejoin highway 2 only a couple of kilometres up the road from where you left it.

Kongsvinger makes a good base for exploring this south-eastern corner of the country. Between here and the Swedish border about 30km away there is an area of rolling hills and forests with hundreds of kilometres of walking trails. The hills are all about 400m to the east but start to get taller as you go north. There are many little roads criss-crossing the area and cycling is another good way of getting about. Kongsvinger, which spans the Glomma as it sweeps round from the north, has plenty of accommodation including campsites and cabins to hire. Of interest are the fortress dating around the 1680s with its many fine old buildings, the fortress museum and town museum.

The route then heads north on highway 3 following the eastern bank of the river which is very wide with many islands. The area around Namnå was devasted by floods in 1789 when the Glomma burst its banks and swept away scores of farms. The railway runs parallel with the road as far as Røros, and both follow the River Glomma which has its source in the mountainous lakeland area north of the mining town.

At **Elverum** (not to be confused with the village of the same name on the E6 in Troms county) there is a memorial to King Haakon VII marking his rejection in April 1940 of a German ultimatum to ratify a new government led by Quisling. The centre of the village was destroyed by German bombing. The village has a forestry museum parts of which are connected to the Glomdalmuseet, the third largest open-air museum in Norway, with its large collection of more than eighty well-preserved old buildings. The local tourist office will be able to give specific opening times.

Elverum makes another good touring base if you enjoy walking holidays. There are a number of hotels and guesthouses, cabins to rent and a campsite. You can also hire boats and there are many good bathing and fishing spots. The church was built in 1738 and has a number of ornate carvings in Regency style.

Highway 25 runs west from Elverum to connect with the E6 at Hamar. The road goes through Midtskogen scene of a battle on 9 April 1940 when local partisans forced back German troops on their way to Elverum to arrest the king and government. A side road south takes you to **Løten**, home of Norway's famous aquavit. Løten church dates from the early twelfth century. Just before highway 25 runs into Hamar you go through **Vang** where the early nineteenth-century church has a medieval tower and decorations by the painter Hugo Lous Mohr.

If you really want to get away from it all you can take highway 25 which runs east from Elverum through dense forests. This route then heads north on highway 26 through Trysil and skirts Lake Femunden, the third largest in Norway, before rejoining highway 30 at Nora about 15km south of Røros.

This is wild country with a few isolated farms but the walking is wonderful and there are spectacular views along the way. The route goes through **Nybergsund** which was heavily bombed on 11 April 1940 by the Germans as the late King Haakon VII and Crown Prince Olav sheltered there. Just to the north there is a very good campsite at Klara and then you arrive at **Innbygda** with Mount Trysilfjell to the west and Brattås to the east. There is also an open-air museum with many fine houses from the Trysil district. It is open to the public but check with times with the local tourist office. There are good camping sites along the river, many bathing and fishing spots and lots of opportunities for walking through the forests.

The road runs past Lake Engeren to Drevsjø where highway 218 heads east across the Swedish border. Stay on highway 26 past a number of good campsites at **Femund** and **Femundsenden** to **Isterfossen** at the foot of Lake Femund. The route now heads north past Bårfjell to the west and a string of mountains to the east starting with Bottølen and Bjørneberga. This whole area is a fisherman's paradise and boats can be hired by lake anglers. There is a lovely campsite by the River Småå at Joten and Joten Farm has rooms decorated in traditional style with paintings dating from the early eighteenth century. The road passes Sømådal chapel and then runs through the mountains via Tufsingdal to Nøra where it rejoins highway 30 south of Røros.

If you stay on highway 3 the road runs north from Elverum along the western bank of the Glomma to **Rena**, a winter resort and small industrial town and railway centre. The station has a collection of stuffed animals and birds from the district. There are good campsites at Rena and the Østerdalen tourist centre a few kilometres to the north. You can pony trek from here as well. The road now travels through the Østerdalen valley.

At **Messelt**, named after a legendary bear hunter, where there is a centuries old farmstead, the famous Birkebeiner road runs west over the mountains to Lillehammer. The route through heavily forested mountains, climbs to 1,090m and goes via the winter ski and summer walking resort of **Nordseter**, south of Neverfjell with a wooden mountain church.

At Nordstumoen you can either stay on highway 3 driving to Tynset via Alvdal where there is a youth hostel and open-air folk museum at Husantunet, or you can detour via Koppang and take highway 28 through Øvre Rendal into Tynset. This is a much more attractive route.

Koppang is on the eastern banks of the Glomma which has created scores of islands. The road runs east until it reaches Lake Storsjøen and then it travels north past Ytre Rendal with its mid-eighteenth-century church to the head of the lake at Otnes. The scenery along Rendalen is beautiful. **Øvre Rendal** church also dates from about 1750 and the village has a museum commemorating the writer Jacob Bull. There is a fantastic mountain road linking Øvre Rendal and Hanestad which takes you through Hanestadkjølen. The highest point along the road is about 750m and there are magnificent views. You can also detour off to the east along the narrow mountain road to the old fishing village of **Fiskevollen** beside Lake Sølensjøen. It is Norway's largest inland fishing village.

Another spectacular drive is to take the mountain road from Midtskogen to Barkald on highway 3 which passes the 5km long, 165m deep canyon Jutulhogget.

Highway 28 continues through **Tylldal**, where there is a church which dates from 1736 with fascinating leaf decorations, and then descends steeply in a series of sharp bends to the mountain village and tourist centre of **Tynset**. There is an open-air museum and an early eighteenth-century octagonal church. It is a very popular holiday area and there are a number of hotels and guesthouses, campsites and cabins to rent. Whether you arrive in Tynset on highway 3 or 28, it is worth the detour along the toll road to Tron for the fantastic views from the summit.

Highway 3 runs north-west from Tynset for Ulsberg where it connects with the E6 and Trondheim, but follow route 30 through Tolga and Os into Røros. **Tolga** is another mining community whose fortune was based on copper. The village dates from 1670. There used to be a number of smelters processing the copper brought down from Røros and there are a number of old miners' cottages. The church dates from 1840 and there are many old farms in the area including Lensmannsgården (the Sheriff's Farm), noted for its decorated Baroque figures. The Toljefossen falls are in the centre of town and just down river is a stone bridge built in 1762. **Vingelin** to the west is a charming mountain village with a museum that is worth a small detour.

Highway 30 then passes Hummelfjell to the east with Gråhøgda in the distance, before entering Os. It is still a farming area with a number of very interesting old estates. There is a very well preserved farm complex at **Oddentunet**, which was built at the beginning of the nineteenth century in Trøndelag Baroque style. It also served as a wayside inn. The interior was painted by local artist Sønvis Olssøn Holemoen (1782-1841). This is another popular year-round tourist centre with a 1,150m long ski tow up Hummelfjell. There is very good walking and in the summer you can hike the well marked trails to try to spot the grazing herds of reindeer. There is good fishing, riding

Nidaros Cathedral, Trondheim; one of the largest Gothic buildings in Scandinavia

and walking, and nowhere are you far from the Copper Trail which links Os with Røros, about 15km to the north.

Røros is a gem tucked away in the mountains. An old mountain town it has been wonderfully preserved and restored and its uniqueness is recognised by being listed by UNESCO in its World Heritage list of the greatest cultural treasures of the world.

The town was established after copper had been discovered in the mountains. The mines closed in 1977 and today Røros is a living museum. Unlike many other Norwegian towns Røros has not suffered any great fires over the centuries and so most of the old log buildings, many 300 years old, have been preserved. You can stroll around the mine workings past the rows of miners' cottages with their turf roofs, which stand in the shadows of the smelting works and slagheaps.

The first smelter was ready for use in September 1646 in the area known as Malmplassen. Ever since there has been a smelter on the site and up to eleven operating in the region. Although the town has been spared, the Smelters frequently caught fire and were destroyed. The last working smelter was closed after a fire in 1953 and was totally destroyed in another blaze in 1975 although the stone foundations and access ramp were saved. The new building was copied from the plans of the smelter erected in 1888 and houses the mining museum.

The Copper Trail ran from Røros to Falun deep in Sweden, more than

Heidal church has an unusual chequered roof

400km away. Norwegian mining apprentices were trained at Falun. Ore used to be shipped from the mines by rail, and now there is a modern highway linking the two towns.

Røros church was built in 1650. Originally wood it became too small for the rapidly expanding town and a new stone church, which took 5 years to build, was consecrated in 1784. It dominates the landscape towering over the log buildings.

About 13km north-east of Røros, the **Olavsgruva** mines have been reopened for tourists. Wearing a miner's helmet (and sturdy shoes) you can descend 500m into the mountain and discover the conditions under which miners had to work centuries ago with the atmosphere heightened by special sound and lighting effects. The complex consists of two mines, Crown Prince Olav's Mine and the Nyberget Mine, the second oldest having opened in the 1650s. In the summer there is folk music and dancing in the largest chamber of the Olav mine, where the temperature is a constant 5°C.

Other things to see in the region include the old mine at Folldal to the south, and the open-air folk museums at Haltdalen and Ålen to the north, and the Great Wall war memorial at Stormuren. The huge structure was built more than 100 years ago for the area's first railroad and partially blown up by Norwegian resistance fighters in 1944.

Røros is not only popular for its mines, it is a great base for an activities holiday in the surrounding mountains. There is skiing in the winter and during the summer there is fishing and hiking, cycling, riding and canoeing. There are boats for hire and numerous organised tours — also you can enjoy mini cruises on Lake Femund which runs daily during the summer season.

From Røros highway 30 heads north past Glåmos, and follows the railway line to Unsholtet where there are the spectacularly deep Killingdal copper pyrites mines. There are the remains of an old foundry at Eidet and the road then goes through the Svølgja gorge. Highway 30 then swings round to the west through Gauldalen where there is a very good campsite at Klokker–haugen beside the River Gaula. A little further up the road at **Singäs** is a sixth-century burial mound topped by a 5m high stone. The road connects with the E6 at Støren which you take for the 45km drive into Trondheim.

Additional Information

Places of Interest

Trondheim

Archbishop's Palace
☎ (07)52 12 53
Open: 15 June to 15 August weekdays 9am-3pm, Saturday 9am-2pm and Sunday 12noon-3pm.
Guided tours daily.

Art Gallery
Open: June to August daily 11am-4pm.

September to May daily 12noon-4pm. Closed Monday.
☎ (07)52 66 71

Civil Defence Museum
Tempeveien 37
For guided tours
☎ (07)54 70 51 / 55 94 30

Munkholmen
26 May to 2 September: boats depart daily from Ravnkloa, every hour on the hour from 10am-5pm.

*Museum of Applied Art and Craft
   (Nordenfjeldske Kunstindustrimuseum)*
Munkegt 5,
☎ (07) 52 13 11
Open: 20 June to 15 August weekdays
9am-5pm. Sundays 12noon-5pm, 16
August to 19 June weekdays 10am-3pm,
Thursday 10am-7pm, Sundays 12noon
to 4pm.

Nidaros Cathedral
Open: summer, Monday to Friday
9.30am-5.30pm, Saturday 9.30am-2pm,
Sunday 1.30-4pm. Winter, Monday to
Friday 12noon-2.30pm, Saturday
11.30am-2pm, Sunday 1.30-3pm.
The tower is open from 15 June to 20
August. ☎ (07) 52 12 53

Olavskirken
Open: 15 May to 15 September, Monday, Tuesday, Wednesday and Friday
8.15am-3pm, Thursday 8.15am-5pm.

Ringve Botanical Gardens
Conducted tours by appointment.
☎ (07) 92 16 60

Ringve Museum
Lade Allé 60
Open: Visitors to the museum must be
accompanied by the museum's guides
on conducted tours.
☎ (07) 92 24 11

Stiftsgården
☎ (07) 52 24 73
Guided tours every half hour from
11am-2pm on weekdays from 1 June to
31 August. Closed Sundays.

Trøndelag Folk Museum
Sverresborg
☎ (07) 52 21 28
Open: 20 May to 1 September 11am-
6pm. Conducted tours, 11.15am, 1pm,
3pm and 4.30pm. Bus no 8 and 9 from
Dronningens gate to Wallumsgården.

Trondheim's Sjøfarts Museum
☎ (07) 52 89 75
Open: daily all year round, 9am-3pm.
Sunday 12noon-3pm. Closed Saturdays
during winter months.

Tyholt Tower
☎ (07) 51 31 66
Open: 11.30am-12pm. Sunday and
public holidays 12.30-7pm.

This tower can be reached by taking bus
no 20 and 60.

University of Trondheim Museum
Open: May and September Monday to
Saturday 12noon-3pm. June to August,
Monday to Saturday 11am-3pm,
Wednesday 6-8pm, Sunday all year
12noon-3pm.

Vår Frue Kirke
Open: 10am-2pm Tuesday to Friday,
June, July and August. Saturdays 11am-
2pm.

Gjøvik
Eiktutnet Museum of Cultural History
Open: during the summer 10am-4pm.

Hamer
Railway Museum
Open: daily 10am-4pm, except October
to April. Closed Sunday.

Hunderfossen
Amusement Park
Open: daily 1 June to mid-August.
☎ (07) 74 222

Kristiansten Fort
Open: June, July and August 10am-3pm,
Saturday and Sunday 10am-2pm.
For guided tours ☎ (07) 51 51 11, ext 182

Lillehammer
Lillammer Municipal Art Gallery
Kirkegt
☎ (062) 51 944
Open: Tuesday to Friday 11am-4pm,
Saturday 10am-2pm, Sunday 12noon-
4pm.

Maihaugen Open-Air Folk Museum
☎ (062) 50 135
Open: May and September 10am-4pm.
June to August 10am-6pm.

Norwegian Museum of Vehicle History
Lilletorget
☎ (062) 56 165
Open: June to August 10am-6pm,
September to mid-June, Monday to
Friday 10am-2pm, Weekends 10am-
4pm.

Røros
Church
Open: June to September, Monday to
Friday 10am-2pm, Saturday 10am-
12.30pm.

Olavsgruva (mines)
Open: guided tours only mid-June to mid-August, six daily. Rest of June, August and September, one to three tours a day.

Trondheim Useful Information

Consulate
Great Britain
Sluppenveien 10
☎ (07) 96 82 11

Emergencies
Fire ☎ 001
Police ☎ 002
Ambulance ☎ 003
Casualty Hospital ☎ (07) 59 88 00
Chemist Emergency Service, St Oláv
Vaktapotek ☎ (07) 52 31 22
Taxis ☎ (07) 52 76 00
Norwegian Automobile Association
(NAF) — Directions and information concerning conditions of roads, routes etc. ☎ (07) 96 62 88

Parking
Parking in the centre of Trondheim is subject to parking zone regulations. There are parking zone signs at all entry points.

Police Station
Kongens gate 87
☎ (07) 51 44 11

Post Office ·
Main Post Office, Kjøpmannsgt 34
☎ (07) 96 47 11
Open: weekdays from 8am-5pm, Saturdays from 9.30am to 1pm.

Kalvskinnet Post Office,
Erling Skakkes gate 25
☎ (07) 52 52 95
Open: weekdays from 8.30am to 5pm, Saturdays from 9am to 12noon.

Travel

Airport
Trondheim Airport is at Værnes, 35km north-east of the city.

The early eighteenth-century, octagonal church at Tynset

SAS: ☎ (07) 82 49 22
Braathens SAFE: ☎ (07) 82 60 22
Widerøe: ☎ (07)82 56 88
Good connections by air everywhere in
the country. A direct flight from
Trondheim to Copenhagen daily except
Sundays.

Bus to Ringve
Bus No 1 from stops in the city centre.
Conducted tours at Ringve Museum.

Car Ferries
Flakk-Rørvik, frequent departures from
Flakk, 10km west of the city on road
715.

Coaches to Værnes
Coaches leave from the Coach Terminal,
Erling Skakkes gate 40, 75 minutes
before the time of departure for SAS
Braathens SAFE flights, driving via the
Braathens SAFE terminal at Royal
Garden Hotel, Kjøpmannsgate 73.

Coach Terminal, Leüthenhaven
Erling Skakkes gate 40. All coaches
connecting Trondheim to outlying areas
(including the passenger service to
Værnes airport) depart from/arrive at
the Leüthenhaven coach terminal.
Waiting room, kiosk, cafeteria, bank,
multistorey car park. For information
☎ (07) 52 44 74 or (07) 52 73 22

Fjord and Coastal Routes
The coastel steamer: southbound at
10.15 (quay 16) northbound at 12 noon
pier 2 (quay 7). Please note: These times
of departure may be altered. Catamaran
to Vanvikan, departure from Skansen.
Catamaran to Fosen, Hitra, Frøya and
Sula, depart from Fosen quay opposite
the railway station. For information
concerning these routes
☎ (07) 52 79 60

Railway Station
Day and night trains to Oslo and Bodø.
Day train to Sweden (Storlien). Trains to
intermediate points. Left luggage, kiosk,
cafeteria, pub and restaurant. For
information ☎ (07) 52 64 69 or 52 10 00

Taxis
24-hour service ☎ (07) 52 76 00. Taxi
ranks at: Torvet (the market square),
Søndre gate, Nordre gate, the Railway

Station, the Royal Garden Hotel and
Ilevollen.

Train: Daily train connections to Oslo,
Trondheim and Åndalsnes. Literature
and excursion suggestions can be
obtained at the Tourist Office.
Train Enquiries ☎ (07) 53 046

Lillehammer
Useful Information

Bank (Money Exchange)
Den norske Creditbank
Storgt 55
☎ (062) 57 000

Sparebanken Østlandet
Kirkegt 74/Storgt 56
☎ (062) 73 000

Banks
Open: Monday to Friday 8.30am-3.30pm
Thursday 8.30am-5pm
Saturday closed.

Bus Transport
LITRA Buss As, Jernbanegt 2
☎ (062) 66 600

Bus: The district is covered by a comprehensive bus network, and there are
daily connections to Sjusjøen, Nordseter,
Gjøvik, Gudbrandsdalen and Valdres.
Excursions by bus are arranged the
whole year. In winter there is a bus
service between Oslo and Lillehammer/
Nordseter/Sjusjøen.

Long Distance Bus Service:
Lillehammer-Gjøvik-Hønefoss: daily.
Lillehammer-Dokka-Fagernes: Monday
to Saturday.
Lillehammer-Otta-Bjorli: Monday to
Saturday.
Lillehammer-Otta-Stryn-Måløy: Mon-
day to Friday.

Car Rental
AVIS-Hamar Bilutleie
avd. Lillehammer
Storgt 136-138
☎ (062) 55 311

Stavseth Bilutleie AS
Hertz, Industrigt 24-26
☎ (062) 53 145

Chemists Shops
Monday to Friday 8.30am-4.30pm
Saturday 8.30am-1pm.
Mesna Apotek is on duty Sunday and
holidays 5-7pm.

Emergencies
Police, Storgaten 120
☎ (062) 58 800

Fire
☎ 003

Casualty Department
☎ (062) 51 450

Post Office
Monday to Friday 8am-4.30pm,
Saturday 9am-1pm.

Railway Station
☎ (062) 53 046

Taxi
☎ (062) 53 100

Useful Addresses

Regional Tourist Boards
Hedmark Tourist Board
Grønnegt 11
N-2300 Hamar
☎ (065) 29 006

Oppland Tourist Board
Kirkegt 74
N-2600 Lillehammer
☎ (062) 55 700

Local Tourist Offices
Offices marked with an asterix* are
staffed during the summer only.

Hamar
Reiselivskontoret for Hamar-Regionen
Boks 318, N-2301 Hamar
☎ (065) 21 217

Lillehammer
Destinasjon Lillehammer
Boks 181, N-2601 Lillehammer
☎ (062) 59 299

Elverum Reiselivslag*
Postboks 327
N-2401 Elverum
☎ (064) 14 963

Norheimsund Turistinformasjon
N-5600 Norheimsund
☎ (05) 55 17 67

Oppdal Næringsforening
Postboks 50
N-7341 Oppdal
☎ (074) 21 760

Otta
Sel-Rondane Reiselivslag
Boks 94
N-2671 Otta
☎ (062) 30 365

Ringebu Reiseliv A/S
N-2630 Ringebu
☎ (062) 80 533

Røros Reiselivslag
Bergmannspl Boks 61
N-7460 Røros
☎ (074) 11 165

Sjusjøen Turist A/S
N-2612 Sjusjøen
☎ (065) 63 565

Tolga Reiselivslag*
N-2540 Tolga
☎ (064) 94 505

Trondheim Turistinformasjon
Boks 2102
N-7001 Trondheim
☎ (07) 51 14 66

Gjøvik ☎ (061) 71688

Kongsvinger ☎ (066) 15210

Koppang ☎ (064) 60703

*Løten ☎ (065) 92600

Nordseter ☎ (062) 64012

*Rena ☎ (064) 40200

Tynset ☎ (064) 80000

11

HEADING FOR THE LAND
OF THE MIDNIGHT SUN

Trondheim is the 'gateway to the north' and the drive up into the Arctic Circle is still a great adventure. Like all adventures, it has to be planned carefully. Having arrived in Trondheim from Oslo you have still only covered half the journey to the Arctic Circle. It is almost 2,000km from Trondheim to Kirkenes close to the Russian border in the far north.

The road north hugs the coastline and is often narrow and twisty. In many places it follows the line of the fjords so you have to drive long distances even though your destination may be only a couple of kilometres away across the water. In other places you have to take ferries and each day's driving should be planned around important ferry connections. The further north you travel the worst the roads become. In many places the roads are unmetalled but they still carry a lot of traffic and pose no problem providing you drive carefully and your vehicle is in good condition. There are many detours to be made and the time for these must be added to your schedule when planning but also take into account the long hours of sunlight each day in summer. It is a good idea to adopt the Midnight Sun philosophy of travelling when you feel fit and stopping when you feel tired, no matter what the time of day or night. Plan a schedule that allows you the time to see as much as possible.

The trip north is only really feasible in the summer months and even then you can run into bad weather so you should be prepared. Carry extra fuel and essential motoring spares, emergency rations and camping equipment. Do not be put off because it really is the adventure of a lifetime.

The E6 runs eastwards out of Trondheim following the southern banks of Tronheimsfjorden through Malvik and Muruvik to **Hell** which is a major rail link with Sweden. You should stop here to see the early Stone Age rock drawings, signposted 'Helleristninger'.

The road then goes through **Værnes** with its modern airport and medieval church. The church is famous for its highly decorated beam ends. **Stjørdalshalsen** is a pretty little town at the mouth of the River Stjørdal. Here the E75 heads off east for the Swedish border through the beautiful Stjørdalen valley and Hegra where there are a number of rock drawings at least 2,500 years old. The E6 continues north and just beyond Tiller you can see a small island on which stands the ruined castle of Steinviksholm built around 1530.

At Åsen you can detour left on highway 753 to **Frosta**, a peninsula steeped in history. You can visit the *ting*, the old parliament site marked out by stones on the hillside. It was the meeting place for the Trøndelag council and was used for more than 500 years until the end of the seventeenth century. Aslo

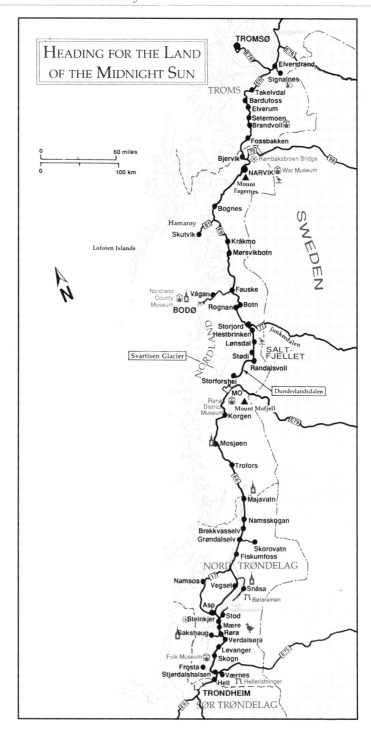

HEADING FOR THE LAND
OF THE MIDNIGHT SUN

worth visiting are the Frosta folk museum, the medieval church at Logtun, and a number of other well signposted ruins and Stone Age rock drawings.

There are more rock drawings just off the E6 at Skjerve. **Skogn** is a noted centre for woodcarving and headquarters of Norway's largest wood processing company. The papermill dominates the landscape and produces newsprint mainly for export. **Alstadhaugh** is worth a visit because of its church, built in the mid-thirteenth century, noted for its medieval murals and frescoes.

Colourful Stone and Bronze Age rock carvings at Bardal, near Steinkjer

Land of the Midnight Sun

Levanger is an old trading town which has a number of fine old wooden buildings around the market place. On the outskirts of the town is Mo Farm whose oldest buildings date from around 1830. There is plenty of accommodation in and around the town including a summer youth hostel (☎ 076 81 638).

About 10km up the road is **Verdalsøra** which has grown rapidly in recent years because of the oil boom. It has several agriculture-based industries and one of Europe's largest yards for building oil rigs although the down turn in the oil industry is affecting the town. Two kilometres north of the town is the turn off for **Stiklestad** where King Olav was killed in battle on 29 July 1030. The king's death is still commemorated annually by religious plays performed at the end of July. The church was built in the early twelfth century on the battlefield site.

Birdwatchers are recommended to turn on to highway 755 and drive into the **Inderøy Peninsula** at **Røra**. The peninsula has a wealth of bird life and there are two Middle Age churches at **Hustad** and **Sakshaug**. If taking this detour you can turn north on to highway 761 at Straumen which swings round Borgenfjorden to rejoin the E6 just before Steinkjer.

Remaining on the E6 the road passes **Mære**, an ancient sacrificial site on which a church was built in the twelfth century. It is noted for its weird animal carvings.

Steinkjer is Norway's largest agricultural centre with agriculture and timber as its main industries. Visit the open-air museum, Steinkjer church with its decorations by Jacob Weidemann, and the chapel decorated by Henrik Sørensen.

There are many reminders of the Vikings presence in this area, as well as ancient burial mounds, stone circles and rock drawings. It is worth a detour to see Norway's most famous rock drawing, the **Bølareinen** (the Reindeer of Bøla). Take highway 763 from Steinkjer which runs through Stod and along the eastern bank of Lake Snåsavatnet. The road deteriorates after Binde but you can still drive on it. Follow the railway line and the rock drawings can be visited just after Valøy railway station. You can continue along the road which improves after a few kilometres, to Snåsa at the head of the lake. It then swings round to rejoin the E6 at Vegset.

If you stay on the E6 the road continues to **Asp** where you have a choice. You can take highway 17 for a detour which takes in **Namsos**, a popular fishing and water sports centre. Highway 17 follows the northern bank of the River Namsen to Bjøra bru where you take highway 760 to reconnect with the E6 at Grong.

If you do not take this detour the E6 runs along the northern shore of Snåsavatnet to **Vegset** where it is worth the small sidetrip to **Snåsa** with its medieval church and lovely late eighteenth-century rectory. This is an area famous for its trout fishing and there are hundreds of lakes and rivers to try. There are a number of campsites in the area, cabins to rent and a summer youth hostel.

The E6 continues through Fiskumfoss to Grong on the famous Namsen salmon fishing river. The road now follows the Namsen for many kilometres, past the Fiskumfoss falls and its incredible salmon ladder, through rather bleak countryside. At Grøndalselv you can turn off on highway 764 to visit

Skorovatn and Lake Tunnsjøen, and a little further along the E6 you drive under a conveyor belt which runs to the Skorovass mine. The valley starts to narrow and the Namsen runs much faster and there are many rapids and falls. The first of these are at Trongfossen. Follow the E6 through Brekkvasselv and Namsskogan, both very popular fishing centres, across the county border into Nordland.

Nordland is a county steeped in history. Stone Age man has left his mark in the many rock drawings, Iron Age man built his turf huts, there are constant reminders of the Vikings while the Lapps, the original inhabitants, are remembered by sacrificial stones erected many centuries ago. Winters are long and hard and summers short. There are few other places in the world where you can ski in shorts more than 1,000m above sea level in brilliant sunshine at midnight!

The county has more than a million acres of productive forest and the area provides a haven for reindeer, lynx, fox, marten, otter, beaver and eagle. There are seals, porpoise and whales off the coast and more than 28,000 lakes covering 2,039sq km, as well as salmon and trout rivers. Nordland stretches for more than 500km yet at its narrowest it is only 6.3km from the coast to the Swedish border. It has 14,000km of coastline and 12,000 islands.

At the lakeside village of **Majavatn** — noted for its natural beauty and wildlife — there is an interesting Lapp church. This is another very popular fishing area but there is good camping and walking and you can hire boats. The area is full of large lakes teeming with fish, and to the north east is the imposing Børgefjell with its many towering peaks which make up one of the country's most isolated National Parks. A few kilometres beyond the village the road reaches 375m and then runs down into the heavily wooded Svenningdal valley.

At Trofors there is a turning off on highway 73 for Hattfjelldal and a number of small roads which allow you to explore Lake Røsvatn. From Trofors the E6 continues north and it is worth visiting the spectacular **Laksfoss** falls, where you can watch the salmon negotiating the ladder. The falls are by the old E6 but are well signposted from the new road. At **Mosjøen** the aluminium works is the main industry and you should visit Dolstad church, built about 1735 and the oldest octagonal church in north Norway, and the old buildings in Sjøgata.

The E6 now heads inland through the forests with mountain peaks all round you. Away to the east are the high peaks of the Okstindan range. The road passes many large lakes, including Fustvatn, Mjåvatnet, Ømmervatnet and Luketvatnet, and there are several campsites along the way. After passing the massive power station at Korgen, the road runs north along the shores of Sørfjorden to Finneidfjord, and then up to Mo i Rana.

Mo is an industrial town with a steelworks and the world's largest smelter. It was the scene of heavy fighting in May 1940 between British and German troops. Visit the Steinneset open-air museum and the Rana district museum which has a fascinating display about the Lapps.

Mo makes a good touring base and there are a number of things to see in the area. To the north is the Svartisen glacier, the second largest in Norway. You can drive to Svartisvatnet and then take a boat across the lake. It is then a 40 minute walk to the foot of the glacier. There are guided tours on to the glacier. You can take highway 804 to Nesna at the end of the peninsula which looks out over three fjords, and camp out by the sea. Visit the Grønli grotto by turning left off the E6 at Røssvoll. The cave, which is reached after an easy 30 minute walk, was not discovered until 1965 and is full of fascinating dripping stalactites. Waterproofs and non-slip footwear is essential. There is a cable car on to Mount Mofjell which affords wonderful panoramic views.

The E6 now runs north-east following the River Rana and running parallel with the railway past **Reinfoss**, with one of the longest salmon ladders and tunnels in Europe, and Storfossen into **Storforshei** which stands at the entrance to **Dunderlandsdalen**. The valley which is very scenic is also the home of the Rana mine, close to Storfoshei, which supplies the iron ore for the smelter at Mo. The road starts to climb through the trees and there are

marvellous views of the mountains to the west with the glacier behind them. Most of the peaks are well over 1,200m.

Around **Randalsvoll**, the E6 is less than 5km from the Swedish border, and then the road climbs through the Arctic Circle, marked by a number of stone cairns erected by travellers, and a Lapp camp selling souvenirs on the old road, to Stødi, the highest point on the road across Saltfjellet at 707m. The E6 now enters **Lønsdal**, a popular winter resort surrounded by high mountains

Bodø's busy harbour

and with good skiing, especially on Akjektind just to the west. The road is closed during winter storms.

It is worth a small detour on highway 77 from Hestbrinken into the wild but beautiful **Junkerdalen** which runs to the Swedish border. The whole area is now protected as a nature reserve and contains many rare plants. There is a tourist centre and restaurant close to the Swedish border.

Playing Children,
a sculpture by Trygve
Thosen in Narvik

A bird's eye view of
Tromsø from the
cablecar

The E6 continues through **Storjord** with its government plant breeding institute, to the boat building town of Rognan at the head of Saltdalsfjorden. The road then swings round the bottom of the fjord to Botn where there is a military cemetery for the Yugoslav prisoners of war who died of cold and hunger during World War II. Germans are also buried here. The road then follows the eastern coast of Saltdalsfjorden to Fauske.

It is worth another detour on highway 80 following the northern shore of Skjerstadfjorden to Bodø. Stop on the way at **Vågan** where there is a 4,000 year old rock drawing of an elk, and take time to visit the Saltstraumen, off highway 17, where the tide is exceptionally fast and high as it is forced through the narrow channel four times a day.

Bodø is another town that suffered terribly from German aerial bombing in 1940 and had to be largely rebuilt. It is now a bustling trading centre with a busy ice-free port, the terminus for the north-bound railway and the military headquarters for northern Norway. There are a number of boat trips available including visits to the famous bird islands of Værøy and Røst.

The Nordland County Museum has exhibits on fishing, Vikings and local history. Visit the modern Bodø Cathedral, and the medieval Bodin stone church built at the beginning of the thirteenth century. You can also climb to the summit of Rønvikfjellet just outside the town for splendid views over the surrounding sea and countryside. From June to mid-July you can see the Midnight Sun from this peak.

From Fauske the E6 runs round Leirfjorden, an arm of the Sørfolda, through a number of tunnels on a new stretch of road. This stretch of road is fantastic with wild and desolate mountain country to the east and the magnificent Lofoten Islands just off the coast to the west which you might just be able to catch a glimpse of.

There is a marvellous campsite (☎ 081 95118) at Mørsvikboten and then the road goes past Kråkmofjellet and between Nordfoldakslat on the left hand side of the road and Kråkmofjellet to the right. Nobel prize winning author Knut Hamsun wrote many of his novels while staying at Kråkmo Farm and he features many of the local lakes in his works. There is also a summer youth hostel at Kråkmo. Near Tømmernes, on the shores of Sagfjorden, there are more rock drawings, about 3,000 years old. They are clearly signposted.

The road goes through Innhavet and then descends to Ulvsvåg. From here you can take highway 81 to **Skutvik** for the 2 hour ferry crossing to Svolvær in Lofoten. Even if you do not plan to take the ferry it is worth a detour to the island of **Hamarøy** for its beautiful mountain scenery.

The E6 continues to **Bognes** where you catch the ferry across the many-forked Tysfjorden to Skarberget for Narvik, or Lødingen if you want to spend some time exploring the islands. As you sail into Skarberget there are fantastic views of Mount Breiskartind. The road bridges Efjordfen and crosses the peninsula to the small port of Ballangen and then runs over the impressive Skjomen and Beisfjord bridges into Narvik.

Narvik is an amazing town because despite its proximity to the North Pole just 2,420km away, it enjoys a very pleasant climate thanks to the Gulf Stream. The average temperature in January and February is only -4 °C while it is very much colder several hundred kilometres further south. If you do not want to drive to Narvik you can fly into one of the two airports, or arrive by boat, bus or train from Sweden. There are a number of hotels, pensions, cottages and campsites.

The history of Narvik is closely linked with the massive iron ore fields in Swedish Lappland. For centuries Narvik was little more than a small fishing village but in 1898 the united Norwegian-Swedish State agreed to build a railway line linking Kiruna and Narvik so that the iron ore could be shipped from the ice-free harbour. The 168km Ofoten railway line through incredible hostile country was finished in 1902 and officially opened on 14 July 1903. The opening signalled the rapid growth of Narvik. Every year in February or March a week long festival is still held to celebrate the coming of the railway and the navvies who built it. Narvik was granted its town charter in 1902. Its economy is now broad based involving ship building, printing and high tech industries and iron ore shipments are still important.

Narvik was the scene of bitter fighting in 1940 between the Allies and the Germans and much of the town was destroyed. Narvik was invaded on 9 April 1940 under cover of a thick blizzard. A fleet of ten German destroyers entered the harbour, sank the two armoured battleships *Norge* and *Eidsvoll*, and captured the town to control the shipments of iron-ore. A few days later a British naval force reached Narvik and destroyed the German fleet and on 28 May, a combined force of Norwegian, British, French and Polish troops landed and retook the town. It was Germany's only defeat in the first 3 years of World War II. After the Allies left, the Germans re-entered the devastated town and stayed in occupation for 5 years. The War Museum gives a graphic account of the fighting and Narvik's occupation, and the nearby military cemetery which has thousands of graves, bears witness to the ferocity of the fighting.

Worth visiting are the port with its automatic loading equipment, some of the most advanced in the world, and the summit of Fagernesfjellet which can be reached by cable car (March to October).

Other things to do include walking or riding treks along the extensive network of trails and cabins in the mountains close to the Swedish border. These cabins are maintained by the Narvik Touring Association. Keys are at the fire station in Narvik (☎ 028 45 100), who will want a deposit for their use. There are also many ancient monuments and rock drawings in the area. Narvik has become a very popular winter sports resort and it is possible to ski from November until May. It is also popular as a winter fishing area.

From Narvik the E6 swings round Rombaken and then goes over the Rombaksbroen, the country's largest suspension bridge. As you cross the bridge you can look out over the fjord which was the scene of the naval battles in 1940.

The E6 heads north to **Bjerkvik** where you can detour off on highway 19 to explore the Lofoten Islands. It is a delightful journey through beautiful coastal scenery and charming little fishing villages.

From Bjerkvik the road climbs up to 330m and at the top of the hill you cross the border from Nordland into Troms county. Continue through Gratangen and Lapphaugen, both of which have tourist stations, and cross the Spanselv river over the Jordbrua, a natural bridge cut in the limestone. This is a charming route through woods mainly of birch although there are impressive snow-capped peaks all around you.

At Fossbakken you can take highway 84 to follow the coast through Sjøvegan to Sørreisa where you can take highway 86 to explore Senja and the Anderdalen National Park, or you can return on highway 86 to reconnect with the E6 at Bardufoss.

If you stay on the E6 at Fossbakken it swings inland, past the open-air museum at **Brandvoll**, which also has a display of military weapons, to the garrison town of Setermoen (Bardu). You then travel through the Bardu valley, again surrounded by snow capped peaks, to Elverum. As you have to return to Trondheim by virtually the same route, it is a good idea to make as many detours as possible along the way. At Elverum highway 87 runs eastwards to Skjold, past Målselvfossen, and then past Erikbufossen into the charming Tamokdalen which leads to Øvergård.

From **Elverum** the E6 goes to **Bardufoss** where the falls have been harnessed by the power station, and through Moen to **Takelvdal**, where there is accommodation and a lovely campsite. To the south there is Mauken and to the north Blåtind. The road skirts Takvatnet, and then heads north at Heia past Sagelvvatnet, into Storsteinnes at the head of Balsfjorden. The road then skirts the fjord to Nordkjosbotn where you turn left on to the E78 along the eastern banks of Balsfjorden for **Tromsø**. You enter the town over a 300m long bridge.

Archaeological finds have shown that there have been settlements at Tromsø for at least 9,000 years. It was an ecclesiastical centre and the first recorded church was built in 1252. Because of trading restrictions imposed by the Hanseatic League Tromsø did not prosper until 1794 when it received its town charter and the right to trade independently. The period between 1840 to 1890 was a time of great growth and prosperity. The Tromsø shipyard was opened in 1848, the town museum in 1872 and the Mack's Brewery in 1877.

It was an important base for expeditions and Tromsø became known as the 'gateway to the arctic'. The statue of Roald Amundsen near the harbour bears witness to this. In 1927 the Northern Light Observatory was established and it was at Tromsø in 1944 that the German battleship *Tirpitz* was destroyed. The Tromsø Bridge, the link with the mainland, was completed in 1960 and the town's airport at Langnes opened in 1964.

Tromsø is an important port because of its year-round ice free harbour, but also a delightful, sprawling town covering 2,400sq km making it the 'largest' town area in Norway. It has the world's most northerly university, and a wonderful museum at the Folkeparken with displays of old boats, the flora and fauna of the region, and Lapp culture.

Visit the old city centre — the 'Paris of the North' — with its lovely wooden buildings, the new glass-roofed cathedral, also known as the Ice Sea Cathedral with Europe's tallest stained glass windows (23m high), and the old Tromsøya church with its seventeenth-century carvings and altarpiece. Take the cable car ride to Mount Storsteinen (422m) and enjoy some spectacular boat trips and bird watching (information available from the tourist office).

If you decide not to visit Tromsø on this leg of the journey, continue on the E6 to **Elvestrand** where you should really detour down the delightful Signadalen valley. **Signalnes** is one of the most beautiful spots on a fine day with stunning views of the encircling mountains.

Return to the E6 and follow the southern bank of Storfjorden to Skibotn where the road turns north along the fjord to Odden on the point. The E6 then skirts round Kåfjorden to Breivoll, where you can again detour off down Kåfjorddalen, before heading north again into Olderdalen, where you meet the ferry bringing the cars across from Tromsø to continue the journey north.

Additional Information

Places of Interest

Bodø
Nordland County Museum
Prinsensgt
☎ (081) 21640
Open: Monday to Friday 9am-3pm, Saturday 10am-3pm, Sunday 12noon-3pm.

Church
Open: daily June to August 10am-8pm.

Narvik
War Museum (Krigsminne Museum)
Open: daily March to September 10am-2pm. June to August daily 10am-10pm.

Tromsø
Tromsø Museum
Open: daily June to August 9am-6pm September to May, Monday to Friday 9am-3pm, Wednesday 7-10pm, Saturday 12noon-3pm, Sunday 10am-3pm.

Cathedral
Open: Monday to Saturday 10am-2pm and 4-6pm. Sunday 1-7pm.

Useful Addresses

Regional Tourist Boards

Nordland Tourist Board
PO Box 434
Storgaten 28
N-8001 Bodø
☎ (081) 24 406

Troms Reiser
Storgt 63, PO Box 1077
N-9001 Tromsø
☎ (083) 10000

Local Tourist Offices

Offices marked with an asterix * are staffed during the summer only.

Bodø Reiselivslag
Postboks 514
N-8001 Bodø
Visitors: Sjøgt 21
☎ (081) 21 240

Elverum Reiselivslag*
Postboks 327
N-2401 Elverum
☎ (064) 14 963

Frosta Reiselivsnemnd*
N-7633 Frosta
☎ (07) 80 77 60

Levanger Reiselivslag*
N-7600 Levanger
☎ (076) 82 105

Mo i Rana
Polarsirkelen Reiselivslag
Boks 225
N-8601 Mo i Rana
☎ (087) 50 421

Narvik Reiselivslag
Boks 318
N-8501 Narvik
Visitors: Kongens Gate 66
☎ (082) 43 309

Steinkjer Reiselivslag*
N-7700 Steinkjer
☎ (077) 63 495

Inderøy ☎ (077) 53300

Namsos* ☎ (077) 73470

Snåsa* ☎ (077) 81500

12

THE NORTH CAPE

The journey from Tromsø to the North Cape is 500km. Leave Tromsø on the E78 to **Fagernes** and then turn left on to highway 91 which takes you past Stormheimfjell on your right and then Storfjellet and Finnheimfjellet on your left, before arriving at Breivikeidet where you take the ferry across Ullsfjorden to **Svensby**. Follow highway 91 along the northern shores of Kjosen to **Lyngseidet** with its mid-eighteenth-century church and ferry terminal where you take the boat to Olderdalen. This crossing takes you across Lyngenfjord where it divides inland into Kåfjorden and Storfjorden. At **Olderdalen**, where there is a good campsite (☎ 089 171 21), you rejoin the E6 and head north along the eastern shores of Lyngenfjord.

After the cliffs at Kåfjordbergan you pass a number of peaks on your right. The first is Nordmannviktind, with Goattegaissa and Cokkulatgaissa in the distance as you continue along the road. Much closer to the road are Goattejiekke and Sorbmejiekke and then you arrive at Djupvik where it is worth the small detour left to the headland at Spåkenes for the splendid views out over Lyngenfjord.

The road then follows the shore of Rotsundfjord to Rotsundelv and Langslett. From here you can detour north on highway 866, island hopping to Skjervøy. The E6 swings round the head of Reisafjorden through Sørkjosen and Storslett to Nordreisa, at the mouth of the Reisa, a famous salmon river.

A lovely detour from Nordreisa takes you south on highway 865 along the Reisadalen as far as Bilto, about 45km away. The road does continue for a few kilometres beyond Bilto through Saraelv but becomes increasingly rougher. The highlight of this trip is to take a boat from Bilto along the River Reisa to the magnificent Mollesfossen which drops almost 270m.

The E6 continues along the eastern shores of Straumfjord, past the **Sandnes** campsite a short distance from Fosselyfossen. This is a very popular tourist area and there are a number of campsites and cabins to rent along the fjord. At **Mettevoll** the road rises quite steeply to 402m to scale the ridge which is part of the Kvænangstindan. The views from the top of the pass are spectacular. This is an area frequented by Lapps and there are a number of settlements and camps along the road.

The road then drops sharply in a series of bends to **Kvænangen.** The bridge across the Sørstraumen, a very good stretch of fishing water, was opened in 1981. Before that the route had to go round the head of the fjord through Seljevoll.

At **Burfjorddal** there is a small mountain road off to the right which takes you into Burfjorddalen where there is exciting walking and good fishing, and then the E6 runs into **Alteidet**. This is the last community in Troms before you cross over into Finnmark. There is a small road north which takes you to Jøkelfjorden and some charming little fishing villages. It also gives you the chance to explore the Øksfjordjølen glacier which dominates the landscape to the north.

Finnmark is Norway's most northerly county, and at the same latitude as the most inhospitable parts of North Alaska. This is not a land covered by ice, however, and in the summer you can explore by car or foot. The North Cape is the most northerly point in the world accessible by car.

The land of the Midnight Sun is not known for its predictable weather. Summer temperatures can reach 32°C one day and you may be having snow squalls the next. The coast tends to have cool summers and mild winters, although there can be many days on end of warm weather and many hours of sunshine, while inland there are usually warm summers and bitterly cold winters — the record low temperature is -51°C.

The boroughs of Karasjok and Kautokeino, which together cover one third of the county, are Sami speaking. It is the Lapp stronghold where they have their own schools, newspapers and radio and television stations. Anyone interested in the history of the Sami must visit the museums at Kautokeino and Karasjok. There are also a number of Finn speaking Norwegians known as Quænen in Finnmark who have preserved their own culture.

The history of Finnmark stretches back more than 10,000 years and the area was certainly inhabited by 8000BC. Rock carvings at Hjemmeluft, near Alta, date from between 2,000 and 6,500 years old, and in 1985 were added to the UNESCO's list of the world's most important prehistoric monuments.

Norway's only Greek Orthodox chapel is found in Finnmark at **Neiden**, and there are many other old chapels and churches. St George's Chapel in Neiden was built in 1567. The Oscar II Chapel was built in 1809 and stands near the head of the River Jakobselva which marks the frontier between Norway and the USSR.

It is possible to take a trip into the USSR provided you leave enough time for visa clearance. There is a travel agent in Kirkenes which will arrange flights into the Soviet arctic port of Murmansk.

The Arctic Road links Finnmark with Rovaniemi, the capital of Finnish Lapland and the North Cape Route which runs the 5,000km from Rome to Kirkenes, has been attracting visitors for more than 450 years.

The E6 follows the southern shores of Langfjorden to the headland at **Toften**, where the Germans built more gun batteries, before running south along the western bank of Altafjorden to Talvik. This area is famous as the home of the rare poppy Papaver lapponium. The next settlement is **Kåfjord** where a British company mined copper for most of the last century. The settlement is at the head of an arm of Altafjorden and was used by the Germans to hide their battleship, the *Tirpitz*. To the north is **Lille Haldde** where the world's first observatory to study the Northern Lights was built. Some of the original buildings have been restored.

The E6 then rounds the head of the fjord and arrives at **Alta**, Finnmark's largest town although it does not have official municipal status. There is an airport at Alta with direct flights to Oslo.

The area was first settled during the Stone Age about 7000BC and the archaeological excavations of this Komsa culture can be seen from the Komsafjellet. They were discovered in 1929 and the site is the oldest known settlement in Norway. A former whaling town, the main industry is now quarrying and there is a museum at the foot of the mountain which shows how slate is mined. It also has interesting displays on fishing and Sami handicrafts. The Alta is considered by many as the world's best salmon fishing river and it attracts anglers from around the globe, although a special permit is required to fish it.

You must visit the rock carvings at **Hjemmeluft** — the most extensive in northern Europe — and **Amtmannsnes**, both well sign posted, and the neighbouring town of **Bossekop** which gets its name because it was a Dutch trading post in the sixteenth century. During the winter months Lapp markets are held there.

Another detour is to **Savtso**, the deepest canyon in northern Europe. Take highway 93 south out of Alta and after about 8km turn left on to the old road at Tangen. The road is rough but the scenery is beautiful. Follow the road past the mountain hut at Gargia and then you follow the path to the canyon. In places the canyon is almost 600m deep. If you want to continue south, the old road rejoins highway 93 at Suolovuobme. About 18km further on you come to **Masi**, a Lapp community with a fine church, in the heart of excellent walking, fishing and canoeing country.

If you take this route south on highway 93 through Finnmarksvidda you arrive at the Lapp centre of **Kautokeino** travelling along 'The Lapp Road'. The town is the chief Lapp winter camp in Norway and a massive reindeer market is held every year during the spring and autumn. The Sami museum is excellent (check opening times with the local tourist office). It is the largest Sami municipality and a centre for Sami education.

If you turn left on highway 92 you arrive in **Karasjok**, a Lapp town 18km from the Finnish border. There is a Sami museum with many fine old buildings, and a library containing the world's largest collection of books on the Samis and their culture. The church dates from 1807 and is the oldest in Finnmark, and there is plenty of summer accommodation. On both routes you are likely to meet Lapps tending their reindeer herds. Because your travel options are limited on this route, it is better to stick to the E6 from Alta before detouring to visit Hammerfest and the North Cape and then switching to highway 98 for Kirkenes, so that on the return journey you can use the E6 which runs close to the Finnish border back to Karasjok from where you can take highways 92 and 93 back to Alta.

If you head north out of Alta on the E6 the road runs through Stokkedalen and then Sennalandet. This a vast desolate plateau rising to 385m before slowly dropping down past a Lapp chapel (Finnemisjonens kapell) on your left to **Skaidi**, the centre of another very important salmon fishing area. Along the way there are a number of Lapp summer camps.

At Skaidi you can detour off on highway 94 to visit Hammerfest. The road goes through Repparfjorddalen and then follows the southern shores of Repparfjord to Kvalsund and then over the longest suspension bridge in Norway whose 715m span crosses Kvalsundet to the island of Kvaløya. Just after crossing the bridge there is a small road on the right leading to

Stallogargo close to a huge stone column once used by the Lapps as a sacrificial place.

Highway 94 heads west for a few kilometres along the fjord giving you wonderful views of Nordmannsjøkelen and Seilandsjøkelen on the neigh- bouring island of Seiland.

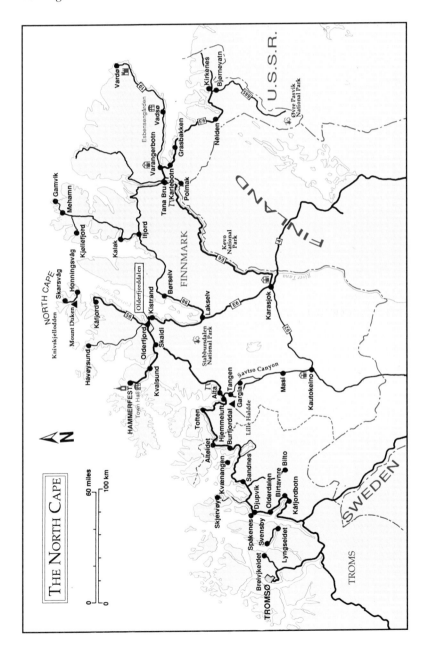

The road is not too good in places but quite passable. There are wild reindeer and elk on the island and you may be lucky to spot them although they tend to keep out of sight. Highway 94 then swings north following the coast past Tyven on the right and then through Rypefjord into Hammerfest.

Hammerfest is the world's northernmost town, and gets its name from *feste* which means a mooring place, and *hammer* a steep cliff. The harbour nestles under the massive mountain wall behind and was for centuries regarded as the best ice-free harbour in northern waters, although it has suffered at the hands of ferocious storms over the centuries.

In February 1825 many houses and boats were smashed by a hurricane, but the worst winter storms were experienced in 1882 when the whole coastline from Troms to Varanger was devastated, with Hammerfest worst hit of all.

The town was rebuilt and in 1890 work started on a hydroelectric station for power but on the night of 21 July fire swept through Hammerfest and two thirds of the town was destroyed. Undeterred, the houses were rebuilt and the power station opened, and in 1892 Hammerfest became the first town in Europe to have electric domestic and street lighting.

Hammerfest developed as a port because of its proximity to USSR and the desire of the Danish-Norwegian government to increase trade with its eastern neighbour. Ships from all over the world used the port in transit to the north Soviet ports. It was also the base for hunting expeditions into the Arctic and from about 1820 for more than 100 years, it was Norway's most important hunting and fishing town.

Hammerfest was occupied by the Germans during World War II and the port converted into a U-boat base. The German battleship *Tirpitz* hid out in nearby Kåfjord while the *Scharnhorst* anchored in Langfjord. When the Germans retreated in the winter of 1944-5 they fired the town and every building, except the chapel in the churchyard, was destroyed.

Today Hammerfest is Norway's main trawler port. Fishing is the major industry although it is an import supply base for the Arctic oil fields, and tourism is becoming increasingly important as well.

The town nestles around the harbour and has good air, sea and bus connections with the rest of the country, more than 600 hotel beds, pubs, cafés and restaurants and discos. It enjoys permanent daylight from 17 May to 28 July, and total darkness from 22 November to 21 January.

Things to see include the new Hammerfest church with its stained glass windows consecrated in 1961. Its form is inspired by the traditional wooden fish drying racks. Hammerfest has had five churches in its history, the first four were destroyed by fire although articles from each have been saved and are kept in the new building, including an altar piece from the first church built in 1623. The Catholic church, the most northerly in the world, was built in 1885 and rebuilt in 1957 after being destroyed during the war. The Town Hall is also the headquarters of the Royal and Ancient Society of Polar Bears and you can join only by personally calling at the office. The skin of the largest polar bear ever shot is also on show in the town hall.

Also of interest is the fountain with its group of figures Mother and Children, presented to the town by the former USA Ambassador to Norway Charles Ulrick Bay, whose mother was born in Hammerfest. The Meridian Column (Meridianstøtten) was built on the Fuglen peninsula to commemorate a 33 year-long survey by a combined Norwegian, Swedish and Russian team of scientists to determine the exact shape and size of the world. The column is capped by a large bronze globe.

It is worth driving up to the summit of Salen on the fringe of the town for the views. You drive along the zig zag road. The road was the idea of the Bishop's curate Simonsen who wanted to build a road through the Salsfjellet mountains. The money was raised by a lottery organised by the women of the town during the winter of 1892-3. Close to the summit stands the beacon built by the young people of the town during the same winter because there was little else to do. The Germans destroyed it but it was rebuilt in 1983-4 partly with funds donated by West Germany. On the southern outskirts of town stands the Mid Day Pole, erected at the end of the last century. The pole is capped by a cannon ball fired when two English warships attacked the town in 1809 during the Napoleonic Wars. The following year the battery at Skansen was built on the headland at Fuglenes but it never saw action. When the shadow from the pole points directly to the Meridian Column it is 12noon.

The Music Pavilion in the park, opposite the stone monument to composer Ole Olsen, was erected as part of the town's bicentenary celebration. In the winter the gardens of Hammerfest prove a great attraction for the wild reindeer foraging for food.

You have to retrace your route from Hammerfest along highway 94 to Skaidi where you rejoin the E6 and cross the Porsanger peninsula to Olderfjord. The road climbs up to a high point of 240m with Stuora Hatteras on your left before running through Olderfjorddalen to the sea.

At **Olderfjord** you can take a side tour on highway 889 to the fishing village of Slotten and then to Skavvik where you can catch a ferry or drive to **Havøysund**, which boasts the most northerly fishing cabins in the world. Alternatively you can follow highway 95 from Smørfjord through the 3km long Skarvberget tunnel to Kåfjord where you catch the car ferry (about 45 minutes) for the very busy fishing port of Honningsvåg on the island of Magerøy, before going on to the North Cape.

Honningsvåg is one of Norway's busiest ports and every year it is visited by thousands of foreign trawlers. It was completely destroyed when the occupying German troops pulled out in 1944. There is a passenger ferry to Honningsvåg which takes about 20 minutes and if there is a long queue for the car ferry, it is worth taking the passenger ferry and then catching one of the many buses for the 34km trip to the North Cape. There are also many boat trips from Honningsvåg around the North Cape.

The **North Cape** was named by Richard Chancellor, an English explorer who was searching for the North East Passage to China in 1553. The North Cape Hall has a restaurant with fantastic views, and the world's most northern champagne bar. It also houses a post office where you get your letters stamped. The building is housed in a cave blasted out of the rock and there are windows in the cliffs allowing you to look out over the Arctic Ocean. If visibility is poor there is even a cinema showing what the views would be like if the weather was better. Louis Philippe of Orleans who visited the North Cape in 1795, donated a statue of himself to be placed looking out to sea. The original disappeared during World War II and the present statue is a copy.

The Cape is very desolate and the elation you feel is in actually reaching it,

rather than the place itself. Camping at the Cape is not allowed but there is a campsite near Nordmannset (☎ 08475113). Although the North Cape is billed as the most northerly point in Europe, you have to walk if you want to reach the actual most northerly point, which is **Knivskjellodden**, to the west of North Cape on the other side of Sandfjorden.

On the way back take a look at the strange white **Mount Duken** on the left hand side of the road near Magerøy. Its outer rock surface is chalk and the mountain looks like it has been covered in a giant tablecloth — *duken* is Norwegian for cloth. You can take a small detour to the very picturesque **Skarsvåg**, the world's most northerly fishing village.

Having retraced your steps to Olderfjord, a popular tourist spot on the shore of Porsangenfjord with plenty of accommodation, the E6 heads south through **Kistrand** to **Lakselv** at the head of Porsangenfjord. Lakselv is a port and fishing harbour with a small airport with regular flights to Oslo and Kirkenes. The E6 now heads south through an area of woodland and lakes but becomes boggy and much bleaker as you approach Karasjok close to the Finnish border, but this route switches to highway 98 and continues east to Kirkenes, returning to Lakselv via the E6.

Highway 98 runs north along the eastern bank of Porsangen to **Børselv**, a Finnish speaking fishing village and a reminder of the massive Finnish influx in the eighteenth and nineteenth centuries, and then heads inland climbing through the Børselvdalen and past the Silfarfossen — the second largest canyon in northern Europe — up on to the windswept Børsfjell plateau. The road crosses the plateau rising to 190m where there is a summer Lapp camp, and passes between many peaks. The mountains are steeper to the south and there are plenty of signs of reindeer husbandry.

The road drops down to Laksefjorden and follows the head of the fjord round to Ifjord where route 88 heads north. A new road is under construction and due to be opened in 1991 linking Kalak and the villages of Kjøllefjord, Mehamn and Gamvik.

The whole Ifjord region is noted for its fine salmon rivers. Highway 98 continues eastwards across the plateau, and past Ifjordfjellet to Rustefjelbma on the wide River Tana which flows into Tanafjorden to the north.

The road then drops south the 31km to Tana Bru, an important crossing point linking east and west Finnmark. The Tana is Norway's third longest river, running more than 325km and one of the country's richest for salmon. It holds the world record for the largest rod caught salmon which weighed in at 36kg. This is a popular area because you can explore both sides of the river easily without having to make massive detours. There is plenty of accommodation in the area including campsites and cabins to rent.

Having crossed the suspension bridge over the river, the road divides. Highway 890 runs north through the very rugged and desolate mountain plateau of Varanger to the fishing villages of Berlevåg and Båtsfjord while the

Previous page   (Top left) Hammerfest church; (Bottom left) A sleigh ride with a difference, Finnmark; (Top right) The North Cape at 1pm; (Bottom right) A summer day in Norway's northernmost community, the fishing village Skarsvåg, North Cape.

E6 runs for about 4km to a road junction before heading east along the
southern shores of Varangerfjorden. At this junction highway 895 continues
to run south of the Tana as far as Polmak with its church dating from around
1850 on the border and then on into Finland.

At **Varangerbotn**, with its open-air Lapp museum, highway 98 follows the
northern shores of Varangerfjorden to **Vadsø**, the capital of Finnmark, where
there is an interesting open-air museum containing Finnish architecture and
the Esbensengården, a nobleman's house built about 1840 and the only one of
its kind in Finnmark. The modern 'Arctic' church was built in 1958 and the two
towers outside the front entrance have been built to resemble huge blocks of
ice. Their real purpose is to shelter the congregation by blocking the wind. The
road then takes you through Kiberg to the fortified town of **Vardø**, Norway's
most easterly town. It was given municipal status in 1789 but was mostly
destroyed during World War II. A 2.8km long underwater tunnel connects the
town with the mainland. It was the first of its kind built in Norway and is 88m
below sea level at its deepest point. The fortress — the most northerly in the
world — was built in the 1730s with four bastions. It was the third on the site,
the first having been built around 1300, and the second about 120 years later.
There is a district museum and the nearby bird island of Hornøya is Norway's
most easterly point.

Vardø was the scene of Norway's worst witch hunt and between 1621 and
1692 eighty women were found guilty and burned there. The women were
supposed to have met the devil on the Domen Mountain. During the Middle
Ages this most northerly region — Ultima Thule — was thought to be the
empire of the Devil. The tourist office is inside the only hotel, Norten Hotel
Barents.

Just south of Varangerbotn on the E6 you come to **Karlebotn** where a large
Stone Age settlement with almost 100 huts has been discovered along the
shores of the fjord. There is a similar but smaller settlement at **Grasbakken**,
14km further along. Just after Gandvik there is a turning off to the left which
will take you to the fishing village of Bugøynes on the southern headland of
Varangerfjorden. The E6 continues south heading for the Soviet border with
glorious views out over Varangerfjorden and the islands to the left with
Kirkenes in the distance.

At **Neiden** there is Norway's only Greek Orthodox chapel built in the
sixteenth century. It has not been used for services since 1917 but you can look
inside by borrowing the key from the nearby huts. Just south of the village is
the Skoltefoss. There is a small road from Neiden which runs deep into
Finland past the massive Lake Inari while the E6 skirts round Munkfjorden
and into **Kirkenes**, a mining town on the border with the Soviet Union. The
mine at Bjørnevatn is the largest in Norway and the ore is shipped by rail to
Kirkenes where it is smelted or exported. From Tromsø to Kirkenes the
distance is 850km.

At the turn of the century the town had mainly a Sami population but this
has mixed with immigrants from around the globe as the smelting works and
port facilities expanded. The town was bombed by the Germans on several
occasions during World War II and completely destroyed in 1944. Interesting
detours are to take highway 885 south along the border to Nyrud from where
you can explore the Øvre Pasvik National Park. The road passes close to the

border and at Skoltevatn you can look out over the Soviet village of Nikkel and the tundra beyond.

You can also take highway 886 east to Bjørnstad and then take the small road north to the village of Grense Jakobselv where the protestant King Oscar II built a chapel in 1896 on the frontier.

From Kirkenes you have to return along the E6 to Tana Bru. Then you can either take highway 98 to Lakselv, or return by the E6 which follows the border — close to Finland's Kevo National Park — to Karasjok and then swings north to Lakselv. Another alternative is to take highway 92 from Karasjok and cross Finnmarksvidda on highway 93 which heads north into Alta where you again pick up the E6 for the long journey south.

Additional Information

Places of Interest

Hammerfest
Royal and Ancient Society of Polar Bears
Town Hall
Open: Monday to Friday 8am-6pm,
Saturday and Sunday 10am-3pm.

Hjemmeluft (rock carvings)
Open: mid-June to mid-August 8am-8pm.

Karasjok
Sami Museum
Open: daily June to August 9am-6pm.
Rest of year Monday to Friday 9am-3pm, weekends 10am-3pm.

Useful Addresses

Regional Tourist Boards

Finnmark Tourist Board
Postboks 1223, N-9501 Alta
☎ (084) 35 444

Troms Reiser
Storgt 63, PO Box 1077
N-9001 Tromsø
☎ (083) 10000

Skaidi ☎ (084) 16280

Tana Bru ☎ (085) 28281

Local Tourist Offices

Offices marked with an asterix* are staffed during the summer only.

Alta Reiselivslag*
Boks 91 Bossekop
N-9501 Alta
☎ (084) 35 041

Hammerfest og Omegns
Reiselivsforening
Postboks 226
N-9601 Hammerfest
☎ (084) 12 185

Kautokeino Turistinformasjon*
N-9950 Kautokeino
☎ (084) 56 203

Lakselv Reiselivslag
N-9700 Lakselv
☎ (084) 61 644

North Cape:
Nordkapp Reiselivslag
Postboks 34
N-9750 Honningsvåg
☎ (084) 72 894

Reisetrafikklaget for Valdres og Jotunheimen
Rådhuset
N-2900 Fagernes
☎ (063) 60 400

13

SVALBARD

Svalbard is a high Arctic archipelago, 657km north of the most northerly point on the Norwegian mainland. It is situated between 74° and 81° latitude north and between 10° and 35° longitude east, and consists of number of islands — Spitsbergen, Nordaustlandet, Edgeøya, Barentsøya, Kong Karls Land, Kvitøya, Hopen and Bjørnøya.

The archipelago covers more than 61,700sq km of which Spitsbergen accounts for more than half, extending to just over 39,000sq km.

The islands consist mainly of mountains and steep sided fjords and valleys although there are some wide lowland plains. Almost two thirds of the land is covered with glaciers which break up on and release icebergs when they reach the sea.

During the thaw there is water everywhere and the rivers are constantly changing course. The rivers reach flood levels and their lower reaches form flatlands which create large deltas out into the fjords. In the winter many of the river beds are dry. The fjords are mostly on the western coasts. Isfjorden on Spitsbergen is the one most widely used by shipping because of its many tributaries. Many of the fjords are very scenic, especially Kongsfjorden and Magdalenefjorden. The longest is Wijdefjorden which runs 120km inland. The massive Storfjorden, which separates Spitsbergen from Edgeøya and Barentsøya is often full of ice. The highest peaks, Newtonoppen and Perriertoppen, (both 1,717m) are in the north-eastern part of Spitsbergen.

The islands offer the outdoor adventure holiday of a lifetime for those experienced in mountain, snow and ice terrains, and even if you do not want to explore, a flying visit is highly recommended to see at first hand how communities exist in such a remote and often harsh environment.

The Norwegian authorities issue detailed information for people planning extended trips to Svalbard which includes invaluable advice. All general enquiries to the Ministry of Justice, The Polar Department, Postboks 8005, N-0030 Oslo 1.

History

The Dutch seafarer Willem Barents 'discovered' Svalbard in 1596 and called the islands Spitsbergen, although there are references in the sagas to the islands of Svalbard. In 1194 there is a record of 'the country with the cold coasts which had been discovered by the Vikings', and another that reported that the distance from Iceland 'to the country north of Havsbotn was four days' sailing'. The Vikings believed the archipelago was a continuation of Greenland and archaeological digs have unearthed evidence that indicates the islands may have been inhabited as far back as the Stone Age.

Following its re-discovery at the end of the sixteenth century, the archipelago became the centre for a massive whale hunting operation led by the Dutch and British but with countries throughout Europe cashing in. The Greenland whale was driven away from its traditional grounds close to the fjords but whale hunting continued out to sea for more than 200 years until all the whale populations in Svalbard waters had been exterminated.

Different nations maintained settlements on the islands during the whaling season and there was constant fighting between them. The Danish king claimed sovereignty because it was still assumed the islands were part of Greenland and he tried to get the foreign nations operating there to pay dues.

When the whale hunting ended most of the settlements closed down and by the early eighteenth century the population largely consisted of Russians sent from the monasteries on the Russian Arctic Ocean coast to hunt, trap for furs and gather eggs. The life was harsh and settlements lasted only 20 years or so.

By the end of the eighteenth century Norwegians started sealing on Svalbard and this reached its peak at the end of the nineteenth century. The island's fortunes turned at the beginning of this century when coal was discovered.

The Norwegians, Russians, Germans, British, Americans and Dutch all disputed land rights but at the Treaty of Svalbard in 1920 Norway was granted sole sovereignty, although this was not recognised by Germany until 1925 and the Soviet Union until 1935.

During World War II hostilities broke out on the island and in 1941 the mining population was evacuated by the British, who also destroyed the power supplies and radio station. Spitsbergen was subsequently occupied by the Germans but they were driven out by a combined Norwegian-British force. In 1943 the mining settlements were destroyed by bombardment from a large fleet of German warships.

Today mining is still the major industry, although seal hunting and sea fishing are still important. There are two Soviet mining communities — at Barentsburg and Pyramiden — with their own consulate. The Norwegian and Soviet mining operations extract about 900,000 tons of coal annually. There has been a lot of exploration for oil but no finds of any commercial value have yet been made. Tourism has been on the increase but lack of accommodation hinders this. Most of the tourists come on the cruise ships and many go on walking tours.

Svalbard is administered by a governor, the *sysselman*, who is responsible to the Polar Department under the Norwegian Ministry of Justice, because he also acts as commissioner of police, magistrate and public notary.

Geology

Svalbard is a protrusion of the continental shelf in the Barents Sea. For almost all its existence it has lain submerged in the sea subject to a continuous process of sedimentation. The large number of fossils trapped in the sedimentary strata makes it geologically very interesting because it provides an easy-to-follow diary of the world's evolution. Between Randfjorden, Wijdefjorden and Isfjorden there are massive stratified formations of red sandstone and schists containing fossils of primitive fish and other forms of marine life from the early Silurian and Devonian periods. These are overlaid with continental sediments, mostly sandstone and shale, containing fossils and a coal layer from the Lower Carboniferous period, followed by marine limestones and siliceous rock types with many fossils from the Upper Carboniferous and Permian times. Above these are Triassic and Jurassic strata of mainly marine shale and marl slates full of fossils of bivalves, ammonites, fish and early lizard-like reptiles. The geological layers continue to build up with the coal deposits being laid during the early Tertiary period.

On a number of occasions these strata have been subject to enormous pressures which produced the mountain chains. The most important period for this was between 400 and 500 million years ago, during the Caledonian orogenesis, when granite magmas were thrust up from deep in the earth's core. Land movements have also resulted in a large number of fissure zones, running north to south. A volcanic eruption about 5,000 years ago occurred among the most westerly fissure zones and pools of warm springs that still exist today are a reminder of this violent activity.

Climate

An arm of the Gulf Stream flows northwards off the west coast of Spitsbergen which leaves a wide opening in the sea ice even in winter. Another arm flows into the Barents Sea and this coupled with a lot of cyclonic activity results in Svalbard having a milder climate than its northern situation would indicate.

On the west coast of Spitsbergen the average temperature during February and March, the two coldest months, is between -8°C and -16°C with temperatures below -30°C—quite rare, although frequently recorded on the mainland far to the south. The hottest month is July when the temperatures on the west coast range between 1°C and 10°C, with an average of about 5°C. The highest temperature recorded is 17°C. Precipitation is between 300 and 400mm.

The interior has a more continental climate, about 2°C to 3°C colder in the winter and 1°C to 2°C warmer in the summer. The lowest temperature recorded is -40°C and the hottest 18°C. There is less precipitation but more wind.

The climate has warmed since the beginning of the century and new vegetation on the mountain sides shows that the glaciers have diminished in recent times. Experience shows, however, that the glaciers could suddenly start to move forward again and rates of progress of 30m to 40m a day are possible if conditions change.

In the summer there is a lot of fog. In Longyearbyen the Midnight Sun is visible from 21 April to 21 August, and the sunless period lasts from 28 October to 14 February.

Ice conditions

There are three sorts of ice in the sea and fjords of Svalbard. **Calved ice** consists of icebergs which break away from the glaciers as they hit the sea. They usually melt before they become a danger to shipping. **Winter ice** forms in the fjords and sea. It is rarely more than $1^1/_2$m thick and breaks up around May to June except in enclosed fjord arms. **Drift ice** comes up from the north-east all through the year and in bad years can prove a threat to shipping.

Plant and Animal Life

Vegetation is sparse because of the climate. There are about 170 indigenous species of plants and a few others that have been introduced by man. There are no trees or large bushes except for dwarf birches. Due to the cold current from the north-east, vegetation is much sparser in the eastern part of the archipelago than the west. Vegetation is rich beneath the bird colonies with carpets of moss, flowers and grass.

The only three land mammals are reindeer, polar bear and polar fox. The reindeer had almost been exterminated at the beginning of this century but there are now more than 10,000. The Svalbard reindeer is smaller than its mainland relative with shorter legs and a more shaggy coat. The polar fox is very common but thrives best around the bird colonies. The polar bear stock is estimated at between 1,500 and 2,000, mostly in the east and north-east. The musk ox was introduced from Greenland in 1929 and thrived initially but

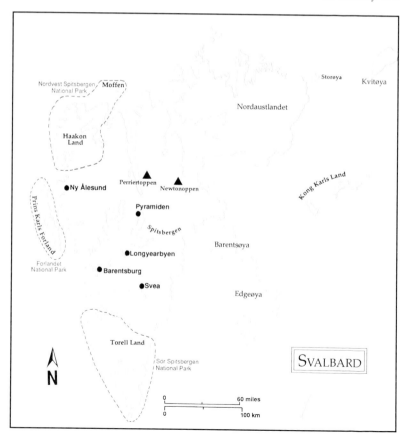

stocks have declined rapidly and it is now very scarce. Marine mammals include ringed and bearded seal, walrus, and white whale.

Bird life is prolific in the summer but only ptarmigan winter on the islands. There are 109 bird species recorded of which 30 breed regularly, mostly gulls, auks, duck, geese and waders. The largest bird cliffs are on Bjørnøya and along the west coast of Spitsbergen. Most numerous species are little auk, Arctic guillemot, kittiwake, Arctic petrel, puffin and black guillemot. The eider duck is common everywhere and there are large numbers of barnacle and pink-footed geese.

Only one species of fish, the char, is found in the rivers and streams, but the seas are rich in fish, especially cod, capelin, haddock, Greenland halibut and redfish. There are also considerable quantities of shrimp.

The whole of Svalbard is covered by a nature conservation scheme and there are fifteen bird reserves along the west coast of Spitsbergen, two nature reserves, and three national parks — South Spitsbergen, Forlandet and north-west Spitsbergen. More than 27,000sq km of the Svalbard area is protected against technological encroachment, pollution, traffic, hunting and fishing.

Settlements

Longyearbyen, a mining community containing the administrative centre for Svalbard, Svalbard airport and Svalbard radio, with about 1,100 inhabitants. There is a bank, post office, telegraph and telephone office, and church. This is where the governor has his office. Some supplies of oil, paraffin, methylated spirit, petrol and other kinds of fuel can be obtained in Longyearbyen.

Ny Ålesund is a small community, formerly a Norwegian mining centre. Today it is the most important scientific research station run by the Norwegian Polar Institute. This settlement has a small landing strip, and postal and telegraph service.

Svea, a Norwegian mining community where coal mining and exploratory mining for coal are carried out. Small landing strip and postal service.

Isfjord Radio, a radio and weather station on Cape Linne with postal service.

Hopen, a radio and weather station.

Bjørnøya (Bear Island), a radio and weather station.

Barentsburg, a Soviet mining community. The headquarters of Soviet activity on Svalbard with Soviet consulate and helicopter landing pads.

Pyramiden, a Russian mining camp with about 1,000 inhabitants.

Additional Information

On arrival all equipment is checked by the local authorities. If it is not considered adequate, admission will be refused. The authorities will also require details about your planned routes so that a rescue can be launched if you are overdue. The weather can hinder rescue attempts and it is essential to have good equipment, emergency provisions, signal light etc.

Svalbard is an arctic area with a specially vulnerable natural environment which needs protecting. Visitors are urged to make themselves familiar with the environmental conservation regulations and be conservation-minded at all times when travelling in Svalbard.

The Ministry of Environment, Post Box 8013 Dep, Oslo 1, issues a pamphlet which lists all the regulations. The aim is to protect terrain, flora and fauna and prevent pollution. All historical sites are protected and it is prohibited to remove or damage historical remains. Any finds should be reported to the governor (see p221 for the telephone number).

It is little use burying refuse because the frost pushes it up again. Burn as much as possible and take the rest with you.

The weather on the islands is subject to swift changes. Visitors who have not reserved accommodation must have suitable equipment for camping out. There are no hotels open to the public in Svalbard, and no supplies of provisions are available. What you need you have to take with you.

Accommodation and Food

There is a campsite with washing facilities and toilets near the airport and about 8km outside Longyearbyen. Camping elsewhere around the settlement is forbidden. There is also a campsite near Ny Ålesund but it has no facilities.

Spi Tra arranges nearly all the accommodation for visitors, administrating rooms of varying standards. To book a room telephone Spitsbergen Travel ☎ (080) 21 811.

There are guest houses in Barentsberg and Pyramiden, and are run by Trust Arktikugol. To book overnight accommodation in the Soviet Settlements contact the Spitsbergen Travel Agency. Private and publicly owned cabins are all over Svalbard. In emergencies the publicly owned cabins can be used but they are sometimes lent to residents of Svalbard. The cabins cannot be used for overnight accommodation.

Lufthavnhotellet is close to the airport but is usually reserved for civil servants and other people on special missions to the island. No food is available here, except at the airport café which is open in connection with most arrivals and departures.

Tourists can buy basic meals at the Busen café as well as tax free cigarettes and alcohol. If you need special light weight food for excursions, check in advance whether this can be bought locally at Proviantlageret (provisions store) at Longyearbyen.

Communications

From June to August there is a weekly sailing to Svalbard from Honningsvåg to Longyearbyen and Ny Ålesund and back via Tromsø. SAS operates flights from Tromsø to Svalbard airport up to twice a week between mid-April to mid-September and up to three times a week during the summer. The Russian airline Aeroflot has a monthly flight from Moscow via Murmansk. A number of cruise ships also visit the island.

Internal traffic is primitive. The Soviets have landing facilities for helicopters which is their main form of transport. Occasionally light aircraft can be hired from Longyearbyen to fly to Ny Ålesund, which has an 800m landing strip, or to Svea, which has an even shorter runway. It is possible to find a taxi in Longyearbyen but there are no roads outside the settlements. You can hire transport locally. Tour operators arrange boat trips during summer. For details contact Spitshergen Reisebyrå (Spittshergen Travel Agency).

Further Reading

A list of publications on Svalbard may be obtained from:

The Norwegian Polar Research Institute
Rolfstangvn 12
PO Box 158
N-1330 Oslo Lufthaven

The Fridtjof Nansen Institute at Polhøgda
Fridtjof Nansens vei 17
N-1324 Lysaker

Maps

The Norwegian Polar Institute prepares maps of Svalbard which can be bought from the following places:-

Norsk Kartverk
N-3500 Hønefoss

The Norwegian Polar Research Institute
9170 Longyearbyen, or
Rofstangyn 12
PO Box 158
N-1330 Oslo Lufthavn

The Norwegian Tourist Association
Stortingsgt 28
N-0161 Oslo 1

The Svalbard Museum
9170 Longyearbyen

The Svalbard Shop
9170 Longyearbyen

Radios

The use of a radio transmitter, receiver or walkie-talkie requires a licence which can be obtained by applying to the: Norwegian Telecommunications Administration, Postboks 6701, St Olavs Pass, N-0130, Oslo 1.

Time Zones

Svalbard follows Norwegian time, which is 1 hour ahead of GMT. The Soviet communities, however, follow Moscow time, which is 3 hours ahead of GMT.

Useful Telephone Numbers

Svalbard is connected to the direct dialling system. The district code is 080.

A/S Lufttransport
☎ 21160

Braathens SAFE
☎ 21922

Governor's Office ☎ 21400
  - duty telephone ☎ 21222
  - mobile telephone ☎ 21855

Kailageret (Wharf warehouse)
☎ 21300

Lufthavnhotellet (Airport hotel)
(Civil Aviation Administration)
☎ 21305

Nordic Restaurant/café
☎ 21275

Post office
☎ 21604

Resepsjonen
(Reception — room booking)
☎ 21811

SAS ☎ 21650

Sparebanken (Bank)
☎ 21801

Spitsbergen Travel, administration
☎ 2300

Spitsbergen Travel Agency
☎ 21160

Store Norske Spitsbergen
Kulkompani A/S
☎ 21300

Svalbardposten (newspaper)	Svalbard Næringsutvikling A/S
☎ 21200	☎ 21300
Svalbard Museum	Taxi
☎ 21384	☎ 21375
Svalbard Samfunnsdrift A/S	Rental vans
☎ 21300	☎ 21573

WARNING. Polar bears prefer to frequent the eastern and northern areas during the summer but stray bears may be encountered on the west coast during the warmer months. They are likely to be hungry and very dangerous. Keep a safe distance from them.

Do not encourage a bear by leaving out food. A polar bear will attack without warning. Deposit refuse at least 100m from your dwelling or tent and ideally in a straight line from the tent door so that you can spot a prowling bear in good time.

Rabies: Svalbard is a rabies-infested area so avoid all contact with wild animals. If bitten, thoroughly cleanse the wound immediately and seek urgent medical help. Vaccine against rabies is available at all times from the hospital in Longyearbyen.

The last two warnings should in no way deter you from travelling to Svalbard if you have time. Attacks by polar bears are very rare as are bites from rabid animals. Svalbard does, however, offer you a chance to visit the most remote and most exciting outpost in Europe.

To explore the islands you must be properly equipped

14

THE HURTIGRUTEN ROUTE NORTH

This is perhaps the best way of seeing the west and north of Norway and is certainly an option to be considered if you have plenty of time. The coastal steamers run round the coast from Bergen to Kirkenes in the far north close to the Soviet border. The timetables are arranged so that you have time ashore before the boat sails again but if that is not enough you can find accommodation and explore until you want to move on. The ferries take the 'inner passage' along the coast sheltered for the most part by the thousands of islands between them and the open sea.

You can island hop by ferry from Stavanger if you like but the famous coastal steamers, the *Hurtigruten* sail from Bergen and this is where the real cruise through the western fjords and islands begins. The ships sail daily and the latest editions to the fleet can carry up to forty cars so you could always sail north and drive back. The round trip to Kirkenes and back of more than 3,800km, takes 11 days and all the ships have berths and round the clock cafeterias.

The round trip fare includes berths, meals and service. These are not cruise liners but working ships delivering mail and packages. The standard on board is quite acceptable, however, the food good and the crew friendly. On summer sailings a tour guide accompanies the ship and arranges shore excursions. There are 11 steamships operating the route — *Finnmarken, Harald Jarl, Vesterålen, Nordnorge, Polarlys, Nordstjernen, Ragnvald Jarl, Midnatsol, Lofoten, Kong Olav* and *Narvik*.

From Bergen the northbound route takes in Florø, Måløy, Torvik, Ålesund, Molde, Kristiansund, Trondheim, Rørvik, Brønnøysund, Sandnessjøen, Nesna, Ørnes, Bodø, Stamsund, Svolvær, Stokmarknes, Sortland, Risøy-hamm, Harstad, Finnsnes, Tromsø, Skjervøy, Øksfjord, Alta, Hammerfest, Havøysund, Honningsvåg, Kjøllefjord, Mehamn, Gamvik, Berlevåg, Båtsfjord, Vardø, Vadsø and Kirkenes. The ships retrace the same route back to Bergen.

The journey takes in the most westerly, northerly and easterly points of Norway, much of it is inside the Arctic Circle and in the summer there are spectacular sights to be seen at any time of day or night because you are in the land of the Midnight Sun.

Along the way you will pass towering snow capped peaks, and glaciers, roaring rivers and waterfalls, flower-filled meadows and Arctic tundra. There are islands to explore with picturesque fishing villages and cities with medi-eval quarters and modern hotels, shops and restaurants.

Many of the places visited by the *Hurtigruten* have already been described in the various road routes, but there are many places that you can never see by car, and many isolated island communities that rely heavily on the steamers for their lifeline with the mainland.

As you leave **Bergen** (chapter 6) you steam through Hjeltefjorden with a myriad of small islands on both sides of the ship. You pass the island of Holsnøy on your right. As the ship heads into Fedjefjorden, you pass the Hellisøy light on the island of Fredje on the starboard side while ahead of you stands the island of Sula at the mouth of the magnificent 200km long Sognefjorden. The steamer skirts between the islands of Sula and Ytre Sula and you are now close to the most westerly point of Norway. The steamer continues north picking its way through the islands and past Åfjorden, Dalsfjorden and Førdefjorden to its first port of call at the neat shipbuilding town of **Florø**, Norway's most westerly borough and the only town in Sogn og Fjordane. The white-painted lighthouse built on the rocks is a beacon on a busy shipping route not only for vessels travelling the coast but for those sailing to Førde, about 70km from Florø at the head of Førdefjord.

The catamaran express from Bergen to Selje also calls at the port twice a day connecting with the many local boat services plying between the mainland and the scores of little islands. There is also a small airport linking the town and district with Oslo and Bergen.

Main attractions are the Central Coastal Museum (open daily but check times locally), the twelfth-century Roman style church on the neighbouring island of Kinn and the Svanøy Estate, which is known as the 'Pearl of the Sunnfjord'. The Ausevik rock carvings are also well worth visiting. They show hundreds of animals and hunting scenes dating from the Stone and Bronze Ages.

From Florø you sail north along the coast into Froysjøen and then across the mouth of Nordfjord. The huge mountain on the left which towers up out of the sea is Hornelen on the island of Bremangerlandet.

The Nordfjord stretches inland 100km from the West Cape to the village of Stryn. On the northern banks of the fjord lies Nordfjordeid, the largest equestrian centre in northern Europe where they specialise in breeding and training the famous fjord horses.

After crossing the fjord the steamer docks at the fishing village of **Måløy**, site of a famous British commando raid in December 1941. The waters along this stretch of coast are busy and can also be very treacherous in bad weather, especially around the Stadlandet peninsula and boats often used to run for shelter in the small fishing harbours at Selje and Vågsøy.

Travelling north the steamer swings out to sea to skirt the islands and then pops into the fishing village of Torvik before docking at the 'fishing capital' of **Ålesund** (chapter 9). The town is famous for its Art Nouveau architecture having been completely rebuilt after a devastating fire in 1904. As the steamer nears the town you pass a cluster of islands famous for their birdlife including the internationally recognised ornithological site of Rune. The islands play host to hundreds of thousands of sea birds.

You then set sail again cutting between the mainland and the islands for the 'rose town' of **Molde** (chapter 9) on the far side of the mouth of Romsdalsfjorden. This part of the country is Møre og Romsdal and eight large fjords dissect the county, the most impressive and famous of which is Geirangerfjorden.

From Molde the steamer heads out to sea again to swing round the islands into a channel of water known as the Hustadvika which leads to Kristiansund, the main port along this stretch of coast. As you near the port you can spot the famous Grip Lighthouse 14km out to sea on your left.

Grip used to be a thriving fishing village of 400 people on one of the scores of very small islands dotting this stretch of sea. There was even a medieval stave church. The area is noted for its ferocious storms and twice — (1640 and 1802) the island was completely inundated by the sea and only the church remained standing. People continued to live there round the year, however, until 1974 when the island was finally abandoned. It is now used only in the summer.

Kristiansund (chapter 9), often referred to as the 'Venice of the North', is the capital of Nordmøre province and a modern, bright port sprawling over three islands. Its prosperity was based on fishing and then the oil boom, but now that this is declining slightly, fishing is once again of major economic importance. The Varden Tower in the centre of town gives magnificent views out across the sea and provides a good focal point as you steam into port.

From Kristiansund the steamer cuts between the islands along a stretch of water called Trondheimsleia, and then crosses the headland by the Agdenes light into Trondheimsfjorden for **Trondheim** (chapter 10). Explore this bustling city with its magnificent cathedrals and old buildings, street markets and museums.

Shortly after sailing from Trondheim you pass **Munkholmen** which was the site of Norway's first monastery founded in 1028 and then the ship heads out to sea, past Austråt Castle at the mouth of the fjord on your right. The castle was the sixteenth-century home of Lady Inger, immortalised by Ibsen.

The steamers now follow the line of the coast squeezing through the narrow sound of Stokksund between the mainland and the island of Stokkøya, and then it negotiates the skerries which abound offshore.

Shortly after passing the Buholmråsa light at the mouth of Svefjord you enter a sea area known as Folda — one of the few stretches of open water on the trip — which takes you to Rørvik, the next port of call, in the Vikna island group.

Rørvik is a small fishing village standing at the entrance to the Nordland Channel, famous in mythology as the batteground between the giants and the trolls.

The ship sails between the mainland and the island of **Leka** and legend has it that the 422m high mountain is the petrified Leka Maiden. The second largest burial mound found in Norway was also discovered on Leka, and in the south-west corner there is the Solsem Cave with its Stone Age rock drawings.

The next port of call is **Brønnøysund**, a municipality made up of more than 2,050 islands. As you near the port you pass on the left the Torghatten mountain on the island of Torget. Although not that large, the mountain can be seen from a great distance because of a massive hole which was formed by the action of ice and waves before the mountain was heaved out of the sea. The hole is now 160m above sea level. This whole coastline was settled very early on and settlements dating back to the Stone Age have been found in limestone caves close to the town.

The next port of call is Sandnessjøen on the island of Alsten. Tjøtta to the south of the island used to be the centre of a huge farming estate consisting of

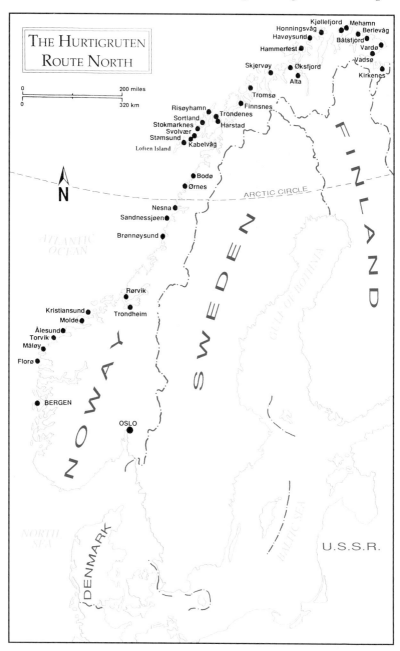

THE HURTIGRUTEN
ROUTE NORTH

0   200 miles
0   320 km

more than 250 farms. In 1929 it was bought by the Ministry of Agriculture as a sheep breeding station and it is still one of the largest farms in northern Norway. As you sail up the coast of the island you will spot a stone monument erected in memory of more than 7,500 Russians who died while prisoners of the Germans during World War II.

On the southern tip of **Alsten** is a medieval church at Alstahaug and then you pass a monument erected in the memory of the poet priest Petter Dass who lived on the island around the end of the seventeenth century. Inland you can see a series of tall mountains which are known as Sju Søstre. The steamers started to call at Sandnessjøen just before the end of the last century and it is has grown steadily since and is now a thriving port. You steam to Nesna at mouth of Ranafjord and then past Sjonafjord up the coast and between the islands to Melfjorden where you cross the Arctic Circle. Straddling the Arctic Circle is the island of Hestmona. A little further on you pass between the coast and the island of Rødøyløva, with its spectacular 440m high mountain of red serpentine.

Inland the snow capped peaks of the Svartisen glacier are clearly visible, especially **Snøtinden** (1,594m) and **Sniptinden** (1,591m). It is Norway's second largest glacier covering 370sq km and in places up to 100m thick. At the

A popular excursion is to take a trip down one of Norway's spectacular fjords such as this one, Geirangerfjord

head of Holandsfjorden it is only 20m above sea level, which also makes it the lowest lying glacier on mainland Europe. **Ørnes**, the next port of call is a delightful old trading port, dating back to 1794 and it nestles below Mount Spildra.

Bodø (chapter 11) is the next stop after passing the imposing Børvasstindan and then crossing the broad mouth of Saltfjorden. Bodø is the capital of the region and was very badly damaged by German bombing during World War II. The old trading centre of Kjerringøy, lying on the coast to the north is well preserved. The author Knut Hamsen lived here.

Bodø is also the gateway to the Lofoten Islands although to reach them you have to cross the Vestfjorden which is notorious for sudden storms. In the eighteenth century it took the mail boat 3 months to reach Bodø from Oslo and in the nineteenth century four mail boats were lost between 1803 and 1840.

In fair weather it takes about 3 hours to cross Vestfjorden to Stamsund on the island of Vestvågøy.

As you cross over from Bodø you should be able to see the islands of Røst and **Værøy** far out to sea on your left (chapter 11). The two islands play host to millions of sea birds. Here the waters crashing down from the Arctic Ocean are squeezed through a sound into Vestfjorden to produce the legendary maelstrom, known locally as the Moskenesstraumen. In the summer local fishermen offer cruises round the islands, but this depends on the weather. You can charter for a price. There is an even more violent maelstrom south of Bodø at Saltstraumen.

The Lofoten Islands and the Vesterålen chain are really worth exploring. The Lofoten range is made up of the world's oldest rock, reckoned to be almost 3.5 billion years old. At Andøya in Vesterålen is Norway's youngest visible rock, a mere 150 million years old, and is geologically very exciting because it contains many fossils of the early plant and animal life of the region. Norway's only coal seams are found here.

The Lofoten chain of more than eighty islands is a wall of jagged mountains which in places seems to rise sheer out of the fjord. It runs for more than 180km parallel to the coast and acts as a huge sea wall protecting the waters in between although in the winter these can still be very treacherous and rough.

Vestvågøy was certainly settled in the Stone Age and one of the largest houses from the Viking age was discovered by archaeologists at **Borg**. The house, possibly the home of the Lofoten chieftain Tore Hjort, measured 74m by 8m and contained many articles brought back from England and France. Several boat houses from the same period have also been found. **Vågen** on the north of the island was ranked equally with Bergen and Trondheim in the fourteenth century because of its lucrative fur trade with the Lapps.

Although not long, the fjords of the two island chains are very impressive. The cliff faces of the $2^1/_2$km long, 150m wide Trollfjord are so steep that the coastal steamers dare not sound their ships' horns for fear of starting a rockfall. Fishing is still the mainstay of the islands although the waters do not attract distant trawlers quite so much.

Stamsund is the major fishing village in the western Lofotens and has a hotel and summer youth hostel (☎ 088 89 166), and nearby at Hol there is the wreck of a Viking ship, but the steamer only docks here for a short time before heading for Svolvær on **Austvågøy. Henningsvær** is on the southern tip of the island, and now has the Lofotens largest fishing fleet. Towering behind it is Vågekallen. You then sail past **Kabelvåg**, the Lofotens oldest village where the first church was built in 1120. It used to be the largest fishing village as well and King Øystein had the first rorbuer built here in the early Middle Ages. The village is the site of the Lofoten Island Museum (open: summer Monday to Friday 9am-3pm, Saturday and Sunday 11am-3pm) which concentrates on the fishing activities of the islands over the centuries.

Svolvær is now the administrative centre for the eighteen fishing villages on the islands. It is now developing a reputation as a centre for arts because of its galleries and the number of artists who live there or who travel to paint the amazing mountain scenery. You can watch many of them at work in the Artists' House. It is open throughout the summer as a working studio, but it depends on which artists and craftsmen feel like working.

All the main islands of Lofoten are now linked by road bridges although boats are still needed to travel between the smaller skerries. Highway 19 wriggles its way through the islands of the Lofoten and Vesterålen chains all the way down to the tiny fishing village of Å. Along the way there are some marvellous beaches — especially at Flakstad and Ramberg — although the water may take a little getting used to, and some wonderful picturesque fishing villages such as Nusfjord where many of the houses date from the eighteenth century.

After Svolvær the steamer heads through the Raft sound for **Stokmarknes** on Langøya in the Vesterålen Islands. The small town is famous for its market which has been held for more than a century. It is also the headquarters of the steamship company which started the coastal service in 1881.

After a 2 hour stop over, the steamer continues along the southern shore of the island to **Sortland,** the capital of Vesterålen. There are bridges connecting Sortland with the main islands in the chain — Langøya, Hinnøya, Norway's largest island, and Andøya. Sortland is now a busy little fishing village and trading centre and its long history stretches back to the time of the sagas.

Europe's only whale safari takes place in Vesterålen every summer. There is usually a nursery of sperm whales off Andøya although many other species of whales can be spotted as well. To the west of Andøya lies the bird island of **Bleiksøya**. It is forbidden to land on the islands where the hundreds of thousands of arctic sea birds nest, but there are incredible close-up views from the boats.

Risøyhamn is the next port of call on Andøya and then the steamer takes the Toppsundet between the islands of Hinnøya and Grytøya with its impressive mountain of Nona, before docking in Harstad. The town grew quickly last century because of the rich herring fisheries and received municipal status in 1904. Fishing is still important but it has become a major supply centre, especially for foreign trawlers. It is also the base for oil exploration off the islands. The town hosts two important festivals each year, music and theatre in June and deep sea fishing in July. At **Trondenes** about $3^1/_2$ km north of the town, there is a lovely Gothic medieval church built in the mid-thirteenth century.

From Harstad the steamer heads out across Vågsfjord. Away to the left you might catch sight of the island of Bjarkøy, home of tens of thousands of eider ducks and a main source of eiderdown from Norway.

After steaming up Solbergfjorden you land at Finnsnes which is now linked by bridge to the island of Senja with its spectacular mountain scenery and dramatic Ånderdalen National Park. The steamer then negotiates Gisundfjorden before crossing Malangen and entering Balsfjorden for Tromsø, where you have a couple of hours or so to explore. **Tromsø** (chapter 11) is the main town along the northern coast and is in a lovely location on the fertile island of Tromsøya. The statue of Roald Amundsen on the harbour front is a permanent reminder of the many explorers who set sail from Tromsø.

The steamer then sail under the massive bridge linking Tromsø with the mainland and set a course for the Grøtsundet channel which runs between the mainland and the islands of Ringvassøy and Reinøy. The channel enters Ullsfjorden and if you look to the right you can see the magnificent peaks of the Lyngen range towering up to 1,833m.

The steamer skirts the mainland close to Lyngstuva and then crosses the mouth of Lyngenfjord for their next port of call — Skjervøy, where there have been settlements since Stone Age migrants first explored the area. The coastal steamers then head out along Kvænangen into a stretch of open sea called the Lopphavet. It gets its name from the small island of Loppa, which means the flea.

The small fishing village of **Øksfjord** is the next stop. Øksfjord faces the Øksfjordjøkelen, which towers to 1,204m. across the sound. The steamer then sails for Alta at the head of Altafjorden and then it is full steam ahead for Hammerfest. The steamers travel between the islands of Stjernøya and Seiland, with its imposing glaciers, to the east and Sørøya to the west before docking at Hammerfest on the island of Kvaløya.

Hammerfest (chapter 12) is the world's most northerly town although there is not much time to explore before the steamer heads out to sea again for **Havøysund** on the northerly tip of the Porsanger-halvøya peninsula. You approach this small fishing village by sailing through the Breisundet which separates the mainland and the bird island of Hjelmsøya. If the weather is good the steamers will sail around the North Cape to give you fantastic views of the 300m high cliffs, but if the weather is poor, the captain may take the ship through the Magerøy sound which separates Magerøya from the mainland, before docking in the fishing and shipping town of Honningsvåg, the largest community in west Finnmark.

The steamer then sails eastwards passing the broad mouth of Porsangerfjorden and the high rock face of Sværholtklubben, at the most northerly point of the Svaerholt-halvøya pensinsula. Huge colonies of birds, especially kittiwake, live on the rocks. The steamer then crosses the mouth of Laksefjord for the small fishing port of Kjøllefjord past the cliffs of Finnkirken.

The steamer has to round the headland of Nordkinn-halvøya, calling in at Mehamm before sailing past the Slettnes light, which is the most northerly point on the European mainland. South of the light, the steamer calls at Gamvik before crossing the mouth of Tanafjorden for Berlevåg where the huge breakwaters now allow the ships to dock safely. In the old days passengers had to be transferred to smaller boats at sea to be ferried ashore.

(opposite) Sunset over the harbour at Alesund

Båtsfjord is the next port of call. This important fishing village was one of the few in the north to escape destruction when the Germans retreated in 1944 and after a short stop in the early hours of the morning, the steamer heads round the coast for **Vardø** (chapter 12), Norway's most easterly town. The next stop is at **Vadsø** (chapter 12), the rather diminutive capital of Finnmark, which has flourished as a trading centre. The final leg of the journey takes you across Varangerfjorden into Bøkfjorden for Kirkenes, the end of the line.

Additional Information

Useful Addresses

Local Tourist Offices

Sør-Helgeland Reiselivslag
Boks 315
N-8901 Brønnøysund
☎ (086) 21 688

Sortland
Sortland Nerdic Hotel
☎ (088) 21 555

Florø ☎ (057) 42010

Main Cruise Operators

Finnmark Fylkesrederi og Ruteselskap
Box 308
N-9601 Hammerfest
☎ (084) 11 655

Nordenfjeldske A/S
Box 87
N-7001 Trondheim
☎ (07) 52 05 00

**Ofotens & Vesteraalens
 Dampskibbsselskab A/S**
Box 57
N-8501 Narvik
☎ (082) 44 090

Troms Fylkes Damskibsselskap A/S
Box 548
N-9001 Tromsø
☎ (083) 86 088

NORWAY FACT FILE

Accommodation

Camping

Camping is allowed almost anywhere provided it is not close to someone's home, or in an area clearly marked as private. There are more than 1,000 campsites in Norway, most equipped to a very high standard, with hot water and electricity. Sites are usually awarded one, two or three stars, depending on the facilities. There is no standard price and rates do vary. Reservations are not necessary.

Many campsites have self-catering chalets which can be rented for one or more nights. These usually accommodate four or six people and are reasonably priced. Most have fully-equipped kitchens and all you need to take is bedding.

The Norwegian Tourist Board publishes an annual guide covering every campsite in Norway, with addresses and telephone numbers, and symbols indicating facilities, but not prices.

The FICC camping carnet is valid in Norway, but is not obligatory. Norges Campingplass Forbund (the Norwegian Campsite Association) also sells a pass called Norsk Campingkort. It costs NOK 10 for a family and gives a fortnight's credit, so that you can pay for your entire holiday's camping all at once. You can purchase and use it at any site affiliated to the NCF. For a list, contact: Norges Camping plass forbund, Dronningensgt 10-12, N-0152 Oslo 1 ☎ 010 47-2-421203.

Camping gas is not freely available in Norway. Norges Automobilforbund publishes its own campsite guide, *Camping Norge*, which you can buy from bookshops in Norway. For further information contact NAF, Storgt 2, N0155 Oslo 2 ☎ (02) 34 14 00.

If you wish to set up tent bear in mind that you are free to do so on any uncultivated land, provided it does not lie directly next to the owner's residence. It is not permitted to pitch a tent or park a caravan closer than 150m from a house/chalet. Caravans may not be parked on lay-bys or picnic sites. It is forbidden to have an open fire — which includes a camping stove — in forests or on open land, between 15 April and 15 September.

Hotels

There are international hotels in all the main cities but even in the countryside there are small hotels. Many of the hotel chains operate voucher schemes which are paid for in advance, giving a 25 per cent discount on accommodation.

Mountain hotels are a Norwegian speciality offering all facilities and providing an excellent base for walking holidays. Local tourist offices can provide addresses of private homes taking in guests.

All hotels offer reduced rates in summer. The majority of establishments allow children under 3 to stay in their parents' room for quarter price, and those up to 12, or sometimes 15, for half price. Guesthouses in Norway are called *Pensjonat* or *gjestehus*, and are cheaper.

There are also a number of pass schemes, giving considerable reductions. Leaflets called the *Scandinavian Bonus Pass*, *Fjord-Pass*, and *Hotelcheque Scandinavia*, are available from the Norwegian National Tourist Office. A card may be purchased at modest cost, giving discounts to two adults and any children under 15 at participating hotels.

The Norwegian Tourist Board can supply a list of all hotels, motels and guesthouses in Norway. There is no star categorisation system in Norway.

Your local travel agency should be able to provide a booking service. You can book yourself by post or telephone; practically everyone in Norway speaks English. If travelling in the high season (mid-June to mid-August), it is advisable to book ahead. Local tourist offices in Norway often have a reservation service, charging a small fee.

Huts

These are another Norwegian speciality. They can vary from a simple pine cabin consisting of one room, to luxury homes with two or three bedrooms, bathroom, fully fitted kitchens with fridges and so on. All provide facilities for cooking as well as utensils and crockery, and plenty of space for children. *Hytter* come in various sizes, but they normally house four to six people. Signposts to the huts (*hytter*) can be spotted throughout the main tourist areas. If you are looking for accommodation, ask at the reception desk if they have any vacancies. On some sites you drive round until you see a key in the door of one of the huts. This means the hut is available, so take the key to the reception and check in. For *hytter* write to the following addresses and ask for brochures:

Den norske Hytteformidling A/S
Postboks 3207 Sagene
N-0405 Oslo 4
☎ (010) 47-2-356710

Fjordhytter
Jon Smørsgt 11
N-5011 Bergen
☎ (010) 47/5/23 20 80

Youth Hostels

To stay in a youth hostel, you must be a member of your own national Youth Hostel Association or you can join in Norway. To find out more contact:

Norske Vandrerhjem, Dronningensgate 26, N-0154 Oslo 1.
Monday to Friday 8.30am-1pm ☎ 02/421410

Travel Section:
Terra Nova Travel, Dronningensgate 26, N-0154 Oslo 1
☎ 02/421410. Terra Noval Travel, Strandgaten 4, N-5013 Bergen
☎ 05/322377

Concessions
For information on all travel services, apply to the Travel Sections:
Terra Noval Travel, Dronningensgate 26, N-0154 Oslo 1 ☎ (02) 42 14 10
and Terra Noval Travel, Strandgaten 4, N-5013 Bergen ☎ (05) 32 23 77.

Admission Charges - Museums
50 per cent reduction at the following: Norsk Folkemuseum, Maritime
Museum (Norsk Sjøfartsmuseum), The Viking Ships, Resistance
Museum (Norsk Hjemmefrontmuseum) in Oslo, Musical History
Museum (Ringve Museum) in Trondheim.

Sightseeing
Båtservice, Oslo: 50 per cent reduction on sightseeing tours. Bergen: 25
per cent reduction on sightseeing tours by coach or motor vessel.
(Tickets obtainable only at Terra Noval Travel, Bergen).

Sea Travel
Fred Olsen Lines: Kristiansand/Egersund-Hirtshals/Hanstholm vice
versa Bergen/Stavanger-Hirtshals vice versa. Oslo-Hirtshals vice
versa. 10 per cent reduction on ordinary fare for those under 26 years
of age.
Larvik Line: Larvik-Frederikshavn vice versa. 10 per cent off ordinary
passenger fare. Reduced tickets obtainable from any travel agent.
DFDS Seaways: Oslo-Copenhaven vice versa. 10 per cent of basic fare.
Norway Line: Bergen/Stavanger-Newcastle vice versa. 10 per cent
reduction on sleeperette fare.
Stena Line: 10 per cent reduction on ordinary passenger fare on: Oslo-
Frederikshavn vice versa, Gøteborg-Frederikshavn vice versa, Moss-
Frederikshavn vice versa and Gøteborg-Kiel vice versa. Reduced tick-
ets obtainable only at NUH Travel. Valid for travel Mondays to Thurs-
days June to August; no restrictions September to May.
Flaggruten (coastal express service): Bergen/Haugesund-Stavanger
vice versa 25-30 per cent reduction.
Car ferry 'Kystveien': Bergen-Stavanger vice versa 20 per cent reduction on adult fare.

Arrival and Customs

Norway operates red and green channels for customs — red for
something to declare, and green for nothing to declare. Because of the
strict drinking laws, you might be stopped on entry and asked what
drink you have bought. Travellers aged 20 and over are allowed to
take 1 litre of spirits and 1 litre of wine or fortified wine into Norway.
If no spirits are taken, the allowance is 2 litres of wine and fortified
wines. In addition, 2 litres of beer are allowed. People aged 16 and over

can also take in 200 cigarettes or 250g of other tobacco. Additional alcohol may be taken in, but it will be taxed and the extra duty on fortified wine, sparkling wine and spirits is very high.

There are very strict rules banning the importation of a wide range of agricultural produce, including meat, fruit and berries, in order to prevent the spread of plant and animal diseases. It is also prohibited to bring in eggs and potatoes, milk and cream from non-Scandinavian countries, mammals, birds, plants for cultivation, drugs, medicines, weapons and ammunition. Small quantities of medicines for personal use are exempt, as are small bunches of flowers or pot plants intended as gifts.

Customs posts between Norway and Sweden are often unmanned. UK visitors need a valid passport but there are no visa requirements unless you are planning a long stay, or intend working. Other nationals should consult the Norwegian embassy or consulate.

Banks

All towns and most large villages have one or more banks which will exchange currency. Some will also exchange cash against major credit cards. Banks are usually open between 8.15am and 3pm during the week, with an extension on Thursdays to 5pm. Branches in rural areas may have shorter opening hours. There are usually facilities to exchange currency at airports and ports, and in most hotels.

Chemists

Chemists are called *Apotek* and open during normal shopping hours, with some operating an emergency duty at night and weekends.

There are strict controls on drugs and strong medicines are only available through a chemist, usually only on prescription. Mild painkillers and insect bite creams can be bought in general stores.

Currency and Credit Cards

The currency is the Norwegian Krone which is usually written as Nkr or NOK. The krona consists of 100 øre. Coins are 10 and 50 øre, as well as 1, 5 and 10 kroner pieces. Notes are 50, 100, 500 and 1000 NOK. Foreign currency and travellers cheques can be exchanged at banks and hotels and most adopt a standard exchange rate. Travellers entering the country are allowed to bring in an unlimited amount of foreign currency but are not allowed to take out more than they had on arrival, or more than 5,000 NOK in notes and coins. Fuel stations do not accept travellers cheques. All major credit cards are generally accepted in hotels, stores and restaurants; cash may be preferred in isolated areas.

Electricity

Operates at 220 volts AC. Round ended, two pronged continental adaptors are needed for UK appliances.
NOTE: Some ferries and coastal steamers have 220 V DC electrical supplies and this could damage electric razors, hairdryers etc.

Embassies and Consulates

The main Norwegian embassies and consulates are:

Australia
Royal Norwegian Embassy
17 Hunter Street, Yarralumla
Canberra ACT 2600
☎ (62) 733 444

Canada
Royal Norwegian Embassy
Royal Bank Centre
90 Sparks Street, Suite 532
CDN Ottawa
Ontario KIP 5B4
☎ (613) 238 6570

USA
Royal Norwegian Embassy
2720 34th Street NW
Washington DC
20008 USA
☎ (0101) 333 6000

Norway
British Embassy
Thomas Heftyesgate 8
N-Oslo 2
☎ (02) 55 24 00

United States Embassy
Drammensun 18
Oslo 2
☎ (02) 44 85 50

UK
Royal Norwegian Embassy
39 Eccleston Street
London SW1
☎ (071) 730 9900

Facilities for the Disabled

Disabled people are generally well catered for in Norway. By law, all public buildings must be accessible to disabled people. Many trains have special facilities for the disabled, including hydraulic lifts for people boarding in wheelchairs. The Norwegian Association for the Handicapped publishes the *Travel Guide for the Disabled* (in English). This 192-page comprehensive survey includes transport facilities, accommodation and points of interest which are especially accessible for disabled persons. You can obtain a copy from the Norwegian Tourist Board, or Norges Handikapforbund, PO Box 9217 Vaterland, N-0134 Oslo 1 ☎ (02) 17 02 55.

Health Insurance

Because of reciprocal agreements, UK citizens can receive free medical care while in Norway although a charge may be made for some specialised services, which can often be reclaimed when you return home. An E111 form is needed to be eligible for this and the forms are obtainable from post offices. Other nationals should ensure they have adequate travel and health insurance before leaving home.

Maps

Good road maps can be bought at stationers, bookshops and many garages. Walking maps and guides can be bought at tourist offices, hotels and hostels and bookshops. Regional and municipal tourist offices can often provide street maps and local maps. The following maps are useful: Cappelens Road Hiking and Survey maps of Norway 1:325,000, Hallwag Map of Norway 1:1,000,000, Norwegian Highway Authority (Norske Vegkart) 1:250,000 (21 maps covering the whole country). If you have difficulty then contact the map specialists; Stanfords, 12-14 Long Acre, Convent Garden, London WC2E 9LP, ☎ (071) 836 1321.

Measurements

The metric system is used in Norway. Conversions are:
1 kilogram (1,000 grams) = 2.2lb
1 litre = $1^3/_4$ pints
4.5 litres = 1 gallon
8km = 5 miles

Medical Treatment

This can be obtained from doctors and dentists surgeries during treatment hours, or from hospital casualty wards outside these times. Most hotels have doctors on call and will put you in touch in an emergency. Doctors and dentists are paid cash which is reclaimed by medical insurance or reciprocal health agreements. Ambulance travel and hospital in-patient treatment is free, as are tooth extractions.

Some charges may be partially refunded by Norway's social insurance scheme. Obtain a receipt for payment and claim at the district social insurance office called *trygdekontor*.

Emergency numbers:

Oslo	☎ (02) 201 090	Stavanger	☎ (04) 533 333
Bergen	☎ (05) 321 120	Tromsø	☎ (08) 383 030
Trondheim	☎ (07) 598 800		

Pets

Because of strict disease control laws, it is not permitted to take pets into Norway. The country is rabies-free and all animals entering Norway must have a permit issued by the Norwegian Ministry of

Agriculture and must spend a minimum 4 months in quarantine. For further information contact: Veterinæravdelingen i Landbruks-departementet, PO Box 8007 DEP, N-0030 Oslo 1 ☎ (02) 34 90 90.

Post Offices

Usually open: Monday to Friday at either 8am or 8.30am and close at 4pm or 5pm and Saturday 8am to 1pm.

Public Holidays

New Year's Day	May Day
Maundy Thursday	Constitution Day
Good Friday	Ascension Day
Easter	Whit Monday
Easter Monday	Christmas Day and Boxing Day

There are also a number of flag days. These celebrate religious festivals, important dates in the country's history, and the birthdays of members of the royal family. These are:

New Year's Day	**2 July** (birthday of King Olav)
21 February (birthday of Crown Prince Harald)	**4 July** (birthday of Crown Princess Sonja)
Easter	**20 July** (birthday of Prince Haakon Magnus)
May Day	**29 July** (St Olav's Day)
8 May (Liberation Day, 1945)	**22 September** (birthday of Princess Märtha Louise)
17 May (Constitution Day)	
Whit Monday	
7 June (Dissolution of the Union 1905)	**Christmas Day**

Shopping

In most towns and cities the larger shops open: Monday to Wednesday from 9am to 5pm and stay open till 7pm on Thursday and Friday. On Saturday they open from 9am to 3pm.

State alcohol shops are open Monday to Wednesday 10am-4pm, Thursday 10am-5pm, Friday 9am-4pm, and Saturday 9am-1pm. In the summer months of June to August some shops may operate shorter opening hours. There is a returnable deposit on all bottles of wine bottled in Norway.

Tax Free Shopping
This is available in stores throughout Norway which can be recognised by stickers in their windows. At least 300 NOK must be spent to qualify for the VAT refund. Goods purchased must not be used in Norway and must be taken out of the country within 4 weeks of purchase. Tax-free shopping is not available to Scandinavian nation-

als and a passport is needed as proof of residence. The receipt will have to be produced at the airport, ferry port or station before you leave, in order to claim back the VAT. For further information contact: Norway Tax Free Shopping, Østerrndalen 27, Postboks 48, 1345 Østerås ☎ (02) 24 97 84 or the Norwegian Tourist Office.

Shopping is expensive but items worth considering are knitwear, pewterware, silver jewellery, wooden carvings, reindeer goods, and food and fish.

Smoking

This is banned in all public buildings, and on domestic air routes.

Sports and Pastimes

Canoeing

Only the most experienced canoers should venture into the open sea. The Telemark Canal (Telemarkskanalen) runs from Dalen, where canoes can be hired, for 110km to Skien. There are eighteen locks, many of them close to waterfalls which should always be approached with great caution

For further information contact the canoeing association: Norges Kajakk-og Kanoforbund, Hauger Skolevei, N-1351 Rud ☎ (010 47) 2 51 88 00.

Cycling

The National Cyclists' Association (Syklistenes Landesforening, Nedregt 5, N-0551 Oslo 5) produces a map with twenty-two suggested routes covering the whole country. All the routes are linked so that you can move from one to another if you have time. The map also shows which roads are not suitable for cyclists, usually because of tunnels from which cyclists are banned. Good lights are essential because not all tunnels are illuminated, and where access to cyclists is barred, diversion signs indicate the route to follow.

Cycles can be carried on all trains except express trains and there is a charge. You must arrive at the station at least 30 minutes before departure, and the cycle must carry a label with name, address and places of destination and departure.

Buses in rural areas have provision for carrying bikes but space is limited. They are carried on ferries free of charge.

Diving

The warm waters of the Gulf Stream which flow around Norway provide excellent conditions for underwater exploration.
Here is a selection of diving clubs in Norway.

Oslo Froskemannskole
Gøteborggt 27B
N-0566 Oslo 5
☎ (02) 71 75 60

Bergen Froskemannsenter/-skole
Lyder Sagensgt 12
N-5008 Bergen
☎ (05) 32 62 07

Kristiansund Dykkerklubb
Postboks 293
N-6500 Kristiansund N
☎ (073) 77 190

Havsport A/S
Kjøpmannsgata 41
N-7011 Trondheim
☎ (07) 51 19 16

Polardykk A/S
Snev 11
N-8000 Bodø
☎ (081) 60 922

Dykkerservice A/S
Dronningensgt 99
N-4610 Kristiansand S
☎ (042) 24 124

Fishing

Fishing licences are readily available locally from sports suppliers, kiosks, tourist offices, hotels, and campsites etc and can be either for one stretch of water or a collection of lakes and rivers. They can cover a day, a week or a season and the price depends on duration and the quality of the fishing. As a rule, a separate licence is needed for net or otter fishing. To protect the fisheries, all equipment brought into the country must be disinfected.

A licence is not needed for sea fishing although the inland regulations and conservation measures regarding salmon, trout and sea char also apply at sea. For further information contact The Hunting and Fishing Society, Hvalstadåsen 5, N-1364 Hvalstad ☎ (02) 78 38 68.

Fishing seasons vary from district to district — ask at the local tourist board, get in touch with the regional *lensman* (county sheriff), or contact the Directorate for Wildlife Administration (Direktoratet for naturforvaltning), Tungsletta 2, N-7000 Trondheim ☎ (07) 91 30 20.

Golf

Golf is played from May to September and there are courses in Oslo, Blommenholm, Kolbotn, Sarpsborg, Borgenhaugen, Fredrikstad, Hov, Røyken, Tøonsberg, Skien, Arendal, Kristiansand, Stavanger, Bergen and Trondheim. Guest or day membership can be arranged and clubs can be hired. Contact the Golf Association for a list of golf courses at Norges Golfforbund, Hauger Skolevei, N-1351 Rud ☎ (02) 51 88 00.

Horse Riding

There are many riding centres and a number of farms also hire out horses which can be hired for a short period, a day or you can set out on organised tours lasting a week or more. For further information contact Norsk Rutterforbund, Hauger Skolvei 1, N-1351 Rud ☎ (02) 51 88 00.

Mountaineering

There are many ranges and peaks to explore, especially in the north with the Lofoten and Vesterålen mountains and the ranges on the Lyngen peninsula in Troms. The Norwegian Mountain Touring Association (DNT), Sportinsgt 28, Postboks 1963 Vika, N-0125 Oslo 1 ☎ (02) 40 80 20, organises the sport and arranges courses and expeditions.

Skiing

There are excellent winter downhill and cross country facilities in many areas, and it is possible to ski during the summer in Oppland, Hordaland, Sogn og Fjordane and Nordland. For information contact Skiforeningen (Ski Society), Kongeveiens, Oslo 3 ☎ (02) 14 16 90.

There is also skiing in the summer and the Norwegian summer skiing season lasts as a general rule from June to September. Contact:

Stryn Sommerskisenter
N-6880 Stryn
☎ (057) 71995/72070
June-September: (090) 56109/56110

Galdhøpiggen Sommerskisenter
N-2687 Bøverdalen
☎ (061) 19711

Finse Skisenter & Alpinanlegg
Postboks 12
N-3590 Finse
☎ (05) 526 711

Sommerskisenter Folgefonna
Jondal Kommune
Ordførerens kontor
N-5627 Jondal
☎ (054) 68531

Ski Vargebreen Sommeralpint
Geilo Turistservice
Postboks 85
N-3581 Geilo
☎ (067) 86300

Swimming

Swimming is possible almost anywhere, but the water may be cold. The inland lakes and their islands provide very safe bathing. Even above the Arctic Circle it is possible to swim in the lakes on very hot days and after a hot spell the water temperature can be acceptable. Official bathing sites are usually clearly marked. There are many swimming pools run by hotels and municipalities.

Walking

There are hundreds of miles of well-marked trails in and around Oslo, and every community can give you details of walks in its area. Tourist offices often have guides of walks in their districts which contain details about things to see along the way, time taken and difficulty.

There are many guided walks, especially on the mountains and across glaciers. Glacier walking, however, should never be attempted without an experienced local guide. During summer organised glacier walks take place daily from the Leirvassbu, Glitterheim, Spiterstulen, Juvasshytta, Krossbu and Sognefjell mountain touring huts.

Mountain maps can be obtained from the Mountain Touring Association (Den Norske Turistforening). If going into the mountains you must be fit, have the right equipment and know how to use it, check the weather forecast and make sure someone knows where you are going and when you plan to return.

Den Norske Turistforening works closely with local mountaineering clubs and together they run a network of 286 cabins and hostels, ranging in size from just four beds to more than a hundred. They are generally open from mid-February to the end of September. There are three types of hostel: serviced hostels with full board (S), self-service cabins with groceries on sale (SS), and unserviced cabins where you have to carry in everything you need (NS). You have to be a DNT member to use the cabins, or be accompanied by one, and must provide your own sheet sleeping bag or sleeping bag. The cabins are all linked by paths which are easy to follow and usually marked by a red 'T'.

Information about DNT and how to join can be obtained from Den Norske Turistforening, Stortingsgt 28, Postboks 1963 Vika, N-0125 Oslo 1, Norway ☎ 83 25 50.

Taxis

Taxis (*drosje*) can be hailed in towns and cities but may need to be booked in advance in rural areas and at night. Fares are reasonable although there are supplements for nights and weekends. Taxis generally accept a tip of 10 per cent.

Tourist Offices

The main Norwegian tourist offices are:

UK
Norwegian National Tourist Office
Charles House
5 Lower Regent Street
London SW1Y 4LR
☎ (071) 839 2650

USA and Canada
Norwegian Tourist Board
655 Third Avenue
New York, USA
NY 10017
☎ (1212) 949 2333

Norway
Norwegian Tourist Board
PO Box 499 Sentrum
N-0165 Oslo 1
☎ (02) 42 70 44

Norwegian Tourist Association
Storgingsgt 28
N-0161 Oslo 1
☎ (02) 83 25 50

Travel

BY SEA
Getting to Norway from Britain by sea can be a holiday in itself. The North Sea ferries operated by Fred Olsen, Norway Line and Scandinavian Seaways are like mini-liners offering excellent restaurants, bars with entertainment, comfortable cabins, sun decks and discos.

Fred Olsen Lines, which operates out of Harwich, sails to Oslo weekly all year round, and also to Kristiansand during the peak summer period. At other times of the year passengers can travel to Kristiansand via Hirtshals and use the connecting Skagerak Express Service. The crossing from Harwich takes 36 hours, including two nights. Sleeping accommodation on board consists of two- and four-berth cabins, all with shower and toilet.

The Harwich-Oslo route is a useful one if you plan to start your trip in the capital, and it is an exciting arrival as you steam up the Oslofjord.

Norway Lines operate between Newcastle, Stavanger and Bergen. The crossing is much shorter, taking about 21 hours between Newcastle and Stavanger, and a further 5 to 6 hours for Bergen. There are three sailings a week from Newcastle during the summer season. Accommodation ranges from reclining seats which need to be booked in advance during peak periods, and de-luxe two berth cabins.

Scandinavian Seaways operate out of Newcastle and Harwich and sail to Gothenburg in Sweden and Esbjerg in Denmark. The Harwich-Gothenburg crossing takes about 24 hours (the return journey is a little quicker), Harwich-Esbjerg takes about 21 hours, and Newcastle to Gothenburg about 24 hours. There are four sailings a week from Harwich to both Gothenburg and Esbjerg during the summer. Accommodation ranges from four-berth couchettes to single de-luxe cabins. If you want to start in the south, or by visiting Denmark or Sweden first, this is a useful route. There are frequent ferry crossings between the three countries. For further information contact:

Scandinavian
Seaways Travel
Centre, 15 Hanover Street
London W1R 9HG
☎ (071) 439 1019

Fred Olsen Lines
Crown House
Crown Street, Ipswich
Suffolk IP1 3HB
☎ (0473) 233044

Fred Olsen Lines
PO Box 82
Kristiansand
☎ (042) 26500

Norway Line
PO Box 4004
N-5015 Dreggen/Bergen
☎ (05) 322 780

Norway Line UK
Tyne Commission Quay
North Shields NE29 6AE
☎ (091) 296313

BY AIR

There are daily flights by a number of airlines from Britain and other European countries to Oslo. SAS flies from Aberdeen to Stavanger with connections to Bergen and Oslo, Glasgow to Stavangar, London Gatwick to Stavanger, London Gatwick to Bergen and London Heathrow to Oslo. British Airways operates Heathrow to Oslo and Heathrow to Stavanger and Bergen. Dan Air flies from Newcastle to Bergen, Oslo and Stavanger, with connecting flights from Gatwick and Manchester. Air Europe flies Gatwick to Oslo and Edinburgh to Bergen and Stavanger. Air UK operates flights between Aberdeen and Bergen and Stavanger, Norwich and Stavanger, Edinburgh and Stavanger. Scar Tours of Scandinavia run charter services from Gatwick to Oslo, Bergen and Trondheim. Birmingham Executive Airways flies Birmingham to Oslo three times a week.

British Airways
Speedbird House
PO Box 10
Heathrow Airport
Hounslow TW6 2JA
☎ (081) 897 4000

Dan-Air Services Ltd
Davies & Newman Holdings, plc
New City Court
20 St Thomas Street
London SE1 9RJ
☎ Linkline (0345) 100 200

Air UK	Air Europe	SAS Scandinavian
Stansted Airport	52 Grosvenor Gardens	Airlines
Essex	Victoria	52-3 Conduit Street
CM24 8QT	London SW1 0AU	London W1 0AY
☎ (0279) 755950	☎ (0345) 444 737	☎ (071) 734 4020

BY ROAD

Breakdown

Help from Norway's motor rescue patrols — Norges Automobilforbund (NAF) — is free to members of the RAC, AA, and the American AAA. NAF patrols cover all the major roads and mountain passes during the peak holiday periods. There are also NAF emergency phones in many mountain areas.

If more extensive repair work is required you will have to pay for any tow-in and garage charges. There is a very efficient system of moving spare parts around the country, often using overnight mail trains, so even major breakdowns can be tackled quite quickly. You must carry a red warning triangle in the event of a breakdown. Norway's major motoring clubs are:

NAF Storgt 2
N-0155 Oslo 2
☎ (02) 34 14 00

Kongelig Norsk Automobilklub
(KNA) Drammensveien 20c
N-0255 Oslo 2 ☎ (02) 56 19 00

If you do need help, look in the telephone directory for *redningstjeneste*. In some major towns these are:

Oslo
Falken Redningskorps
☎ (02) 23 25 85

Stavanger
Falken Redningstjeneste
☎ (04) 58 60 20

Bergen
Viking Redningstjeneste
☎ (05) 29 22 22

Trondheim
Viking Redningstjeneste
☎ (07) 93 90 00

Caravans

Caravans are not suitable on some roads, and a free map available from the Norwegian Tourist Board indicates which routes can be taken, permitted axle loads, permitted length of vehicles, roads open to caravans, and tunnels. Cars towing caravans must be fitted with large caravan mirrors, which should be folded or removed when the caravan is not on tow. The maximum speed limit for a caravan with brakes is 80kph (50mph), or 60kph (37mph) if it weighs more than 300kg and no brakes. Touring caravans 2.3m wide are allowed, and may be up to $2^1/_2$m wide provided the towing vehicle is at least the same width. The length of car and caravan must not exceed $18^1/_2$m.

It is possible to hire caravans in Norway. For further information on caravan hire contact:

Majorstuen Autoservice
Marcus Thranesgt 2
N-0473 Oslo 4
☎ (02) 38 19 61

Bislet Bilutleie
Pilestredet 70
N-0354 Oslo 3
☎ (02) 60 00 00

Interrent A/S
Frysjaveien 31
N-0883 Oslo 8
☎ (02) 23 66 85

There are two caravan clubs in Norway:

Norsk Caravan Club Landsforbund
Solheimveien 18
N-1473 Skårer
☎ 02 97 49 20

Norsk Campingbilforening
Postboks 18 - Lysejordet
N-0312 Oslo 3

Norwegian roads are well signposted and most towns and villages have an information board in a convenient lay-by with information on the local tourist office, hotels or campsites, and places of interest.

Car-hire

This is available in most towns and larger villages, as well as at all major airports and ports. Drivers must be aged 21 years or over, have a valid driving licence and some form of identity. A major credit card is the preferred form of payment. Many of the car hire companies offer special deals at certain times of the year and it pays to shop around. For further information contact:

Avis
Munkedamsveien 27
N-0250 Oslo 2
☎ (02) 41 00 60

Hertz
Wergelandsveien 1
0167 Oslo 1
☎ (02) 20 52 12

Driving Regulations

A valid driving licence is required for driving in Norway and it is prudent to have the vehicle's documents with you and check that your insurance affords full cover. Foreign cars must carry the appropriate country identification sticker.

The Norwegians drive on the right hand side of the road and on carriageways the left-hand lane is reserved for overtaking vehicles. A yellow warning line means that it is not safe to overtake and it is illegal to cross a continuous line.

Speed limits are well sign posted. They are generally 50kph (30mph) in built up areas, falling to 30kph (20mph) in some residential areas. Top speed outside built up areas is 80kph (50mph) except on some better stretches of road, where signs indicate it is increased to 90kph (55mph). Cars towing caravans or trailers are still restricted to 80kph (50mph) even in a 90kph (55mph) area.

It is compulsory to wear seat belts in both front and back (if fitted), and children under the age of 4 must have their own safety seat. It is also compulsory to drive on dipped headlights during daylight hours, and this rule also applies to motor cycles and mopeds, whose drivers and passengers must wear crash helmets. Cars from the UK must have the headlights adjusted so that they don't dazzle oncoming traffic in Norway.

The Norwegian drink-drive laws are very tough. The alcohol limit is 0.05% and if you plan to drive it is best not to drink alcohol at all. It is also a serious offence to drive while under the influence of drugs, and this could include some prescribed medicines. In Norway medicines containing drugs which should be avoided when driving are marked with a red triangle.

Heavy vehicles are not allowed on some roads and a map showing permitted axle weights on Norwegian roads can be obtained free from tourist offices.

Fuel
In towns and cities fuel stations are numerous but they are not so common in rural areas. Never let the tank get too low and always fill up when you have the opportunity. Many garages in the country only accept cash. Oil and unleaded petrol is available.

Motorways
There are only motorways in the south-east although the major roads travelling north allow you to keep up a steady speed. There are two types of motorway — Motorvei Klass A and Motorvei Klass B. The first is a two lane dual carriageway, while the second is a two lane road from 7-8m wide with limited access points. Maximum speed on a motorway is 90kph (55mph).

Traffic coming in from the right usually has priority. Red flow signs indicate that traffic entering from the right must be allowed to filter in.

Mountain Driving
This requires a great deal of concentration, especially on the smaller roads which can be quite narrow. Often these roads are only wide enough for a single lane of traffic although there are numerous passing points. These may be indicated by a sign with a white M on a blue background. The rule for mountain driving is take your time. Generally the Norwegians are courteous drivers and will drop back and wait until safe to pass rather than pressure you into driving faster.

Elk signs are a warning to exercise greater vigilance, especially at night. Elk are large creatures and a collision with one can write a car off. Not all mountain passes are open all year round and if you are travelling in spring or autumn, it is vital to check before setting out on your journey.

Major Mountain Passes: Opening Dates
Highway 7: Hardangervidda. Open all year.
Highway 55: Sognefjellsvegen. Closed late December to early May.
Highway 58: Geiranger. Closed early December to mid-May.
Highway 63: Trollstigen. Closed mid-November to mid-May.
Highway 95: Skarsvåg-Nordkapp. Closed mid-November to late May.

Parking
Parking is not allowed on main roads, on bends or in blind spots. Towns and cities may have their own parking regulations forbidding parking on particular sides of the street on some days.

Tolls

Tolls are charged on a number of roads in Norway. There are also a number of private bridge and roads on which tolls are levied, although these are not part of the public highway network. Many of these private tolls bridges and roads operate an 'honesty box' system, with a sign telling you how much you have to pay. Tolls on public roads vary from a few kroner to 30 or 40 kroner. Tolls (15 kroner) are being levied on all drivers travelling into Oslo in a bid to reduce the city's traffic congestion.

Tunnels

Norway has some of the longest tunnels in Europe, many blasted through the mountains. Some of these are not too wide and care must be exercised. The country's longest tunnel is the Svartistunnelen on the R17 in Nordland which is $7^1/_2$km long. There are nine other tunnels which are all more than $4^1/_2$km long.

Useful Road Signs

ferist — cattle grid, *veiarbeide* — roadworks, *kjør sakte* — drive slowly, *løs grus* — loose chippings, *omkjøring* — diversion, *svake kanter* — soft verges.

Winter Travel

It is illegal to drive in snow or ice with summer tyres without chains. Many drivers use studded tyres and these can be hired from Ulrich Gummiservice, Drammensveien 130, N-0277 Oslo 2 ☎ (02) 55 77 18. It is not permitted to use studded tyres between 15 April and 1 November (or in the north 1 May to 15 October) unless you are specifically going into areas of ice and snow.

PUBLIC TRANSPORT

By Air

Because of the size of the country flying in Norway is both convenient and relatively cheap. It is possible to fly into about fifty airports and airstrips throughout the country. The domestic airline system is operated by SAS, Braathens SAFE ALS, Widerøe's Flyveselskap AS, Norsk Air and A/S Norving. Between them they cover the whole country.

Main airports operating international flights are Oslo (Fornebu and Gardermoen), Bergen (Flesland), Stavanger (Sola), Kristiansand, Trondheim, Sandefjord, Tromsø and Fagernes International, the country's new charter flight airport. For further information contact:

British Airways
Karl Johansgt 166
4th floor, 0154 Oslo 1
☎ (02) 33 16 00

Braathens SAFE ALS
Haakon Vlls gate 2
0160 Oslo 1
☎ (02) 59 70 00

Sas Scandinavian Airlines
Fomebuvn 40
Oslo Lufthavn
☎ (02) 59 60 50

Widerøes Flyveselskap
Mustadsveien 1
0283 Oslo 2
☎ (02) 50 91 30

By Bus

Bus services cover most of the country and there are scheduled services over most of Norway's 80,000km of roads. The public transport network is co-ordinated so that there are good connections with trains, buses, boats and planes. Buses service the areas where the trains do not go, and they usually wait at remote stations as the train pulls in.

National timetables are available from tourist offices or bus stations. Like the ferries, the buses follow strict schedules and are rarely more than a few minutes late.

Bus travel is cheap. Children under the age of 4 not occupying a seat travel free, and children between the ages of 4 and 16 travel at half price. Many of the bus companies run their own tours lasting anything from a day to one or two weeks, and details can be obtained at bus stations, or tourist offices.

A new service is Nor-Way Bussekspress, an express bus service of 200 luxury coaches providing a fast link between all the major towns, cities and large villages throughout the country.

Main routes operated include:
Oslo - Gothenburg (5 hrs 30 min)
Oslo - Tyrsil (3 hrs 30 min)
Oslo - Otta - Stryn - Måløy (11 hrs)
Oslo - Minnesund - Gjøvik
  (2 hrs 30 min)
Oslo - Fagernes - Årdalstangen
  (6 hrs 30 min)
Bergen - Aurland - Oslo (13 hrs)
Oslo - Haugesund (5 hrs 30 min)
Oslo - Kongsberg - Rjukan
  (3 hrs 40 min)

Oslo - Notodden - Seljord (4 hrs)
Stavanger - Kristiansand (4 hrs 40 min)
Bergen - Nordfjord - Ålesund
  (10 hrs 50 min)
Bergen - Førde- Trondheim
  (15 hrs 30 min)
Trondheim - Stockholm (14 hrs 30 min)
Trondheim - Støren - Røros (3 hrs)
Trondheim - Molde - Ålesund
  (7 hrs 45 min)
Mosjøen - Brønnøysund (3 hrs 30 min)
Voss - Kristiansand (9 hrs 30 min)

Northern Express services operate between Bodø and Narvik (7 hrs), Narvik and Tromsø (5 hrs 30 min), Narvik via Nordkjosbotn to Alta (11 hrs 30 min), Tromsø to Alta (7 hrs 15 min), and Alta to Kirkenes (10 hrs 50 min).

By Train

The rail network is operated by the Norwegian State Railways NSB, 21-24 Cockspur Street, London SW1 ☎ (071) 930 6666; USA (through Swiss Federal Railway), 608 Fifth Avenue, New York NY 10020 ☎ 212 757 5944. It covers the whole country and some of the journeys through the southern mountains are among the most scenic railway journeys in the world. The Oslo-Bergen line ($6^1/_2$ hours) is a must for anyone with time to do it.

The other main lines are the Sørland line which runs along the south coast from Oslo to Stavanger, the Dovre Line linking Oslo and Trondheim, the Nordland line which runs across the Arctic Circle to Bodø, and the Ofot line, the most northerly railway line in the world which runs from Narvik to Stockholm.

There are a number of different types of train:
Express trains (*ekspresstogene*) are fast, non-stop services running

on the Bergen, Dovre and Sørland lines. They are very comfortable.

Fast Trains (*hurtigtogene*) often operate round the clock, stop at main stations and provide a quick way to travel.

Inter-City trains run from outlying areas such as Halden, Lillehammer or Skien to Oslo.

Local trains (*lokaltogene*) are slow and stop at every station.

Long distance trains often have first class compartments with fares about 60 per cent higher than the second class ticket.

Tickets should be bought at travel offices or stations or, if at an unmanned station, from the conductor. Normal standard tickets for trips over 60km are valid for 2 months and allow you to break the journey as often as you like. If you break your journey, get a special ticket from the conductor or station staff to allow a refund should the rest of the ticket not be used.

One of the best ways of travelling the country is to get a Nordturist ticket. This gives you 21 days total freedom to travel the rail networks of Norway, Denmark, Finland and Sweden (although it is not valid on some local Stockholm trains). There are many cheap and concessionary fares for children, students, senior citizens (67 and over), groups and for off peak travel.

It is sensible to reserve your seat if you plan to travel at busy times, and sleeping cars and couchettes are available on long journeys. These may be booked in advance but you can buy a ticket from the conductor once aboard if any are free.

On express and fast trains and most night services, there are often special compartments with toilet and changing room for people travelling with babies. It is illegal to drink alcohol on the trains, except in a restaurant car.

Ferries

Ferries make travelling around Norway easier, quicker and more enjoyable. The ferries are remarkably efficient and the timetable enables accurate journey planning. The ferries almost always depart on time, apart from peak periods, and you can normally drive into the terminal as the ferry unloads, then go straight on board.

Bookings are only necessary on long distance ferries although in the height of the season there may be long queues for the most popular ferries.

A short ferry crossing can save hours of driving, and moments spent studying the ferry routes and sailings can help you save time. Many ferries simply help to reduce driving distances, while some routes are worth going out of your way for because of the spectacular scenery to be seen from the boat.

Bookings are only necessary on long distance ferries although in the height of the season there may be long queues for the most popular ferries and you may have to wait.

Telephones

A telephone call from your hotel room is convenient but expensive. There are coin-operated telephone boxes in most hotels, restaurants, shops, garages, airports, railway and bus stations, and you can direct dial long distance and overseas provided you have a pocketful of NOK 5 and 10 kroner coins. You can also dial 0115 for the overseas operator and ask for a reverse charge call (collect call) or to make a credit card call. It can take some time to get through to the international operator at certain times of the day, especially if you are ringing from a country area. It is also not unknown for call boxes in outlying areas to be out of order.

To obtain a telephone number in Norway for Britain ring Directory Inquiries on 0180, for all other countries ring 0181. For these last two numbers you must insert a minimum of two 1-kroner coins before you dial for the operator.

To direct dial to the UK from Norway, put the money in the box before dialling 095 44 and then your full STD code (omitting the initial zero) and number. For the USA, dial 095 1 followed by the national dialling code for your local exchange, omitting the first zero, and then the number. A meter shows how much credit is left.

To ring Norway from the UK dial 010 47 followed by the town code (omitting the first zero) and then the number. From the USA first dial 01147. For further information contact Telephone, Telegraph and Telex, Kongensgt 21, Oslo 1 ☎ (02) 40 50 60. For operator assistance in English dial 093.

A Note to the Reader

Thank you for buying this book; we hope it has helped you to enjoy your stay in Norway. We have worked hard to produce a guidebook which is as accurate as possible. With this in mind, any comments, suggestions or useful information you may have would be appreciated. Those who send in the most helpful letters will be credited in future editions.

Please send your letters **Freepost** to:

Tonya Monk (Editor)
Moorland Publishing Co Ltd
Free Post
Ashbourne
Derbyshire
DE6 9BR

MPC The Travel Specialists

INDEX

The European Airline

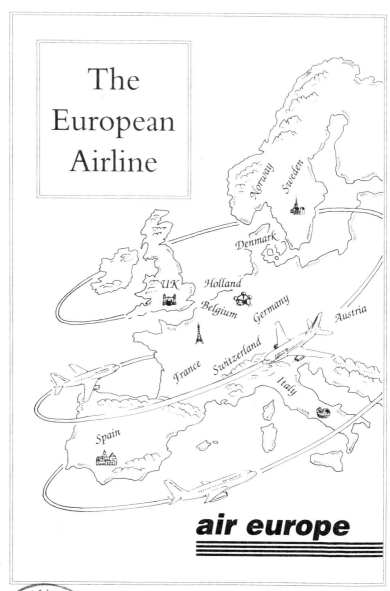

air europe